教材项目规划小组
Teaching Material Project Planning Group

严美华	姜明宝	王立峰
田小刚	崔邦焱	俞晓敏
赵国成	宋永波	郭　鹏

加拿大方咨询小组
Canadian Consulting Group

Dr. Robert Shanmu Chen

Mr. Zheng Zhining

University of British Columbia

Dr. Helen Wu

University of Toronto

Mr. Wang Renzhong

McGill University

中国国家汉办规划教材

NEW PRACTICAL CHINESE READER

(2nd Edition)

新实用汉语课本

4

刘珣 主编

课 本
TEXTBOOK

英文注释
Annotated in English

编 者：张凯 刘社会 陈曦
左珊丹 施家炜 刘珣
英译审订：Jerry Schmidt 余心乐

北京语言大学出版社
BEIJING LANGUAGE AND CULTURE
UNIVERSITY PRESS

（第2版）

图书在版编目 (CIP) 数据

新实用汉语课本：英文注释 . 4 / 刘珣主编 . —2
版 . —北京：北京语言大学出版社，2012.12（2014.5 重印）
ISBN 978-7-5619-3431-9

Ⅰ.①新… Ⅱ.①刘… Ⅲ.①汉语—对外汉语教学—
教材 Ⅳ.① H195.4

中国版本图书馆 CIP 数据核字（2012）第 299257 号

书　　名：	新实用汉语课本（第 2 版 英文注释）课本 4
	XIN SHIYONG HANYU KEBEN (DI-ER BAN YINGWEN ZHUSHI) KEBEN 4
中文编辑：	付彦白
英文编辑：	孙玉婷
责任印制：	汪学发

出版发行：**北京语言大学出版社**

社　　址：北京市海淀区学院路 15 号　**邮政编码**：100083
网　　址：www.blcup.com
电　　话：发行部　8610-82303650 / 3591 / 3651
　　　　　编辑部　8610-82303647 / 3592 / 3595
　　　　　读者服务部　8610-82303653
　　　　　网上订购电话　8610-82303908
　　　　　客户服务信箱　service@blcup.com
印　　刷：北京联兴盛业印刷股份有限公司
经　　销：全国新华书店

版　　次：2012 年 12 月第 2 版　　2014 年 5 月第 3 次印刷
开　　本：889 毫米 ×1194 毫米　　1/16　印张：21
字　　数：348 千字
书　　号：ISBN 978-7-5619-3431-9 / H·12221
　　　　　07200

附录　Appendices

第三十九课
Lesson 39

别总说"亲爱的"，好不好

Please stop saying "亲爱的" all the time, OK?

Ma Dawei is head over heels in love with his girlfriend, Xiao Yanzi. He keeps calling her "honey" and showers her with praise and thanks, but Xiao Yanzi doesn't seem to feel very comfortable about it. Can you figure out why? Do you know how one expresses love in different cultures? This lesson will give you some ideas on this matter.

一、课文 Texts

1 （一）

别总说"亲爱的"，好不好

小燕子：大为，吃饭了。今天请你吃我做的菜。

马大为：亲爱的，你累了一上午，饭终于做好了。[①] 谢谢。你做了这么多好吃的，你真能干！

小燕子：先别夸奖，还不知道味道怎么样呢。你要多少米饭？

马大为：我一看见这么好的菜，就觉得特别饿。我要满满的一碗，可能还不够。

小燕子：你想吃多少就吃多少，米饭多得很。

马大为：菜做得真好吃，你做菜的技术一天比一天好。特别是这个炒

鸡丁，不但好吃，而且样子也很好看。这个菜比饭馆做的好
得多，谢谢你，亲爱的！

小燕子：好了，别谢了。你觉得好吃，就多吃一点儿。

马大为：还有，你炒的这个大虾也好吃得很。我看咱们结婚以后，可
以在美国开一家饭馆，你当厨师，我当经理。咱们一定能挣
很多的钱。

小燕子：哦，你是老板，让我给你打工，我可不干。

马大为：这不是谁给谁打工，而是咱们俩分工合作。你有技术，我懂
管理，咱们一起干，这有什么不好？② 你看，我吃完一碗了。
我还想再来一碗，亲爱的！

小燕子：你怎么一开口就是"亲爱的"？你真是一天比一天话多了。

马大为：我怎么了？③ 你为什么不高兴呢？你不喜欢开饭馆？说实在
的，这个主意很不错啊。你知道，有不少华人在美国开饭馆
挣钱。再说，中国菜世界有名，让更多的西方人吃到你做的
菜，更多地了解中国文化，这不挺好吗？

小燕子：挣钱的办法多得很，不必都去开饭馆。我喜欢做饭菜，可是，
离厨师的水平还差得远呢！厨师必须是专业学校毕业的。还
有，别总说"亲爱的"，好不好？我听着，总觉得别扭。

马大为：好吧，亲爱的——你看，我恐怕改不了了。可是我真不懂，
你究竟为什么不愿意听这三个字呢？

生词 New Words

1. 总（是）	zǒng (shì)	Adv	always	总说，总希望，总是忙，总也没有时间回家
2. 亲爱	qīn'ài	A	dear, beloved	亲爱的同学们，亲爱的老师，亲爱的妈妈
3. 终于	zhōngyú	Adv	finally, eventually	终于到了，终于做好了，终于决定了，终于记住了
4. 好吃	hǎochī	A	tasty, delicious	做得真好吃，好吃得很，不好吃，好吃的
5. 能干	nénggàn	A	able, capable	真能干，能干得很，能干的姑娘，不能干
干	gàn	V	to do, to work	干工作，干事儿，不想干，我可不干，干得好
6. 夸奖	kuājiǎng	V	to praise, to compliment	夸奖她，先别夸奖，夸奖菜做得好，谢谢你的夸奖，得到夸奖
夸	kuā	V	to praise	夸她
奖	jiǎng	V/N	to reward; prize	奖给他；得奖
7. 米饭	mǐfàn	N	(cooked) rice	做米饭，吃米饭
8. 饿	è	A	hungry	特别饿，有点儿饿，饿得很，还不饿
9. 满	mǎn	A	full, filled	满满的饭，坐满了人，写满了汉字
10. 碗	wǎn	N	bowl	饭碗，满满一碗，一碗饭，一碗水
11. 炒鸡丁	chǎojīdīng	N	stir-fried chicken cubes	一个炒鸡丁，一盘炒鸡丁
炒	chǎo	V	to stir-fry	炒饭，炒羊肉，炒大虾，炒蔬菜
鸡	jī	N	chicken	烤鸡，一只鸡
丁	dīng	N	small cube (dice) of meat or vegetables	肉丁
12. 开（饭馆）	kāi (fànguǎn)	V	to operate or run (a restaurant)	开公司，开商店，开网吧，开茶馆，开舞厅
13. 老板	lǎobǎn	N	boss, shopkeeper	当老板，公司老板，饭馆老板

14.	打工	dǎgōng	VO	to do odd jobs, to work for others	给他打工，给公司打工，在饭馆打工
15.	分工	fēngōng	V	to divide work	怎么分工，跟他分工
16.	合作	hézuò	V	to cooperate, to work together	互相合作，跟他们合作，分工合作
17.	华人	huárén	N	Chinese people, foreign citizens of Chinese origin	欧洲华人，海外华人
18.	必须	bìxū	Adv	must, have to	必须努力，必须多练习，必须登记
19.	毕业	bìyè	VO	to graduate	大学毕业，中学毕业，是北京大学毕业的，哪儿毕业的
20.	别扭	bièniu	A	awkward, uncomfortable	觉得别扭，看着别扭，有点儿别扭，这么别扭
21.	改	gǎi	V	to alter, to change, to correct	改错了，改句子，改习惯，改不了，终于改了
22.	究竟	jiūjìng	Adv	actually, exactly	究竟怎么了，究竟为什么，究竟在哪儿

注释　Notes

① 亲爱的，你累了一上午，饭终于做好了。

"Honey, you have been busy (cooking) the whole morning, and now lunch is finally ready."

"亲爱的" (often translated as "dear" in English) is generally used to address someone with whom the speaker has a close relationship. When used as the salutation in a letter, it is commonly applied to one's spouse or lover, parents, children, siblings or intimate friends. In Chinese, when writing a letter to someone for the first time or to someone that one does not know very well, "亲爱的" should not be used. (If necessary, one may use "尊敬的" instead. For example, "尊敬的经理先生" and "尊敬的张教授"). In spoken Chinese, "亲爱的" (translated as "my dear/darling/honey" in English) is rarely used, even among the beloved ones or between husband and wife.

② 你有技术，我懂管理，咱们一起干，这有什么不好？

"You have the skills, and I know about management. Let's work together. What's wrong with that?"

"这有什么不好？" is a rhetorical question, meaning "这样很好".

③ 我怎么了？

"What's wrong with me?"

Here, "我怎么了？" is in the tone of a rhetorical question, the implication being that "我做错什么了？" (Did I do anything wrong) or "我说错什么了？" (Did I say anything wrong).

🎧2　（二）

没有说出的"爱"

王小云给林娜讲了一个故事。

一个 12 岁的男孩儿和一个 13 岁的女孩儿同一年上初中。男孩儿和女孩儿都不太爱说话，他们常常跟几个好朋友一起学习，一起玩儿。女孩儿总是像姐姐一样管着男孩儿，男孩儿也非常愿意让她管。

三年以后，男孩儿和女孩儿都考上了高中。④ 男孩儿记着女孩儿的生日，给她寄去了一封信，祝她生日快乐。他怕女孩儿生气，不敢写上自己的名字。女孩儿给他回了信，也没有写自己的名字。高中比初中忙得多，她和他除了学习以外，没有想别的。

中学毕业了，他们已经是小伙子和大姑娘了。小伙子考上了北京的大学，姑娘考到上海的大学学外语。姑娘去上海的前一天晚上，小伙子来到了她家的门口,但他没敢敲门。⑤ 他,一个小伙子,去看一个姑娘,她家里人会怎么想?姑娘那天晚上也睡得很晚,她在等着跟他说"再见"。

一个月过去了,两个月过去了。姑娘想了很多办法,才打听到了小伙子在学校的地址。一天,小伙子突然收到一封信,是姑娘写来的!信上只有一句话:祝贺你开始大学生活。小伙子高兴得像疯了一样,他每天早上、中午、晚上都要在宿舍里读一遍。第二年,姑娘病了,要休息一年。她一个人回到家里,谁也没有告诉。小伙子一封一封的信寄到她学校,但都没有回信。她为什么不回信呢?姑娘究竟怎么了?小伙子一天比一天瘦了。一年以后,姑娘的病好了,又回到了学校,小伙子才等到了姑娘的回信。他们在信中谈生活、谈学习、谈世界大事,但是他们没有说过一个"爱"字。在小伙子的心里,姑娘是他的理想,是他的梦;他也能从姑娘平平常常的信里读懂她的心。小伙子比姑娘早一年毕业,他在忙着考研究生。姑娘因为实习,总也没有时间回家。

小伙子成了上海一所大学的研究生。那一年的暑假,他们终于见面了。小伙子看着这个又高

又美的姑娘，心里有很多话要说，但是一句也说不出来。他连跟姑娘握一握手也忘了。

那个暑假，他们天天在一起聊天儿，一起散步，一起去公园。一天，小伙子终于对姑娘说了，他心里有一个字，一个最珍贵的字。这个字跟着他到今天……

王小云说，这是三十多年前的故事了。故事里的姑娘是她妈妈，小伙子就是她爸爸。

生词 New Words

1. 初中	chūzhōng	N	junior middle school　上初中，读初中，初中毕业，初中生
初	chū	Pref	preliminary, initial, first
2. 高中	gāozhōng	N	senior middle school　上高中，读高中，高中毕业，高中生
3. 敢	gǎn	OpV	dare　不敢写上名字，不敢游泳，敢说汉语
4. 回信	huíxìn	VO/N	to write in reply; letter in reply　给他回了信，没有回信；等她的回信
5. 敲门	qiāo mén	V O	to knock at the door　没敢敲门，敲他家的门，请先敲门
6. 打听	dǎting	V	to inquire, to ask about (sth.)　打听消息，打听情况，打听一个人
7. 地址	dìzhǐ	N	address　他家的地址，学校地址，打听地址
8. 突然	tūrán	A	suddenly, unexpectedly　突然收到，突然的变化，突然的情况

9. 瘦	shòu	A	thin	瘦了，一天比一天瘦，瘦子
10. 谈	tán	V	to talk, to discuss	谈过去的事儿，谈工作，谈一谈
11. 心里	xīnli	N	in the heart, in (the) mind	在他的心里，心里想，记在心里
心	xīn	N	heart, mind, feeling	了解他的心，读懂她的心
12. 理想	lǐxiǎng	N/A	ideal	他的理想；理想的朋友，理想的工作，很理想，不太理想
13. 平常	píngcháng	A	ordinary, common	平常的信，平常的样子，平常的人
14. 研究生	yánjiūshēng	N	graduate student, postgraduate	读研究生，研究生毕业
15. 实习	shíxí	V	to practise, to do an internship	实习翻译，教育实习，实习医生
16. 暑假	shǔjià	N	summer vacation	那个暑假，放暑假，过暑假
17. 见面	jiànmiàn	VO	to meet, to see	第一次见面，没有见过面，见过一次面，跟他见面
面	miàn		face	
18. 握手	wòshǒu	VO	to shake hands	跟她握手，握了握手，热情地握手
握	wò	V	to hold, to clasp	

补充生词 Supplementary Words

1. 菜谱	càipǔ	N	cookbook	
2. 啰唆	luōsuo	A	long-winded, wordy	
3. 宁静	níngjìng	A	tranquil, peaceful, quiet	
4. 辞	cí	V	to resign, to quit	
5. 宁静致远	níngjìng zhì yuǎn	IE	to accomplish sth. lasting by leading a quiet life	

6. 温暖	wēnnuǎn	A	warm
7. 愚人节	Yúrén Jié	PN	April Fools' Day
8. 蓝色	lánsè	N	blue (colour)
9. 风衣	fēngyī	N	trench coat
10. 引起	yǐnqǐ	V	to give rise to, to cause, to arouse
11. 沉思	chénsī	V	to be lost in thought
12. 允许	yǔnxǔ	V	to allow, to permit
13. 痛苦	tòngkǔ	A	painful, suffering
14. 煮	zhǔ	V	to boil, to cook

注释　Notes

④ 三年以后，男孩儿和女孩儿都考上了高中。

"Three years later, both the boy and the girl passed the entrance examination and were admitted to a senior high school."

In this sentence, "考" means "to take the entrance examination". "考上" means "to have passed the entrance examination and been admitted to a school or a course". For example, "考上北京大学", "考上历史系" and "考上研究生".

⑤ 姑娘去上海的前一天晚上，小伙子来到了她家的门口，但他没敢敲门。

"On the night before the girl's departure for Shanghai, the boy came up to her front door, but did not dare to knock."

"VP/S-PP＋的＋前＋TW" indicates the time before a certain happening. For example, "他考上大学的前一年" (the year before he passed the entrance exam and was admitted to the university), "你到上海的前一星期" (the week before you arrive(d) in Shanghai) and "开车的前一分钟" (the minute before the train start(ed)).

二、练习 Exercises

练习 **与运用 Drills and Practice** 3

核心句 KEY SENTENCES

1. 女孩儿总是像姐姐一样管着男孩儿。

2. 你累了一上午，饭终于做好了。

3. 厨师必须是专业学校毕业的。

4. 姑娘究竟怎么了？

5. 小伙子一天比一天瘦了。

6. 这个菜比饭馆做的好得多。

7. 这不是谁给谁打工，而是咱们俩分工合作。

8. 姑娘去上海的前一天晚上，小伙子来到了她家的门口。

1. 熟读下列词组 Read the following phrases until you learn them by heart

（1）总是问　总是怕　总是担心　总是打工　总是那么着急　总是这么朴素
　　总也不回家　总也学不会　总也不下雨　总也没时间　总也看不见他

（2）终于做好了　终于明白了　终于见面了　　　终于过上好日子了
　　终于习惯了　终于解决了　终于研究出来了　终于干净了
　　终于瘦了　终于便宜了　终于热起来了　　终于安静下来了

（3）必须复习　必须多听多说　必须努力工作　必须是研究生　必须停下来
　　必须他去　必须自己回答　不必写得很多　不必回信　　　不必着急

（4）究竟去哪儿　究竟由谁买单　究竟考不考研究生
　　究竟谁参加　究竟多少钱一斤　究竟什么时间合适

究竟决定了没有　　　究竟哪家商店最便宜

（5）棒得多　　瘦得多　　慢得多　　满得多　　差得多　　能干得多

好吃得多　　稳定得多　　清楚得多　　困难得多　　大方得多　　珍贵得多

（6）一天比一天好　　一天比一天流利　　一天比一天能干　　一天比一天地道

一天比一天糟　　一天比一天凉快　　一天比一天好看　　一天比一天复杂

2. 句子练习　Sentence drills

A. 用所给词语完成句子

Complete the following sentences with the given words and expressions

总（是）

（1）他对工作很不认真，你每次找他帮助解决问题，他总_____。

（说要研究研究）

（2）他学习很努力，也很认真，他的成绩_____。

（全班第一）

（3）北京王府井大街_____。（那么热闹）

（4）他们俩在食堂_____，别人听了觉得很别扭。

（大声地说笑）

（5）他去了好几次北京，_____。

（没时间登长城）

终于

（1）这么多的作业，他　做完了　。（做完）

（2）他很早就想买这本书，今天他　买到了　。（买到）

（3）这个问题已经研究好几次了，这次　把它解决　。（把它解决）

（4）他很早就想参观兵马俑，今天来西安旅游，他　终于　看到了　。（看到）

（5）他打扫了一个上午，房间_____。（干净）

必须（不必）

（1）我们＿＿＿＿＿＿＿＿＿＿＿＿以前到火车站，才能坐上今天八点一刻

去广州的火车。

（2）你＿＿＿＿＿＿＿＿＿＿＿＿＿＿，才能学好外语。

（3）小燕子说＿＿＿＿＿＿＿＿＿＿＿，才能当大饭店里的厨师。

（4）车开不上去了，＿＿＿＿＿＿＿＿＿＿＿。

（5）您＿＿＿＿那么着急，他们一定会帮助您解决问题的。

jiejue

究竟

（1）他们提的意见＿＿＿＿＿＿＿＿＿＿＿？（对）

（2）小燕子做的菜＿＿＿＿＿＿＿＿＿＿＿？（好吃）

（3）我们班＿＿＿＿＿＿＿＿＿＿＿？（考口语）

（4）他＿＿＿＿究竟＿＿＿＿？（参加比赛）

（5）张经理＿＿＿＿＿＿＿＿＿＿？（回公司）

B. 用"一天比一天"改写句子

Rewrite the following sentences, using "一天比一天"

（1）现在是秋天了，上星期28度，昨天26度，今天只有24度了。

现在是秋天了，天气＿一天比一天冷＿。

（2）这儿的苹果真便宜，前天四块钱一斤，昨天是三块五，今天只卖三块

钱一斤了。

这儿的苹果＿一天比一天便宜＿。
（pian yi）

（3）他前天走了半个小时的路，昨天走了35分钟，明天他要走40分钟。

他走路的时间＿一天比一天远＿。

（4）这里吃的东西越来越贵。

这里吃的东西＿一天比一天贵＿。

（5）我们要学的生词越来越多了。

我们要学的生词＿一天比一天多＿。

C. 用 "不是……，而是……" 和所给的词语回答问题

Answer the following questions, using "不是……，而是……" and the words and expressions given

（1）这次口语考试林娜是不是第一名？（第二名）

<u>不是第一名而是第二名</u>。

（2）马大为暑假是去的泰山吧？（黄山）

<u>不是泰山而黄山</u>。

（3）你朋友是今年去悉尼留学吗？（明年）

<u>不是今年而是明年</u>。

（4）他是不是公司的经理？（工作人员）

<u>不是经理而是工作人员</u>。

（5）他是坐火车来的吗？（坐飞机）

<u>不是坐火车而是坐飞机</u>。

3. 根据课文回答问题 Answer the following questions according to the texts

（1）马大为为什么总是夸奖小燕子、感谢小燕子？小燕子觉得怎么样？

（2）马大为对结婚以后的生活有什么打算？

（3）小燕子对马大为的打算有什么看法？

（4）小燕子为什么不喜欢听大为叫她 "亲爱的"？

（5）小伙子（王小云的爸爸）和姑娘（王小云的妈妈）是什么时候开始认识的？

（6）在上初中的时候，小伙子和姑娘是什么关系？

（7）姑娘过生日时，小伙子给姑娘写信为什么不写自己的名字？姑娘回信为什么也不写名字？

（8）姑娘高中毕业以后，考上了哪儿的大学？她学习什么专业？

（9）姑娘去上海的前一天晚上，小伙子为什么不敢敲她家的门？

（10）两人考上大学以后，是谁先写了信？

（11）后来小伙子为什么收不到姑娘的信？

（12）他们是什么时候再见面的？

（13）小伙子是什么时候说出他对姑娘的"爱"的？

4. 会话练习　Conversation practice

会话常用语　IDIOMATIC EXPRESSIONS IN CONVERSATION

这有什么不好？　(What's wrong with that?)

这不挺好吗？　(Isn't that good enough?)

我怎么了？　(What's wrong with me?)

特别是……　(particularly, ...)

还有，……　(furthermore, ...)

【表示必须　Expressing necessity】

（1）A：张师傅，我想向您请教一个问题：怎样才能做好中国菜？

　　B：这个问题不是一两句话就说得清楚的。不过有一点我可以告诉你，做菜也是一种艺术，必须认真地学习。要多读菜谱（càipǔ），自己还得多练。我当了三十多年的厨师了，现在还在研究怎么做新菜。必须不断地研究，这样才能进步。

　　A：还应该向有名的厨师学习吧？看他们是怎么做菜的。我想跟您学，可以吗？

（2）A：都八点了，小英还没回家，她去哪儿了？

　　B：你别着急，孩子可能去爷爷家了。

　　A：给爷爷打个电话问一下吧。

　　B：不必了，一会儿她就回来了。

　　C：爸爸、妈妈，我回来了。

　　A：你去哪儿了，这么晚才回来？以后不能按时回来，必须先给家里打个电话。

　　C：我都这么大了，你们不必为我担心。

【夸奖与回答　Praising and responding to praise】

（1）A：这条裙子是你自己做的？你做得真棒，你真能干！

　　　B：哪里，比你买的这条差得远呢。

　　　A：谁说的？样子比我这条好看得多，颜色也选得好极了。

（2）A：今天主要是请大家聚一聚，没有什么菜。

　　　B：你们准备了这么多菜，真太客气了。

　　　A：都是很一般的，我太太也不会做菜。

　　　B：菜的味道都很好，特别是这个炒大虾，这么好吃，是怎么做的？

　　　A：她是看菜谱学的。喜欢就多吃点儿，来，再来点儿炒鸡丁。

　　　B：谢谢，我吃得太多了，真吃不下去了。

【抱怨与解释　Complaining and giving an explanation】

　　　A：你为什么总是不高兴的样子？

　　　B：没有啊，我怎么了？

　　　A：你怎么一开口就说别人不好？你真是一天比一天啰唆（luōsuo）了。

　　　B：我不是说谁不好，而是告诉你这件事儿的经过。这有什么不好？

　　　A：我听着觉得别扭。别总说这些不愉快的事儿，行不行？

　　　B：我想跟你商量商量，帮我想出个解决的办法。

　　　A：我可不干。这是你们单位的事儿，我不了解情况。

5. 交际练习　Communication exercises

(1) Although Wang Xiaoyun's father and mother had been in love for a long time, they never used the word "love" when talking to each other. Why?

(2) Tell a favourite story of yours, using Text 2 as a model.

　　After the oral presentation, write down what you have said about the above two topics.

阅读 与复述 Reading Comprehension and Paraphrasing

🎧4 宁静（níngjìng）咖啡屋

我辞（cí）掉了公司的工作，自己开了一家小小的咖啡屋。古人说"宁静致远（níngjìng zhì yuǎn）"，我的名字也叫宁静，所以我就把自己开的咖啡屋叫做"宁静咖啡屋"。咖啡屋的桌子、椅子、杯子和墙壁都是咖啡色的，屋里又温暖（wēnnuǎn）又清静。

今年西方愚人节（Yúrén Jié）那天，晚上9点多钟，来了很多客人，他就是那个时候进来的。我现在还记得，他穿一件深蓝色（lánsè）的风衣（fēngyī），选了窗户旁边的一个座位，要了一杯咖啡。在那么多的客人中，他特别引起（yǐnqǐ）我的注意，因为他长得很帅，也很有文化人的特色。

那天，他好像不是在享用咖啡，而是在欣赏墙上挂着的那幅"宁静致远"的字画。可能是他喜欢上我们咖啡屋"宁静"的风格，愚人节后，他差不多每天晚上9点都来。他总是穿着深蓝色的风衣，选那个窗户边的座位坐下，再向我招招手，要一杯咖啡，就坐在那儿静静地沉思（chénsī）。每次走的时候，总要对我说一声"谢谢"。

夏天来了，天气一天比一天热了，他换下了深蓝色的风衣，穿了一件深蓝色的衬衫走了进来。这一次，他又要了一杯咖啡，然后问我："您就是宁静小姐吧？"我说："是的，您贵姓？"他笑了笑，给了我一张名片，没有再说什么，然后就静静地喝他的咖啡。这次以后，他有两个多月没来"宁静咖啡屋"了，可是每天晚上9点，我都在等着他。虽然我对他还不太了解，但心里已把他当成了自己很好的朋友。咖啡屋的两个服务员也常对我说："老板，你是不是爱上他了？"我只是笑了笑，对她们说："谁爱上他了？别开玩笑。"我自己也说不清楚，是不是真的喜欢上他了。有一天，我突然收到了一个包裹，是一把咖啡壶，还有一封短信：

> 宁静：
>
> 　　请允许（yǔnxǔ）我这样称呼你。谢谢你这几个月的咖啡，你的咖啡和你们的咖啡屋让我得到了平静。我以前的女朋友也叫宁静，不过，现在她已经不是我的女朋友了，而是一个大老板的太太。宁静，是你的咖啡让我从感情的痛苦（tòngkǔ）中走了出来。我送给你一把咖啡壶，这是我去欧洲时买的，希望你喜欢。

看完信后，我又惊喜又担心。惊喜的是他终于给我寄来了信；担心的是他可能不会再来了，因为他已经不再为过去的爱情痛苦，以后也不用到咖啡屋来了。

那天晚上，我用他送的那把咖啡壶煮（zhǔ）咖啡。9 点，他突然来了，这次他微笑着走到我的面前，对我说："你好，这是一把不错的咖啡壶吧？用它煮咖啡，味道一定很好。"我也开玩笑地说："味道好极了，你要一杯吗？"他笑着说："当然，这么香的咖啡，这么热情的服务，去哪儿找这样的宁静，我怎么能不要呢……"

三、语法　Grammar

词语 例解　Word Usage and Examples

1　总（是）

The adverb "总（是）" means "always, invariably", expressing the idea that things or actions remain unchanged.

总（是）+ V/A

　　每天上班，他总是来得最早，走得最晚。

　　他总是不愿意多说自己的成绩。

　　丁力波对朋友总是那么热情。

　　他写的小说的女主角总是又美丽又能干。

"总（+也）+ 没 / 不 + V/A" is used in negative sentences, for example,

　　老王找小张找了好几天，总也没有找到他。

　　他很早就想回国看看父母，总也没有时间。

　　他生病很长时间了，总也不好。

2 终于

The adverb "终于" is used as an adverbial, indicating that an expected result has finally been attained. The verb (phrase) following "终于" must consist of two or more syllables.

终于 + V

　　饭终于做好了。

　　他们终于登上了万里长城。

　　他研究了很长时间，这个问题终于解决了。

终于 + A

　　她的病终于好了。

　　书架上的书终于整齐了。

Adjectives applicable in this construction are limited to the ones indicating a change in the state.

3 必须

The adverb "必须" indicates an inevitability in fact or in reason.

必须 + V/A

这么多人在等他，他必须马上回来。

他病得这么厉害，必须住院。

我们是服务员，对客人必须热情。

必须 + S-PP

这事儿别人办不了，必须您自己去。

今天的练习必须每个人都做一遍。

"必须 + S-PP" is used to emphasize the subject.

In the negative sentences, " 不必 " is usually used (One cannot say " 不必须 "), for example,

您这么忙，就不必参加了。

你不必着急，孩子一定会回来的。

明天你不必去了。

4 究竟

Used in questions, the adverb " 究竟 " gives emphasis to the interrogative tone.

究竟 + V/A

这位姑娘究竟怎么了？她总是很生气的样子。

你究竟参加不参加他们的婚礼？

月亮上究竟有没有生命？

这道题做得究竟对不对？

究竟 + S-PP

究竟谁去？

究竟哪家饭馆最好？

"究竟 + S-PP" is often used to form questions about the subject.

句子 结构　Sentence Structure

1 用"A + 得多"表示程度　"A + 得多" denoting a degree or an extent

Placed after an adjective and "得", the adverb "多" emphasizes the result of a comparison.

S + 比 + NP + A + 得多

> 今天我们的生活比过去幸福得多。
>
> 这个炒鸡丁比饭馆做的好得多。
>
> 他的中文书比我的多得多。

2 一天比一天 + A　The construction "一天比一天 + A"

The construction "一天比一天 + A" means "being more... with each passing day", which is used as an adverbial to indicate a comparison. Similar to "越来越" (more and more...), it shows that something intensifies with the passage of time. For example,

> 你做菜的技术一天比一天好。
>
> 大家手里的钱一天比一天多了。
>
> 他的身体一天比一天差。

3 不是……，而是……　The construction "不是……，而是……"

This pair of conjunctive phrases means "not..., but...". It is used to connect and contrast two words, phrases or clauses. It emphasizes the part affirmed rather than the part negated. One may also put the adverb "并" before "不是". For example,

> 这次足球比赛第一名，不是 A 班，而是 D 班。
>
> 在中国北方，节约用水不是一个小问题，而是一个大问题。
>
> 不是我不想参加明天的活动，而是我很忙，参加不了。
>
> 他现在不是老师了，而是爱华公司的经理。

四、字与词 Chinese Characters and Words

1 集中识字 Learn the characters of the same radicals

纟：终 练 经 绍 结 纸 给 绩 继 续 绒 绝 线 红 绿
　　络 级 纪

扌：扭 打 握 抢 护 把 报 挂 授 拐 排 提 抓 撞 拍
　　技 换 挣 摇 挺 抬 指 批 接 搞 按 摆 搬 括
　　

讠：谈 认 识 让 访 议 译 证 词 记 请 说 诉 谢 读 诞
　　话 讲 评 谦 诗 试 谁 谊 课 该 订 设 语 诚
　　调

2 词语联想 Learn the following groups of associated words

学校　　　小学　　　中学　　　初中 高中　　专科学校　大学

工业大学　农业大学　科技大学　学院 医学院　商学院　　工学院

语言学院　外语学院　外交学院　财经学院

教师　　老师　　教授　　讲师　　助教　　工作人员

学生　　小学生　中学生　大学生　研究生　博士生　留学生

教室　　实验室　阅览室　图书馆　宿舍　食堂　　操场　　体育馆

健身房　网球场　足球场　篮球场　排球场

上课　　下课　　学习　　复习　　自习　　预习　　练习

做练习　听录音　念课文　讲语法　练口语

写汉字　看报纸　用电脑　上网

Changes in Chinese People's Views on Love and Marriage

Since the founding of the People's Republic of China, Chinese people's views on love and marriage have undergone several stages of development.

The first marriage law in China came out shortly after the founding of the People's Republic of China. At that time, most marriages were arranged by parents with the help of matchmakers. When a matchmaker, entrusted by the parents, found that a boy and a girl are suitable for each other, she would arrange a meeting for them and their parents. Marriages then were largely under geographical restriction, and people rarely had any dating relationships before marriage.

With the advancement of China's reform and opening-up policy, Chinese people became more open-minded, and matchmakers were no more the only people to seek help from. In early 1980s, matrimonial agencies and lonely-hearts ads began to appear in China, and introduction-based marriages became the main trend.

Since the 1990s, more and more young people have started to pursue the freedom of marriage. They would choose the boy or girl of their own heart and bring him/her home to see their parents after a certain period of time when the relationship is considered mature enough. The parents would generally respect their children's choices.

In the 21st century, as people's minds become more pluralistic each day, their views on love and marriage also break through the traditions and display an increase in diversity. There even have emerged some novel notions such as "flash marriage" and "trial marriage".

In terms of age, people got married younger in the past. Now, young people increasingly want a "late marriage". There are a lot of 30-

year-olds who haven't got married, mostly people with high educational backgrounds. In the countryside, however, people still get married at basically the same age as they did in the past 20 years.

Marriages in old times were generally not based on love, but on common objectives of life. Affection would grow between the couple during the time they got along with each other and could usually last a really long time. Divorces were rare then. Today, both parties in a marriage pay more attention to material factors as well as affection, some even considering material conditions the most important thing in marriage. This is caused by the increasing desire for material comfort among young people on the one hand and the pressures of life after marriage, especially in big cities, on the other. On the contrary, there are also some young people who are much too idealistic and hold a set of strict standards when picking a mate. Most of these people are talented, intelligent and financially well-off, but their failure in finding the ideal partner gradually makes them the so-called "leftover men and women".

第四十课

Lesson 40

"半边天" 和 "全职太太"

Career women and housewives

Do you know what "half the sky" means? As an expression often heard in mainland China, it refers to women and the importance of their social roles. Equality between men and women is a topic that has been debated for over a thousand years. Today it is still an issue. Let's observe Lu Yuping interviewing Ms. Chen and Wang Xiaoyun about this matter.

一、课文 Texts

5 （一）

bàn biān   quán zhí
"半边天" 和 "全职太太"

陆雨平：有人提出妇女结婚以后，特别是有了孩子以后，应该回到家里做 "全职太太"，因为她们要照顾孩子，要做家务。对这个问题，你们有什么看法？

陈老师：这个主意很可能是男人想出来的吧？妇女经过了多少个世纪的努力，终于从家里走出来，得到工作的权利，而且能发挥 "半边天" 的作用。[①] 这是社会的进步。现在怎么又要让妇女回到厨房去呢？

陆雨平：这不只是一些男人的看法，有些妇女也有这样的看法。大家都知道，城市里几乎都是双职工的家庭，丈夫和妻子每天都要在外边工作，他们没时间照顾孩子。没有一个母亲不关心自己的孩子，要是妇女回家，孩子的教育问题就可以解决得更好。这不是看不起妇女，而是为了更好地发挥妇女的作用。

王小云：我认为，照顾孩子和做家务不只是妇女的事儿，也是男人的事儿。应该男女都一样：要是愿意回家照顾孩子，就回家照顾孩子；要是愿意出来工作，就出来工作。

陆雨平：如果大家都愿意回家照顾孩子，不愿意出来工作，怎么办？

王小云：这不可能。不会没有人愿意出来工作。

陆雨平：有人还认为，中国人口太多，就业的问题很大。要是妇女回家，这个问题就比较容易解决了。

陈老师：为了解决就业问题，就必须让妇女回家吗？这不公平。我觉得，现在首先要解决就业中的男女平等问题。比如说，有的工作男女都可以干，可是一些单位只要男的，不要女的。我认为这是很不对的。

陆雨平：你不认为有的工作男人来做更合适吗？

王小云：当然有，但是也有的工作妇女比男人做得更好。重要的是，男女都应该有公平竞争的机会。

陆雨平：最后，我们不能不谈到这个问题：陈老师，您认为究竟怎样才能实现男女平等呢？

陈老师：只有在各个方面男女都享受同样的权利，男女才能平等。

陆雨平：谢谢你们接受我的访问。

生词 New Words

1. 半边天	bànbiāntiān	N	half the sky, women of the new society
天	tiān	N	sky
2. 全职	quánzhí	A	full-time 全职太太，全职教授，全职工作人员
职	zhí		post, occupation, profession
3. 妇女	fùnǚ	N	woman 妇女是半边天，妇女问题，妇女的事儿
4. 照顾	zhàogù	V	to look after, to take care of 照顾孩子，照顾老人，照顾父母，照顾别人
5. 家务	jiāwù	N	housework, household chores 做家务，忙家务，很多的家务
务	wù		affair, business
6. 男人	nánrén	N	man, male 男人的事儿，男人能做的工作
7. 权利	quánlì	N	right 工作的权利，受教育的权利，批评的权利，选择的权利，享受权利
8. 发挥	fāhuī	V	to bring into play 发挥特点，发挥特色，发挥得好
9. 作用	zuòyòng	N	role, effect, function 发挥"半边天"的作用，发挥着重要的作用，发挥妇女的作用，有作用，没有作用
10. 社会	shèhuì	N	society 社会进步，在社会上，社会问题，了解社会，研究社会
11. 不只	bùzhǐ	Conj	not only 不只是一些男人的看法，不只有这些问题
12. 几乎	jīhū	Adv	nearly, almost 几乎都是，几乎都有，几乎忘了，几乎没有买到

13. 双职工	shuāngzhígōng	N	working couple, double-income couple
			双职工家庭，父母是双职工
双	shuāng	A	two, both, double 双喜，双语，双亲
职工	zhígōng	N	staff members, workers 公司的职工，学
			校的职工，女职工
14. 家庭	jiātíng	N	family, household 在家庭里，家庭事
			务，家庭问题，幸福家庭
15. 要是	yàoshi	Conj	if, suppose 要是愿意回家，要是愿意出
			来工作
16. 看不起	kànbuqǐ	IE	to look down upon 看不起妇女，看不起
			别人，看不起自己
17. 为了	wèile	Prep	for, in order to 为了更好地发挥妇女的作
			用，为了实现自己的理想
18. 男女	nánnǚ	N	men and women 男女都一样，男女都可
			以干
男	nán	A	man, male 男生，男老师，男人
女	nǚ	A	woman, female 女生，女老师，女人
19. 就业	jiùyè	VO	to be employed, to obtain employment
			为了解决就业问题，就业不容易
20. 公平	gōngpíng	A	fair, just 公平的决定，公平地解决，办
			得很公平，这不公平
21. 平等	píngděng	A	equal 男女平等的问题，平等的权利，民
			族平等，国家平等
22. 单位	dānwèi	N	unit (as an organization, a department, a
			division, a section, etc.) 工作单位，一些
			单位，在哪个单位工作，是哪个单位的
23. 竞争	jìngzhēng	V	to compete 公平竞争，努力竞争，技术
			竞争，没有竞争

24. 机会	jīhuì	N	chance, opportunity 公平竞争的机会，受教育的机会，有机会跟大家谈谈
25. 只有	zhǐyǒu	Conj	only 只有在各个方面男女都享受同样的权利，男女才能平等
26. 方面	fāngmiàn	N	aspect, respect 很多方面，各个方面，在技术方面，在就业方面
27. 同样	tóngyàng	A	same, equal 同样的权利，同样的机会，同样的地位

注释 Notes

① 妇女经过了多少个世纪的努力，终于从家里走出来，得到工作的权利，而且能发挥"半边天"的作用。

"After many centuries' effort, women have finally obtained the right to work outside the home and are able to play the role of 'half the sky'."

"多少" in the phrase "多少个世纪" is not an interrogative word, but a word expressing an indefinite number/amount. In declarative sentences, the word "多少" sometimes means "many, much", for example,

他用了多少个小时，才完成了这个作品啊！

我以前买过多少本小说，可是现在一本也没有了。

我不知跟他说过多少次，他总是记不住。

"半边天" means "women can hold up 'half the sky'". It is a metaphor for the tremendous strength of women and their important roles in society. In other words, women are equal to men.

🎧 6 （二）

谈谈中国妇女的地位

各位老师，各位同学：

我很高兴有机会跟大家谈谈中国妇女的地位问题。这是一个很大的问题，我想从四个方面简单地谈一谈。

首先，我要谈一下中国妇女的社会地位。

中国人常说妇女是"半边天"。"半边天"是什么意思呢？就是妇女几乎担负着一半的社会工作。她们跟男人一样，对社会的进步和国家的发展发挥着重要的作用。在全中国的职工中，女职工占百分之四十。② 现在中国既有女部长、女外交官、女经理，又有女科学家、女教授、女画家、女诗人……一般地说，男人能做的工作没有妇女不能做的。有的工作，比如纺织工人、护士，几乎都是妇女；中小学教师，大学里的外语老师，也是女的比男的多。大家都知道，在中国两千多年的封建社会中，妇女没有社会地位。她们一辈子要服从自己的父母、丈夫和儿子。③ 她们没有受教育的权利，也不能走出家门到外边去工作，只能在家里做家务，照顾丈夫和孩子。现在情况不同了，妇女能发挥"半边天"的作用，在社会上有了跟男子平等的地位。这是中国社会的进步。

第二，中国妇女在家庭里的地位。

一般地说，妇女只有社会地位提高了，在家庭里的地位才能提高。她们在外边有自己的工作和经济收入，在家里就有了平等的地位。过去，家里的大事常常由丈夫决定，现在丈夫要跟妻子商量。过去，家务事总是由妻子一个人来做，④ 现在丈夫在家里也要发挥"半边天"的作用。很多家庭的家务事都有了分工：常常是丈夫买菜，妻子做饭；丈夫打扫房间，妻子洗衣服；丈夫管孩子的学习，妻子管孩子的吃穿。⑤ 有的外国朋友看到中国男人会做菜，觉得很奇怪。要是你生活在中国人的家里，就会发现丈夫每天也要下厨房，他们的做菜技术就是这样练出来的。当然，总的来说家务事妇女要比男人干得多，而且不做家务的丈夫现在也还有。

第三，职业妇女的困难。

职业妇女在外边担负一定的工作，在家里又担负很重的家务。她们既要做一个好的工作人员，又要做一个好妻子、好母亲，所以生活很不容易，比男人辛苦得多。有的女职工说，一天二十四小时，除了吃饭睡觉以外，几乎没有一分钟是她自己的！她们没有时间学习，没有休闲活动。家庭和事业的矛盾是职业妇女很难解决的问题。

最后我要谈的问题是，现在男女已经平等了吗？

很多中国妇女认为，现在在一些方面还没有完全实现男女平等。比如在就业方面，有的地方对妇女还很不公平，妇女做同样的工作，得到的报酬没有男人高。在一些农村，女孩儿受教育的机会比男孩儿少得多；在科学家、教授、经理中，妇女还非常少。这些情况不但中国有，世界很多地方也都有。总的来说，为了完全实现男女平等，我们还有很长的路要走。

谢谢大家。

生词 New Words

1. 地位	dìwèi	N	position, status	妇女的地位，社会地位，平等的地位
2. 担负	dānfù	V	to bear, to shoulder	担负一半的工作，担负很重的家务
担	dān	V	to carry	担责任
负	fù	V	to shoulder	负责任
3. 占	zhàn	V	to make up, to account for	占百分之四十，占一半，占多少
4. 部长	bùzhǎng	N	minister	教育部长，文化部长，外交部长
5. 纺织	fǎngzhī	V	spinning and weaving, textile	纺织公司，纺织品
6. 工人	gōngrén	N	worker	纺织工人
7. 护士	hùshi	N	nurse	医院的护士，女护士
8. 封建	fēngjiàn	N	feudal	封建社会，封建经济，封建国家

9. 服从	fúcóng	V	to obey, to submit to	服从父母，服从丈夫，服从大家的决定
10. 事业	shìyè	N	cause, undertaking	个人的事业，教育事业，国家的事业
11. 矛盾	máodùn	N	contradiction	家庭和事业的矛盾，丈夫和妻子的矛盾
12. 完全	wánquán	Adv	completely, wholly	完全实现男女平等，完全了解，完全习惯
13. 报酬	bàochou	N	reward, pay	得到的报酬，打工的报酬，工作的报酬

补充生词 Supplementary Words

1. 婚姻	hūnyīn	N	marriage
2. 建筑	jiànzhù	N/V	building, architecture; to construct, to build
3. 伊斯兰	Yīsīlán	PN	Islam
4. 黄牛	huángniú	N	ox, cattle
5. 草房	cǎofáng	N	thatched cottage
6. 欠	qiàn	V	to owe
7. 生产队长	shēngchǎn duìzhǎng		production team leader
8. 勇敢	yǒnggǎn	A	brave
9. 自信	zìxìn	A	self-confident
10. 粮食	liángshi	N	grain, cereals, food (provisions)
11. 副业	fùyè	N	sideline, side occupation
12. 赚	zhuàn	V	to make a profit, to gain
13. 赔	péi	V	to stand a loss, to lose

14. 激烈	jīliè	A	intense, fierce
15. 口袋	kǒudai	N	pocket
16. 培训	péixùn	V	to train
17. 职称	zhíchēng	N	professional title

注释　Notes

② 在全中国的职工中，女职工占百分之四十。

"Women comprise forty percent of all the workers in China."

The verb "占" is often followed by fractions, percentages and other numbers that indicate the proportion of the whole that the subject accounts for, for example,

中国人口占世界人口的五分之一。

我们班女同学占一半。

③ 她们一辈子要服从自己的父母、丈夫和儿子。

"They had to obey their parents, husband and sons all their lives."

In Chinese feudal society, women had to abide by the moral standard "未嫁从父，既嫁从夫，夫死从子" (obedience to father before marriage, to husband after marriage and to son after the husband's death). These were called "三从" (the three obediences), which formed a feudal ethical code that bound and restrained the behaviour of women.

④ 过去，家务事总是由妻子一个人来做。

"In the past, household chores were done by the wife alone."

⑤ 丈夫管孩子的学习，妻子管孩子的吃穿。

"The husband is responsible for the children's studies and the wife for their food and clothing."

Here, "吃穿" refers to "everyday life", for example,

每个月吃穿花的钱不算多。

现在一些地方的人吃穿问题还没有很好地解决。

二、练习 Exercises

练习 与运用 **Drills and Practice**   7

核心句 KEY SENTENCES

1. 城市里几乎都是双职工的家庭。
2. 为了解决就业问题，就必须让妇女回家吗？
3. 在全中国的职工中，女职工占百分之四十。
4. 没有一个母亲不关心自己的孩子。
5. 只有在各个方面男女都享受同样的权利，男女才能平等。
6. 要是你生活在中国人的家里，就会发现丈夫每天也要下厨房。

---

1. 熟读下列词组 Read the following phrases until you learn them by heart

（1）照顾有困难的同学　照顾不同的生活习惯　照顾得很好

（2）几乎都是双职工　几乎把积蓄都花完了　几乎把这件事忘了

几乎没办成　几乎被汽车撞上　几乎忙了一天

几乎都坏了　几乎全班同学都参加了

（3）为了发挥妇女的作用　为了解决就业问题　为了孩子们的幸福

为了保护环境　为了发展国家的经济　为了帮助朋友

为了学习汉语　为了了解中国的文化

（4）参加竞争　跟那家公司竞争　在很多方面竞争

为考上有名的大学竞争

（5）在学习方面　　在工作方面　　在生活方面　　在经济方面

在环境保护方面　在家庭教育方面　在照顾孩子方面　在报酬方面

在哪些方面　　　在各个方面

（6）担负很重要的工作　担负教练工作　担负父母的生活费

认真地担负　　　　不敢担负

（7）占五分之三　占三分之二　占百分之七十　占百分之九十八

占一半　　　占多少　　　占几分之几　　占百分之几

（8）在男人中　　在职工中　　在科学家、教授、经理中　　在社会中

在家庭中　　在沙漠中　　在婚礼中　　在事业中　　　在矛盾中

在练习中　　在实习中　　在访问中　　在合作中　　　在竞争中

2. 句子练习　Sentence drills

A. 用所给词语完成句子

Complete the following sentences with the given words and expressions

几乎

（1）昨天去看足球比赛的人多极了，我们班的同学＿＿＿＿＿＿＿＿。（去）

（2）在我们学校，教外语的老师＿＿＿＿＿＿＿＿＿＿＿＿＿。（女的）

（3）为了买房子，他＿＿＿＿＿＿把一辈子的积蓄＿＿＿＿＿＿＿。（花）

（4）现在的城里人＿＿＿＿＿＿＿＿＿＿，男的女的都忙工作，实在没有

很多时间照顾家庭。（双职工）

（5）星期六回北京的车票很不好买，我＿＿＿＿＿＿＿＿＿＿＿。（回不去）

为了

（1）＿＿＿＿＿＿＿＿＿＿＿＿，妇女就应该回家做家务吗？（就业）

（2）＿＿＿＿＿＿＿＿＿＿＿＿，马大为决定来中国留学。（文化）

（3）＿＿＿＿＿＿＿＿＿＿＿＿，他们都在认真准备。（比赛）

（4）＿＿＿＿＿＿＿＿＿＿＿＿，我们就应该更快地发展教育事业。（经济）

（5）＿＿＿＿＿＿＿＿＿＿＿＿，我们都要重视环境保护的工作。（人类自己）

在……方面

（1）_____，老师和同学对我帮助很大，所以我的口语进步很快。

（2）_____，问题不大，我已经向银行贷款了。

（3）_____，主要由她丈夫管，她只管孩子的吃穿。

（4）_____，男女还不完全平等，有些工作女的也可以做，可是他们不用女的，只用男的。

（5）_____，妇女比男人的机会少得多。

在……中

（1）_____，几乎看不到植物。

（2）_____，新娘常常要向客人敬酒。

（3）_____，她常得到公司老板的夸奖。

（4）_____，男的常常比女的多。

（5）_____，他们互相帮助、互相合作。

（实习　沙漠　婚礼　事业　所有职工）

B. 用两次否定回答问题

Answer the following questions, using double negation

不……不……

（1）他去黄山旅游吗？

他最爱好游览名胜古迹，_____。（会）

（2）马大为知道明天口语考试吗？

这事儿是他告诉我的，_____。（可能）

（3）小王参加明天的聚会吗？

明天的聚会是为小王举行的，_____。（能）

没有……不……

（1）这件事别人知道吗？

这件事我们班的同学_____。

（2）你喜欢唱这个歌儿吗？

这个歌儿年轻人_____。

（3）你会不会骑自行车？

在我们那儿，_____。

C. 用"要是……，就……"完成句子

Complete the following sentences, using "要是……，就……"

（1）要是事先没有说好由谁请客，_____。

（2）要是在城市里办婚礼，_____。

（3）_____，我就去银行贷款。

（4）_____，你就能看到世界第一大坝了。

D. 用"只有……，才……"完成句子

Complete the following sentences, using "只有……，才……"

（1）只有保护好环境，_____。

（2）只有到了黄山，_____。

（3）_____，才能很好地研究中国文学。

（4）_____，才能练好书法。

3. 根据课文回答问题 Answer the following questions according to the texts

（1）陆雨平为什么要来访问陈老师和王小云？

（2）"半边天"是什么意思？

（3）什么是"双职工"家庭？

（4）在全中国的职工中，有多少是女职工？

（5）哪些工作几乎都是由妇女来做的？

（6）为什么说在中国两千多年的封建社会中，妇女没有社会地位？

（7）为什么说现在中国妇女的社会地位提高了？

（8）中国妇女在家庭里的地位有什么变化？

（9）现在中国的男人也做家务吗？

（10）职业妇女的矛盾是什么？

（11）现在男女已经平等了吗？

（12）课文（二）是从哪几方面来谈妇女问题的？

4. 会话练习　Conversation practice

会话常用语　IDIOMATIC EXPRESSIONS IN CONVERSATION

总的来说 (Generally speaking, ...)

重要的是 (The important thing is ...)

大家都知道 (As you all know, ...)

这不公平。(This is not fair.)

有人认为 (Some people think that ...)

对这个问题，你们有什么看法？
(What's your opinions about this problem?)

你不认为……吗？　(Don't you think that ...?)

【表示强调　Expressing emphasis】

A：大家决定明天去西郊玩儿。

B：西郊有什么好？那儿连山也没有。

A：你一次也没去过，怎么知道那儿不好？那儿的植物园特别好，学植物的没有一个不爱去。

B：我就不喜欢去西郊。

A：明天我们班的同学都去，你可不能不去。

【采访 Interviewing people】

A：很高兴终于有机会来访问您。

B：我也很高兴能跟记者朋友们聊聊。

A：我们知道您很忙，正在研究妇女就业问题。这个问题大家都很关心。有人认为……对这个问题，您是怎么看的？

B：这个问题提得很好。简单地说，……

A：您不认为还有别的矛盾吗？

B：当然有。比如说……，但重要的是，……

A：在这方面，您能不能多谈谈？

B：好，总的来说，……

A：您这么一讲，这个问题就很清楚了。让我们再谈下一个问题。

【演讲 Making a speech】

很高兴今天有机会跟大家谈谈妇女的婚姻（hūnyīn）问题。因为时间的关系，我只想从三个方面简单地谈谈我的看法。欢迎大家批评。

首先，我谈第一个问题，……

我谈的第二个问题是，……

最后我谈一下第三个问题，……

总的来说，……

谢谢大家。

5. 交际练习 Communication exercises

(1) Summarize the advantages and disadvantages of women staying at home as discussed in the texts. What ethical issues are involved?

(2) Deliver a speech on the topic "An Ideal Woman".

After the oral presentation, write a short essay on either of the topics above.

阅读 与复述 Reading Comprehension and Paraphrasing

🎧8 女农民企业家

　　从河南省新乡市向西走 30 公里，就到了南小村。人们好像走进了世界建筑（jiànzhù）博览会，看到各种风格不同的建筑，有欧式的、美式的、伊斯兰（Yīsīlán）式的……不过，这不是在城市，而是在农村。建立这个"农村都市"的是南小村的农民，他们办的企业叫"京华实业公司"。全村有 73 户农民，几乎家家住的都是二层小楼。他们的总经理是位妇女，她叫林志华。

　　1972 年，这个村只有四头老黄牛（huángniú），三间破草房（cǎofáng），一辆旧马车，再有就是欠（qiàn）银行 8,000 元的贷款。那时候，管理村里工作的是生产队长（shēngchǎn duìzhǎng）。老队长确实没有办法了，他不想再干了。在这位老队长以前，村里的男人几乎都当过队长，谁也不愿意再担负这个困难的工作了。在这种情况下，林志华，一个普通的农村妇女，勇敢（yǒnggǎn）地站了出来。她很自信（zìxìn）地说："男的不干，我们女人干！为了改变咱们这个穷村，我愿意当队长！"这一年，她带着大家艰苦努力，终于让村里的人吃上了饱饭。他们用了三年的时间，把粮食（liángshi）亩产量提高到了 800 多公斤。她想，只靠种地，农民是富不起来的；只有搞副业（fùyè），农民才能挣更多的钱。可是，当时有人不愿意向银行贷款搞副业，林志华对大家说："赚（zhuàn）了钱是大家的，赔（péi）了钱算我个人的。"靠着 500 元贷款，他们办起了一个小小的工厂，林志华只留 5% 的劳动力种地，让 95% 的劳动力去搞副业。像滚雪球一样，几年以后，他们先后办起了十二个乡镇企业。

　　全国乡镇企业竞争非常激烈（jīliè），林志华把不赚钱的小厂停了，开始搞第三产业，在村里发展旅游业。现在村里的宾馆、游乐园、饭店每天都能赚不少的钱。从搞第一产业到发展第三产业，林志华确实表现出了一位女企业家的才华。

　　林志华常对大家说："我的理想很明确，就是要让农民富起来。我们农民不但要'口袋（kǒudai）富'，而且还要'脑袋富'。"林志华特别重视提高村民的教育水平。十多年来，公司跟大学合作办职工培训（péixùn）班。在全公司职工中，现在有初、中、高级职称（zhíchēng）的人占50%以上。为了让下一代能受到很好的教育，京华实业公司拿出2,500万元人民币用在孩子的教育方面，办起了幼儿园、小学和中学。林志华说："发展农业就要靠科学和教育。"

三、语法　Grammar

词语 例解　Word Usage and Examples

1　几乎

The adverb "几乎" means "very close to, almost" and is synonymous with "差不多". It is frequently used before a verb or an adjective. For example,

　　　全班十几个同学几乎都想去。

　　　参观展览的人几乎有十多万。

　　　他高兴得几乎跳了起来。

　　　他几乎比我重十公斤。

"几乎 + V" sometimes indicates that something was/is on the verge of happening, but did not happen or has not actually happened yet, for example,

　　　他几乎撞上了那辆车。

她几乎忘了这位老同学的名字了。

我几乎找不到陈老师住的地方。

他因为生病几乎参加不了毕业考试。

2 为了

The prepositional phrase "为了……" is used to express purpose. It may be placed before the subject and separated from the rest of the sentence by a comma, for example,

为了更多地了解中国文化，马大为到北京语言学院学汉语。

妈妈为了照顾家庭，不去工作了。

为了能考上一个好的大学，孩子们从小学就开始竞争起来了。

3 在……方面

"在 + NP/VP + 方面", meaning "in the aspect/respect of ...", indicates the specific scope or area that an action pertains to, for example,

丁力波在口语方面比班上别的同学强得多。

在帮助朋友方面，他总是那么热情。

在就业方面，有的地方对妇女还很不公平。

4 在……中

"在 + NP/VP/AP + 中", meaning "in ..." or "during ...", denotes the range, environment, time or course in which an action takes place or a state exists, for example,

在全校的老师中，女老师占三分之二。（range）

在艰苦中，他学会了怎样节约。（environment）

他在两个月中游览了十多个名胜古迹。（time）

他们在合作中互相越来越了解了。（course）

句子 结构 Sentence Structure

1 两次否定 Double negation

Either "不……不……" or "没有……不……" can be used to form a double negation in a sentence. In usage, the double negation is usually an emphatic expression of an affirmative statement, for example,

她是新娘的好朋友，不能不参加这个婚礼。

（她一定要参加这个婚礼。）

这个消息他不会不知道。（他一定知道。）

陈老师跟大家一起去内蒙旅游，全班同学没有一个不高兴的。

（人人都高兴。）

一般地说，男人能做的工作没有妇女不能做的。（妇女都能做。）

2 要是……，就…… The construction "要是……，就……"

This construction means "if …, then …". The conjunction "要是" is used in conditional clauses. It has the same meaning as "如果", and is often paired with "就". This construction is frequently used in spoken Chinese, and "的话" may be added to the end of the "要是" clause. For example,

要是你生活在中国人的家里，就会发现丈夫每天也要下厨房。

要是明天下雨，我们就不去爬山了。

要是你明天没有空儿的话，我们就改个时间跟他们见面。

3 只有……，才…… The construction "只有……，才……"

This construction means "only if …, then …". The conjunction "只有" introduces an exclusive situation. It is used in conjunction with the adverb "才", which appears in the main clause and indicates the subsequent result of the initial condition. For example,

只有在各个方面男女都享受同样的权利，男女才能平等。

妇女只有社会地位提高了，在家庭里的地位才能提高。

只有您去请他，才能把他请来。

只有发展高科技，才能比较快地发展经济。

只有多读、多听、多说，才能学好一种外语。

4　独立语　The detached phrase

A detached phrase is structurally not related to any other part of the sentence in which it appears. It is often used to express a subjective point of view or attitude, to make a speculation, assessment, explanation or illustration, or to call attention to something. The expressions " 总的来说 ", " 大家都知道 " and " 重要的是 " in this lesson, as well as " 我看 ", " 听说 ", " 说实在的 ", " 你看 " and " 比如说 " from the previous lessons, are all examples of detached phrases. They may be placed at the beginning or in the middle of a sentence, for example,

大家都知道，中国的封建社会有两千多年的历史。

总的来说，家务事妇女要比男人干得多。

中国的经济虽然发展得很快，但总的来说，中国还是发展中国家。

重要的是，男女都应该有公平竞争的机会。

一般地说，妇女只有社会地位提高了，在家庭里的地位才能提高。

四、字与词　Chinese Characters and Words

1　集中识字　Learn the characters of the same radicals

女：妇　姑　好　她　姐　妈　妹　娜　娘　姓　婚　嫩　妻　要　妆

木：权　杯　楼　材　村　格　机　极　棵　梯　棒　橄　榄　桥　树　松　样　植　本　术　架

宀：家　寄　宿　宋　定　客　室　它　完　安　寒　实　官　宴　字　容　赛　宜

2 词语联想 Learn the following associated words

家庭　爷爷　奶奶　外公　外婆　爸爸　妈妈　父母　父亲　母亲　公公

婆婆　新娘　新郎　哥哥　弟弟　姐姐　妹妹　夫妻　丈夫　妻子　爱人

岳父　岳母　姑爷　舅舅　舅妈　姑姑　姑父　伯父　伯母　叔叔　婶婶

姨妈　姨夫　表姐　表妹　表哥　表弟　孩子　儿子　女儿　孙子　孙女

亲戚　家务　买菜　做饭　炒菜　洗衣　扫地　打扫　照顾老人

教育孩子　照顾吃穿

Pluralistic Views of "Equality between Men and Women"

"Women can hold up half of the sky", the proclaim of Chinese women after the founding of the People's Republic of China, is also a criticism of the dominant "male superiority" in the patriarchal society, which has existed for thousands of years. According to the Constitution of China, women have the equal rights as men in political, economic, cultural, social and family life.

As a matter of fact, since the founding of the People's Republic of China, women have been playing  an increasingly important role in every aspect, and the idea of "equality between men and women" is reflected more and more evidently in the society. In rural areas, women plant and reap crops just like men do and discuss farming issues together with their husbands. In cities, the proportion of women in most industries keeps increasing. Women are born with their own characteristics and advantages. Although they are not as strong, courageous and pressure-resistant as men, they are more meticulous, patient, persistent and tenacious. In some professions, such as teachers, nurses, secretaries, attendants and salesclerks, women account for a much larger proportion than men. They play an equally significant role as men in promoting social and economic development.

Moreover, women are gaining a higher status in family life. In most urban Chinese families, women and men manage the family income together and have equal say in big decisions.

However, we shouldn't deny the fact that the notion of "equality between men and women" has not yet been fully popularized. In some rural areas, the preference of boys over girls is still in existence, and people still want to have as many boys as they can. Now, the male-female ratio in China is 117:110, showing a severe imbalance. In job markets, many employers still prefer men, some even excluding women completely. Among the staff who make the biggest decisions of the country, the proportion of female officials is much smaller than male ones too.

Nowadays, Chinese women have established many organizations to protect their rights, and an increasing number of men have also joined in the cause of safeguarding "equality between men and women".

第四十一课
Lesson
41

我想自己开个律师事务所

J want to start a law firm myself

Wang Xiaoyun and Song Hua are talking about working after graduation. Their career objectives are very different from those of their parents. How do the two generations differ in their opinions about career objectives? Why are there such great differences?

一、课文 Texts

🎧9 （一）

我想自己开个律师事务所

王小云：宋华，毕业以后，你打算
　　　　干什么？

宋　华：我想先去一个律师事务所
　　　　干几年，熟悉熟悉这方面
　　　　的情况，然后自己开个律
　　　　师事务所。

王小云：这个想法很好啊。在咱们
　　　　国家，律师算是很新的职
　　　　业。①有不少人还很怕打官司，他们也不太了解怎样请律师帮
　　　　助自己打官司。不过，现在大家已经开始注意用法律来保护
　　　　自己的权利了，我想人们会越来越需要律师。

宋　华：可是我爸爸的看法就不一样。他认为我应该去考国家公务员，
　　　　到政府部门工作，我妈妈也让我到国营公司找个工作，他们
　　　　都不同意我当律师。他们说律师靠帮别人打官司挣钱，不像
　　　　公务员那样，有稳定的收入。

王小云: 对，我想起来了，上次去你家的时候，他们说过这个意思。
你同意这种看法吗？

宋　华: 当然不同意。我爸爸希望我找个稳定的工作，也就是说，拿
国家的工资，平平安安地过日子。②

王小云: 他们那一代人，大学毕业以后都由国家分配工作。③ 国家让
你去哪儿就去哪儿。即使自己有些想法，也得服从国家分配。

宋　华: 确实是这样。关于就业的问题，我们跟上一代人的想法不一
样。我们首先想到怎样去做自己喜欢的工作，能不能实现自
己的理想。我们希望生活中有挑战，工作中有竞争。

王小云: 还有，能得到比较满意的收入。

宋　华: 对。我爸爸妈妈听说我打算以后自己开事务所，就更着急了。

王小云: 不管老人怎么看，你都应该努力实现自己的理想。

宋　华: 那当然。现在企业和公司也都需要有自己的律师，所以律师
这个职业一天比一天受欢迎。我想只要努力工作，就一定会
有一个好的前途。小云，你有什么打算？

王小云: 我打算先考研究生。不过，现在我还没有决定。要是有合适
的工作，我就先干起来。

生词 New Words

| 1. 律师 | lǜshī | N | lawyer　当律师，找律师，请律师帮助，公司 的律师 |

2. 事务所	shìwùsuǒ	N	office　律师事务所，自己开个律师事务所
事务	shìwù	N	work, affair, routine　国家事务，个人事务
所	suǒ	N	place, office　派出所，医务所，厕所，场所
3. 熟悉	shúxī	V	to be familiar with　熟悉情况，熟悉这儿的风俗，熟悉技术，熟悉地理，熟悉他的学生
4. 想法	xiǎngfǎ	N	idea, opinion　这个想法很好，有什么想法，正确的想法，奇怪的想法，同样的想法
5. 打官司	dǎ guānsi	V O	to go to court, to engage in a lawsuit　怕打官司，请律师帮助自己打官司，跟他打官司，打一场官司，打赢官司
官司	guānsi	N	lawsuit
6. 法律	fǎlǜ	N	law　用法律来保护自己，熟悉法律，尊重法律，服从法律
7. 需要	xūyào	V	to need, to want, to require　需要律师，需要食物，需要帮助，需要休息
8. 公务员	gōngwùyuán	N	public servant　考国家公务员，当公务员
公务	gōngwù	N	public affairs
9. 国营	guóyíng	A	state-operated　国营公司，国营企业，国营商店
10. 同意	tóngyì	V	to agree, to consent　同意他的看法，同意他的建议，不同意我当律师，只要你同意
11. 靠	kào	V	to lean on, to depend on　靠父母生活，靠帮别人打官司挣钱
12. 平安	píng'ān	A	safe and sound　平安地生活，大家都很平安，祝你一路平安
13. 代	dài	N	generation　这一代人，上一代人；几代人，老一代，年轻的一代

14. 分配	fēnpèi	V	to distribute, to assign 分配工作，服从分配，分配宿舍，分配房间，分配收入
15. 即使	jíshǐ	Conj	even, even if 即使自己有些想法
16. 关于	guānyú	Prep	about, with regard to 关于就业的问题，关于打官司，关于律师事务所
17. 挑战	tiǎozhàn	V	to challenge 有挑战，是很大的挑战，向困难挑战
18. 满意	mǎnyì	A	satisfied, pleased 满意的工作，满意的收入，对他很满意，对生活条件不满意，满意地说，玩儿得很满意
19. 不管	bùguǎn	Conj	no matter (what, how, etc.) 不管怎么样
20. 前途	qiántú	N	future, prospect 有好的前途，考虑自己的前途，影响前途，公司的前途

注释　Notes

① 在咱们国家，律师算是很新的职业。

　　"In our country, lawyer is a fairly new profession."

　　The lawyer system in China was reinstated in 1979 after a period of inactivity. The legal profession has experienced rapid growth since China carried out the policy of "reform and opening up to the outside world". However, the number of lawyers and their work is still unable to meet the current social demands.

② 我爸爸希望我找个稳定的工作，也就是说，拿国家的工资，平平安安地过日子。

　　"My father wants me to find a steady job, or in other words, to work for the government or state-run institutions and live a stable life."

　　"也就是说" (also "就是说" or "这就是说") is often used as a detached phrase to connect the former and latter parts of a compound sentence. The latter part of the sentence explains or supplements the information in the former part, for example,

　　在张山以前，导演已经面试了一百多人，也就是说，可能有一百多人受骗了。

　　他1972年大学毕业以后就到北京工作，这就是说，他在北京已经生活40年了。

③他们那一代人，大学毕业以后都由国家分配工作。

"For their generation, the government assigned jobs to university graduates."

"他们那一代人" refers to the Chinese university graduates of the 1950s and 1960s.

In this sentence, "他们" and "那一代人" refer to the same people. In terms of sentence structure, the two have the equal status in serving as the subject. They are called "appositives". In "律师这个职业", "律师" and "这个职业" are also appositives. Previously, you have learned appositives such as "力波、大为他们". Please look at more examples:

他们年轻人都喜欢看足球比赛。

他回学校看他的老师，一位八十岁的老人。

🎧 10 （二）

招聘男主角

张山大学毕业以后，开了一家广告公司。他带着几个朋友苦干了几年，现在生意越来越好，公司发展得很快，已经有四五十人了。

一天，张山把副总经理叫来。他说："这几年我几乎没有休假。现在，我想去休两个月假。这两个月，公司的事情就交给你了。没有特别急的事儿，不要打电话找我。"副总说："好的，您放心去休假吧。"

张山回到家里，可是他没休息。他有很多爱好，特别喜欢表演，他很想试试自己在这方面的能力。张山每天都看报上的招聘广告。一天，他看到"招聘男主角"的广告。他想，能当一回电影演员多好啊！要是他出了名，对广告公司的发展就有很大的好处。即使不成功，也没关系，他还去当他的总经理。

张山找到招聘演员的地方。招聘考试挺复杂，首先由副导演面试，张山通过了；然后又由导演面试，张山也通过了。导演满意地说："我们试了一百多人了，只有您才跟我想象的男主角一样。祝贺您，男主角就是您了。"

"真的？"张山高兴地问导演。

"当然是真的。只要您同意，我们就这么决定了。不过，您不管怎么样也不能再改变主意了，要是您改变主意，我的损失就大了。所以，您得先在我这儿交一千块钱。两星期以后，我们就开始工作，您能按时来上班，我就把钱还给您。"

张山说："可以。"

"好了，请把您的电话号码给我，两星期之内，我通知您到哪儿上班。"

张山交了一千块钱，高高兴兴地回家等电话通知。

两个星期都过去了，没有人给他打电话。

第三个星期一的早上六点，电话来了。但不是那位导演打来的，而是他自己公司的副总打给他的。副总说有急事请他马上回去。

张山说："不行，我也有重要的事儿。公司的事情由你们讨论决定吧。"

"这个问题非常重要，您不能不参加讨论。"

张山把导演让他当男主角的事儿跟副总说了。

副总说："哦！我明白了。派出所也在打电话找您呢，您说的那位导演已经被抓住了，听说那是个大骗子。"

张山说："啊！大骗子？报纸怎么会给这样的人做广告让大家受骗呢？"

生词 New Words

1. 招聘	zhāopìn	V	to invite applications for a job 招聘男主角，招聘服务员，招聘园艺师
聘	pìn	V	to invite sb. to a post (or job) 聘他当老师
2. 广告	guǎnggào	N	advertisement 广告公司，招聘广告，做广告，登广告，广告费
3. 苦	kǔ	Adv/A	painstakingly, assiduously; bitter, hard 苦干，苦练，苦学；生活很苦，苦日子，受苦
4. 生意	shēngyi	N	business, trade 生意越来越好，做生意，有生意，生意大（小）
5. 副	fù	A	deputy, vice 副经理，副教授，副教练
6. 总	zǒng	A	chief, general 总经理，副总（经理），总教练，总厨师
7. 休假	xiūjià	VO	to have/take a vacation 打算休假，休两个月假，去郊区休假
8. 事情	shìqing	N	affair, matter, thing 公司的事情，重要的事情，这儿的事情

9. 急	jí	A	urgent, pressing, impatient 特别急的事儿，事儿很急，别急
10. 表演	biǎoyǎn	V	to act, to perform 表演京剧，表演地方戏，表演舞蹈，开始表演，喜欢表演
11. 能力	nénglì	N	ability, capability 自己的能力，（没）有能力，能力大，做生意的能力
12. 出名	chūmíng	VO/A	to become famous; famous 出了名，没有出名，出名以后；出名的地方，出名的公司
13. 成功	chénggōng	V/A	to succeed; successful 事业成功，访问成功，得到成功，祝你成功；成功的演奏，办得很成功，成功地举行，成功地解决
14. 导演	dǎoyǎn	N/V	director (of a show, film, etc.); to direct (a show, film, etc.) 电影导演，京剧导演；导演了一部戏
15. 面试	miànshì	V	to interview, to audition 参加面试，由导演面试
16. 通过	tōngguò	V	to pass, to pass through 通过面试，通过考试，通过决定，容易通过，很难通过
17. 改变	gǎibiàn	V	to change 改变主意，改变想法，改变习惯，改变风格，改变环境
18. 损失	sǔnshī	N/V	loss; to lose 损失太大，（没）有损失，经济损失；损失金钱，损失时间
19. 号码	hàomǎ	N	number 电话号码，房间号码，护照号码，账单号码
20. 之内	zhīnèi	N	within 两个星期之内，三个月之内，一年之内
内	nèi	N	inner, within, inside 内外，国内，校内
21. 讨论	tǎolùn	V	to discuss 你们讨论决定，讨论事情，讨论问题，开始讨论，参加讨论

| 22. 骗子 | piànzi | N | swindler 大骗子，抓住骗子 |
| 骗 | piàn | V | to deceive, to fool 骗钱，骗东西，受骗，别骗我 |

补充生词 Supplementary Words

1. 歌王	gēwáng	N	king of folk songs
2. 王洛宾	Wáng Luòbīn	PN	Wang Luobin (name of a Chinese musician)
3. 汉族	Hànzú	PN	the Han ethnic group
4. 少数民族	shǎoshù mínzú		ethnic minority
5. 深	shēn	A	deep
6. 创作	chuàngzuò	V	to create, to write
7. 改编	gǎibiān	V	to adapt, to revise
8. 维吾尔族	Wéiwú'ěrzú	PN	the Uygur ethnic group
9. 哈萨克族	Hāsàkèzú	PN	the Kazak ethnic group
10. 留恋	liúliàn	V	to be reluctant to leave (a place), can't bear to part (from sb.)
11. 张望	zhāngwàng	V	to look around
12. 达坂城	Dábǎn Chéng	PN	Daban City (name of a town in the Xinjiang Uygur Autonomous Region)
13. 石头	shítou	N	stone
14. 圆	yuán	A	round
15. 西瓜	xīguā	N	watermelon
16. 甜	tián	A	sweet, honeyed
17. 辫子	biànzi	N	braid, pigtail

二、练习 Exercises

练习 与运用 **Drills and Practice**   11

核心句 KEY SENTENCES

1. 律师靠帮别人打官司挣钱。
2. 关于就业的问题，我们跟上一代人的想法不一样。
3. 律师这个职业一天比一天受欢迎。
4. 两星期之内，我通知您到哪儿上班。
5. 我妈妈也让我到国营公司找个工作。
6. 副总说有急事请他马上回去。
7. 即使不成功，也没关系。
8. 您不管怎么样也不能再改变主意了。

1. 熟读下列词组 Read the following phrases until you learn them by heart

（1）靠晚上复习　　　靠贷款上学　　　　靠打工生活
　　 靠借债过日子　　 靠开饭馆挣钱　　　靠高科技发展经济
　　 靠法律解决问题　 靠自己的努力得到好成绩

（2）关于男女平等的问题　　　关于招聘的问题　关于法律的问题
　　 关于发展农村经济的建议　 关于李白的诗　　关于怎样保护自然环境
　　 关于怎样实现自己的理想

（3）受教育　受欢迎　受尊敬　　受照顾　　受称赞　　受夸奖
　　 受锻炼　受保护　受骗　　　受苦　　　受损失　　受批评
　　 受污染

（4）学校之内　　球场之内　　小区之内　　这个胡同之内　　街心花园之内

　　三天之内　　半小时之内　　一年之内　　100米之内　　　这个月之内

　　暑假之内　　50公斤之内　　一万元之内

（5）熟悉这方面的情况　　　　　　非常熟悉银行工作

　　互相熟悉熟悉　　　　　　　　对学校的老师熟悉得很

（6）需要休假　　需要作好准备　　　　　需要科学技术

　　特别需要　　需要比较长的时间

2. 句子练习　Sentence drills

A. 用所给词语完成句子

Complete the following sentences with the given words and expressions

靠

（1）画家没有稳定的收入，＿＿＿＿＿＿＿＿＿＿＿＿＿＿来挣钱。（画画儿）

（2）他＿＿＿＿＿＿＿＿＿＿＿＿＿成了有名的书法家。（艰苦的练习）

（3）他们一家人＿＿＿＿＿＿＿＿＿＿＿＿＿＿＿＿生活。（父母的工资）

（4）中国农村要＿＿＿＿＿＿＿＿＿＿＿＿＿＿＿＿发展经济。（科学技术）

（5）她＿＿＿＿＿＿＿＿＿＿＿＿＿＿＿得到了银行的贷款。（自己的信用）

关于

（1）＿＿＿＿＿＿＿＿＿＿＿＿＿，马大为跟那个小伙子的看法不一样。（隐私）

（2）＿＿＿＿＿＿＿＿＿＿＿＿＿＿，大家谈了很多很好的想法。

　　　　　　　　　　　　　　　　　（怎样保护环境的问题）

（3）＿＿＿＿＿＿＿＿＿＿＿＿＿，你们还有什么不同的看法？（妇女的地位）

（4）请大家多介绍一些＿＿＿＿＿＿＿＿＿＿＿方面的情况。（农村教育）

（5）＿＿＿＿＿＿＿＿＿＿＿＿＿，他们一家人还要好好儿地研究研究。

　　　　　　　　　　　　　　　　　（买房的问题）

受

（1）今年气候不好，小云舅舅家的村子＿＿＿＿＿＿＿＿＿＿＿＿＿＿＿＿。

（2）这家企业的管理方式很好，＿＿＿＿＿＿＿＿＿＿＿＿＿＿＿＿。

（3）这个工厂不注意环境保护，旁边的河水＿＿＿＿＿＿＿＿＿＿＿＿＿＿＿。

（4）他的身体不好，＿＿＿＿＿＿＿＿＿＿＿＿＿＿＿＿＿。

（5）汽车工厂越来越多，他们生产的汽车＿＿＿＿＿＿＿＿＿＿＿＿＿＿。

（称赞　照顾　挑战　损失　污染）

需要

（1）他们公司＿＿＿＿＿＿＿＿＿＿＿＿＿＿＿经理。（招聘）

（2）现在我非常忙，很＿＿＿＿＿＿＿＿＿＿＿＿＿＿＿。（帮助）

（3）他要看的书很多，＿＿＿＿＿＿＿＿＿＿＿＿＿＿。（时间）

（4）发展教育，＿＿＿＿＿＿＿＿＿＿＿。（资金）

（5）他现在累极了，＿＿＿＿＿＿＿＿＿＿＿＿＿。（休息）

B. 替换练习
Substitution drills

（1）他让我马上回去 讨论重要的事情。

给公司写封信	打听一下这件事情
下星期二来	面试
到火车站	接一个朋友
填好表	交到办公室

（2）他有急事让她马上回来。

还没有决定	谁演主角
没有钱	女儿上大学
改变了主意	大家只写两遍汉字
打电话	妹妹也来北京

C. 用"即使……，也……"完成句子

Complete the following sentences, using "即使……，也……"

（1）即使大家都不去，我＿＿＿＿＿＿＿＿＿＿＿＿＿＿＿＿。（一个人）

（2）即使我有时间，＿＿＿＿＿＿＿＿＿＿＿＿＿＿＿。（打工）

（3）即使这个工作的报酬很高，＿＿＿＿＿＿＿＿＿＿＿。（干）

（4）即使＿＿＿＿＿＿＿＿＿＿＿＿＿，自己也必须付出努力。（机会）

（5）即使＿＿＿＿＿＿＿＿＿＿＿＿＿，王小云也不会用父母的钱。（贷款）

D. 用"不管……，都/也……"完成句子

Complete the following sentences, using "不管……，都/也……"

（1）不管生活多么困难，小云的妈妈＿＿＿＿＿＿＿＿＿＿＿＿＿＿。

（2）不管下多大雨，＿＿＿＿＿＿＿＿＿＿＿＿＿＿＿＿。

（3）不管＿＿＿＿＿＿＿＿＿＿＿＿＿＿，杰克也开不了口叫爸妈。

（4）不管＿＿＿＿＿＿＿＿＿＿＿＿＿＿，他也要练好书法。

（5）不管＿＿＿＿＿＿＿＿＿＿＿＿＿＿，他每天都要跑步。

3. 根据课文回答问题 Answer the following questions according to the texts

（1）宋华毕业以后马上就要开律师事务所吗？

（2）王小云为什么认为在中国，人们会越来越需要律师？

（3）宋华爸爸为什么不同意宋华当律师？

（4）宋华爸爸为什么会有这样的想法？

（5）现在年轻人认为什么是理想的工作？

（6）王小云毕业后有什么打算？

（7）张山大学毕业以后做了什么工作？

（8）他的广告公司的生意怎么样？

（9）张山打算休多长时间的假？

（10）张山为什么每天都看报上的招聘广告？

（11）张山为什么对"招聘男主角"很感兴趣？

（12）张山是怎样参加招聘面试的？

（13）导演面试完了以后，跟张山说什么了？

（14）张山为什么没有当上男主角？

4. 会话练习　Conversation practice

> ### 会话常用语 IDIOMATIC EXPRESSIONS IN CONVERSATION
>
> 也就是说 (in other words, ...)
>
> 那当然。(Of course.)
>
> 这个想法很好。(This is a good idea.)
>
> 确实是这样。(It is true indeed.)
>
> 看法不一样 (... have different opinions)
>
> 不管怎么样 (in any case)

【表示同意　Expressing agreement】

（1）A：你同意他的想法吗？

　　　B：那当然，这个想法很好，我完全同意。

（2）A：他关于实习问题的建议，你同意吗？

　　　B：这个问题比较复杂，我得想一想。

　　　C：我觉得他提出的实习单位很好，但是我不同意实习的时间。

【补充说明　Making an additional explanation】

　　　A：毕业以后，你打算找什么样的工作？

　　　B：我喜欢教书，特别是教中学生汉语。

A：也就是说，你想当中学汉语老师？你觉得教汉语的工作机会多吗？

B：现在还不太多。不过，咱们国家跟中国在经济、文化方面的合作一年比一年多，社会需要很多懂汉语的人，也就是说，学汉语的人会越来越多。

A：你说得很对。还有，很多中学生认为学汉语是一种挑战，他们喜欢这种挑战。

【顿悟　Expressing a sudden realization】

（1）A：老师，人们常说"桂林山水甲天下"，"甲"是"第一"的意思，"天下"呢？

B："天"和"下"这两个字你都认识，你再想想。

A："天的下边"，哦，我明白了，是不是"世界"的意思？

B：你说得对。有时候"天下"也指中国，这儿说的是"桂林山水是中国第一"。

A：哦，是这样。

（2）A：丈夫和妻子都是职工，为什么叫"双职工"呢？

B："双"不是"两个"的意思吗？

A：哦，我想起来了，第 38 课我们学过"红双喜字"。

5. 交际练习　Communication exercises

(1) Discuss your ideal future career plans with your classmates.

(2) Write a letter for Zhang Shan to the local police station and talk about how he was swindled out of his money.

After the oral presentation, write a short essay on either of the topics above.

阅读 与复述 Reading Comprehension and Paraphrasing

🎧12 西部歌王（gēwáng）

　　王洛宾（Wáng Luòbīn），人们称他西部歌王，他的歌不但在中国大陆、香港、台湾很有名，在海外华人地区也非常受欢迎。很多人都是唱着他的歌长大的。

　　王洛宾是北京人，汉族（Hànzú）。他年轻时就来到了新疆，在新疆少数民族（shǎoshù mínzú）居住的地方生活了五十多年。他深（shēn）深地爱上了那儿的民族和音乐，创作（chuàngzuò）和改编（gǎibiān）了几百首新疆的爱情歌曲。维吾尔族（Wéiwú'ěrzú）人把他叫做"咱们维吾尔族的音乐家"。王洛宾也说："没有新疆少数民族的优美的音乐，就没有今天的王洛宾。"他与少数民族建立了深厚的感情。

　　《在那遥远的地方》是一首哈萨克族（Hāsàkèzú）民歌，王洛宾改编以后几乎成了人人都会唱的爱情歌曲：

　　　　在那遥远的地方，
　　　　有位好姑娘，
　　　　人们走过她的帐房，
　　　　都要回头留恋（liúliàn）地张望（zhāngwàng）。

　　　　她那粉红的笑脸，
　　　　好像红太阳。
　　　　她那活泼动人的眼睛，
　　　　好像晚上明媚的月亮。
　　　　……

《达坂城（Dábǎn Chéng）的姑娘》是王洛宾的又一首有名的歌曲。达坂城的生活环境很艰苦，六十年代，王洛宾来到这里。他住在农民家里，跟农民一起生活，一起放羊，跟维吾尔族老人一起唱歌，跟年轻人一起跳舞。他把那儿的男女老少看成是自己的亲人，那儿的人也把他看成是自己的兄弟。老人们知道他是音乐家，就把自己民族的歌曲一首一首地唱给他听。王洛宾听了很多民歌以后，改编出《达坂城的姑娘》：

达坂城的石头（shítou）圆（yuán）又大呀，

西瓜（xīguā）大又甜（tián）呀，

达坂城的姑娘辫子（biànzi）长呀，

两只眼睛真漂亮。

你要是嫁人，不要嫁给别人，

一定要嫁给我。

……

这首歌唱出了达坂城人民的爱情，达坂城这个小镇也因为这首歌出了名。

1993年秋天，这位西部歌王再次回到达坂城时，他已是七十多岁的老人了。达坂城的各族人民又一次热情地欢迎他。

三、语法 Grammar

词语例解 Word Usage and Examples

1 靠

The "靠 + O" construction is used to introduce the method, means or basis that an action depends upon. It is often used in front of another verb-object construction to form a sentence with serial verb phrases, for example,

律师靠帮别人打官司挣钱。

他们靠自己的一双手生活。

老王靠这封信打赢了官司。

丁力波的好成绩是靠他的努力得到的。

2 关于

The object of the preposition "关于" refers to the thing or domain an action or behaviour pertains to. It is used as an adverbial and is always placed at the beginning of a sentence, for example,

关于就业的问题，这是大家都很关心的大事。

关于神女峰，有很多美丽的传说。

关于怎样保护环境，大家都提了很多好建议。

Note that when the prepositional phrase with "关于" is used as an attribute, "的" is usually added. For example, "关于男女平等的问题", "关于妇女地位的课文".

3 受

The verb "受" means "to receive, to obtain", such as "受欢迎", "受尊敬" and "受教育". It also means "to suffer something unpleasant", such as "受骗", "受批评" and "受损失". For example,

他不愿意受大家照顾。

张山接到副总的电话，才知道自己受骗了。

今年雨下得特别多，种蔬菜的农民受了很大损失。

那几年他们家生活很困难，爸爸、妈妈受了不少苦。

4 之内

"之内" refers to a range within a certain limit. "NP＋之内" often refers to a range within a certain scope, a period of time or a quantity, for example,

东校区之内不能停放汽车。

这些报酬不在工资之内。

今年之内他不会来北京。

他现在还搬得动二十公斤（kilogram）之内的东西。

● 句子 结构　Sentence Structure

1 连动兼语句　Sentences with serial verb phrases and a pivotal word

Serial verb phrases and a double-functional word construction (a pivotal word construction) are often used in the same sentence. Through the use of this structure, which is relatively simple, it is possible to express complex ideas and meanings. Sometimes, the double-functional word construction appears first, for example,

S_1 +	V_1 +	$O_1(S_2)$ +	V_2 +	O_2	+ V_3	+ O_3
我妈妈	让	我	到	国营公司	找	个工作。
	怎样请	律师	帮助	自己	打	官司？
他	让	丁力波	去	商店	给他买	光盘。
老师	叫	我们	用	中文	写	个故事。

Sometimes, the serial verb phrases appear first, for example,

S_1 +	V_1 +	O_1 +	V_2 +	$O_2(S_2)$ +	V_3 +	O_3
副总	有	急事	让	他	马上回去。	
他	没有	钱·	请	大家	吃饭。	
我	打了	个电话	叫	他	下午来。	

2 即使……，也……　The construction "即使……，也……"

In this construction, which means "even if, even though", "即使" is used to suggest a supposed compromise, which is followed by a conclusion unaffected by the initial supposition. "即使" is often used in conjunction with the adverb "也", for example,

即使明天下雨，我们也要去参观。

即使自己有些想法，也得服从公司安排。

即使有别人帮助，也得靠自己努力。

3 不管……，都／也…… The construction "不管……，都／也……"

The conjunction "不管" is used in clauses containing interrogative pronouns or affirmative-negative phrases. It means that regardless of the situation, the result will never change. The adverb "都" or "也" is often used in conjunction with "不管". This construction is common in spoken Chinese, for example,

不管困难有多大，你都应该努力实现自己的理想。

您不管怎么样也不能再改变主意了。

不管你有什么困难，我都愿意帮助你。

不管他去不去，你都要打电话告诉我。

四、字与词　Chinese Characters and Words

1 集中识字　Learn the characters of the same radicals

亻：亿　什　化　付　代　们　他　伟　传　休　件　价　体　但　作
　　低　你　住　位　件　便　俩　修　保　俄　俭　俗　信　债　借
　　候　倍　健　做　偷　假　停　傻　像

彳：行　往　律　很　得　街　德

氵：汉　汗　污　江　沙　汽　没　法　河　油　注　泳　波　洗　活
　　济　洋　洲　海　酒　深　湖　游　满　漠　漂　清　流　涮　演
　　澡　派

2 词语联想　Learn the following groups of associated words

公务　　公务员　部长　司长　处长　科长　主任　专员　科员

办事员　法律　　法官　法院院长　　律师事务所　律师　官司

打官司　国营　　私营　公司　企业　商店　商场　商品　超市

经理　　总经理　经济师　总经济师　工程师　总工程师　会计

总会计师　技术　技术员　营业　营业员　售货　售货员　保管

保管员

前边　后边　里边　外边　上边　下边　左边　右边　东边　西边

南边　北边　旁边　东北边　西北边　东南边　西南边　中间

前面　后面　里面　外面　上面　下面　左面　右面　东面　西面

南面　北面　东北面　西北面　东南面　西南面　中心

东部　西部　南部　北部　东北部　西北部　东南部　西南部　中部

前方　后方　正前方　东方　西方　南方　北方　东北方　西北方

东南方　西南方　方向　方位

学唱中文歌
Sing a Song

草原上升起不落的太阳

Cǎoyuánshang shēngqǐ bú luò de tàiyáng

The Never-Setting Sun Rises over the Prairie

Allegretto (♩ = 96) 开阔、明朗地　　　　　　　　　　　　　美利其格词曲

1. 蓝 蓝 的 天　上 白 云 飘，　　白 云 下 面
2. 要 是 有　人 来 问 我，　　"这 是 什 么
3. 这 里 的 人　们 爱 和 平，　　也 热 爱

马 儿 跑，　　　　挥 动 鞭 儿
地 方？"　　　　我 就 骄 傲地
家 乡，　　　　草 原 上

响 四 方，　　百 鸟 齐 飞 翔。
告 诉 他，　　这 是 我 们 的 家 乡。
升 起 不 落 的 太

阳，　　　　草 原 上

升 起 不 落 的 太 阳。

Changes in Chinese People's Conception of Career

Chinese people's conception of career has changed from "inheriting a career from one's father" to "accepting a career assigned by the government" and then to "getting a job through a two-way choice".

At the time when the People's Republic of China was newly founded, people didn't have a strong sense of career. It was quite common that children would do the same jobs as their parents. When workers in a factory reached retirement age, their son or daughter would take over the position and succeed their career in the factory. "Inheritance" was one of the career choices for people in those days.

After the restoration of the national college entrance examination in 1977, college graduates, few in number, were valuable talents for the country, so they were assigned jobs by the government according to different needs and wouldn't lose their jobs unless they made big mistakes.

As the number of college graduates kept growing since 1990s, the centralized job placement system seemed more and more infeasible, and its neglect of students' individuality also led to some unsuitable job allocations. In addition to that, with the continuing development of the market economy, there emerged an increasing number of companies wanting talented people. As a result, college graduates began to choose careers according to their own wishes, and employers would choose from the candidates according to their own needs. In that way, the "two-way choice" has become the major method for college graduates to get a job.

When hunting a job, some people still want to find a stable "iron bowl", which is why professions like teacher, doctor and civil servant are so popular. These jobs, however, are not suitable for everyone. Public institutions and government offices where these jobs are found usually lack vitality, while

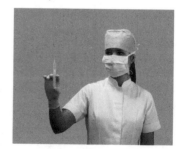

more and more young people are craving for jobs which are highly-paid, with more freedom, promising, challenging and fulfilling. Therefore, some state-owned, foreign, and private companies are also popular among job-hunters.

Meanwhile, there are also more and more young people who choose to set up their own businesses. As compensation for the risk and the amount of money, time and energy it takes to start a business, the entrepreneurs may also enjoy high profits, independence, freedom and the sense of fulfillment and achievement.

第四十二课
Lesson
42

洋姑爷在农村过春节

A foreign son-in-law celebrates the Spring Festival in the countryside

After marrying Yulan, Jack celebrates the Spring Festival in a Chinese village for the first time. He learns many customs associated with the festival and finds it very interesting to celebrate the Spring Festival in the countryside.

一、课文 Texts

🎧 13 （一）

洋姑爷在农村过春节

玉兰爸：欢迎杰克和玉兰回家过春节。咱们全家人能在一起吃年夜饭，

我跟你妈特别高兴。来，咱们先干一杯！

玉　兰：祝爸爸、妈妈身体健康！

杰　克：恭喜发财！①

玉兰爸：好，好。恭喜恭喜！祝你们新年万事如意。杰克，你要是觉

得别扭，就还叫我先生，叫她太太。怎么叫都行，这没什么，②

我知道你们有你们的习惯。

杰　克：您不会生气吧？

玉兰妈：你说到哪儿去了？我不但不生气，反而挺高兴。我也成"太

太"了！吃菜，吃菜，要不菜就凉了。

玉　兰：你尝尝这个红烧鱼。

玉兰爸：多来点儿。杰克，我们吃年夜饭的时候，除了鸡和肉以外，

总要有一条鱼，你知道这是为什么吗？

杰　克：鸡、鸭、鱼、肉都是好吃的菜啊，难道还有别的意思吗？

玉　兰：有啊。因为"鱼"的发音跟结余的"余"一样，"有鱼"就成

了"有余"，意思是希望在新的一年里大家生活得更好，家家

都"有余"。

杰　克：哦，我知道了。有的人喜欢手机号码、汽车号码带"8"这个

数字，不是"188"，就是"518"，可能也是这个想法吧？

玉　兰：对啊。因为有些南方人念"8"跟念"发财"的"发"声音差

不多，念"5"跟念"我"也差不多。所以"188"和"518"

就成了"要发发"和"我要发"。他们希望"发"，所以喜欢

"8"。后来，别的地方的人也这样做了。

玉兰妈：咱们的洋姑爷还知道不少中国的事儿呢。吃完了年夜饭，咱

们一边看电视，一边包饺子。

杰　克：都吃完晚饭了，为什么还包饺子？难道还有客人要来吗？

玉兰爸：这是咱们北方的风俗。今天除夕，旧的一年快要过去，新的一年就要开始，所以家家都睡得很晚，这叫"守岁"。守岁的时候，北方人一般要包很多饺子，好在新年慢慢地吃。

玉　兰：杰克可不会包饺子。杰克，守岁的时候，你干什么呢？

杰　克：我随便，我觉得干什么都很有意思，应该入乡随俗。

玉兰妈：不会包饺子没关系，让他跟孩子们一起到外边去放鞭炮。

玉　兰：那他太高兴了。③北京城里禁止随便放鞭炮，城里人过春节越来越简单，哪有农村热闹？

玉兰妈：现在春节放长假，怪不得很多城里人不是到外地去旅游，就是到农村来过节。

玉兰爸：我们这儿不但不禁止放鞭炮，反而放得比以前更多了。今年咱们家就买了不少大鞭炮、小鞭炮，到12点的时候，你们去放吧。现在我们农

村过春节是比城里热闹得多。除了吃年夜饭以外，我们还写春联、贴窗花、扭秧歌，④还有各种表演和比赛。你们就在这儿多住几天吧，看看我们村是不是也可以发展旅游事业，尤其是文化旅游。

生词 New Words

1. 洋	yáng	A	foreign	洋姑爷，洋酒，洋房
2. 农村	nóngcūn	N	rural area, countryside	在农村过春节，中国农村
3. 年夜饭	niányèfàn	N	family reunion dinner on the Spring Festival's Eve	吃年夜饭，准备年夜饭
年夜	niányè	N	the Spring Festival's Eve, the Lunar New Year's Eve	
4. 健康	jiànkāng	A	healthy	身体健康，祝你身体健康，为大家的健康干杯
5. 发财	fācái	VO	to get rich, to make a fortune	恭喜发财，发了大财
发	fā	V	to make a fortune	
财	cái	N	wealth, money	
6. 万事如意	wàn shì rúyì	IE	to realize all one's wishes	祝您万事如意
7. 反而	fǎn'ér	Adv	on the contrary	反而挺高兴，反而比以前更多了
8. 尝	cháng	V	to taste, to try the flavour	尝尝这个菜，尝尝味道
9. 红烧鱼	hóngshāoyú	N	fish braised in brown sauce	尝尝这个红烧鱼，做红烧鱼，来一个红烧鱼
红烧	hóngshāo	V	to braise in soy sauce	
鱼	yú	N	fish	
10. 肉	ròu	N	meat, pork	红烧肉，烤肉，涮肉，炒肉，尝尝这个肉
11. 难道	nándào	Adv	*used in a rhetorical question for emphasis*	难道还有客人要来，难道你们俩打算干到明天吗

12.	发音	fāyīn	N/VO	pronunciation; to pronounce 这个字的发音，正确的发音，发音清楚；发音方法
13.	结余	jiéyú	V/N	to remain; surplus 这个月结余800块钱；有结余
	余	yú	V	to remain 有余，余两张票，余80块钱
14.	手机	shǒujī	N	mobile phone 手机号码，打手机，买手机，手机上网
15.	饺子	jiǎozi	N	Chinese dumpling 包饺子，吃饺子
16.	除夕	chúxī	N	the Spring Festival's Eve, the Lunar New Year's Eve 今天除夕
17.	守岁	shǒusuì	VO	to stay up all night on the Spring Festival's Eve 守岁的时候，守岁到很晚
18.	随便	suíbiàn	A	any, no matter (what, when, how, etc.) 我随便，随便吃
19.	放鞭炮	fàng biānpào	V O	to set off firecrackers 跟孩子们一起放鞭炮
	放	fàng	V	to set or let off
	鞭炮	biānpào	N	firecrackers
20.	禁止	jìnzhǐ	V	to prohibit, to ban 禁止放鞭炮，禁止吸烟，禁止游泳
21.	怪不得	guàibude	Adv	no wonder, so that's why 怪不得城里人到农村来过节
22.	外地	wàidì	N	parts of the country other than where one is 到外地去旅游
23.	春联	chūnlián	N	Spring Festival couplets 写春联，贴春联
24.	窗花	chuānghuā	N	paper-cut for window decoration 贴窗花
25.	尤其	yóuqí	Adv	especially 尤其是文化旅游，尤其是那个小伙子

注释 Notes

① 恭喜发财！

"May you be prosperous!"

"恭喜恭喜" and "恭喜发财" are expressions of congratulation that people greet each other with during the Spring Festival. "恭喜 + V" is usually used for extending warm wishes during the Spring Festival. Sometimes the structure can also be used for congratulation on other occasions, for example, "恭喜生了个女儿".

② 怎么叫都行，这没什么。

"Whatever you call it is fine; it doesn't matter."

"怎么 + V + 都行" means "doesn't matter" or "don't mind". One may also say "怎么都行". For example,

你怎么做都行，我没意见。

他怎么选择都行，这事儿由他自己决定。

怎么都行，你们商量吧。

③ 那他太高兴了。

"He will be very happy to do it."

Used at the beginning of the sentence, the pronoun "那" refers to "让他跟孩子们一起去放鞭炮" in the previous line of the dialogue. It plays a connective role in the text.

④ 除了吃年夜饭以外，我们还写春联、贴窗花、扭秧歌。

"Besides having a family reunion dinner on the Spring Festival's Eve, we also write Spring Festival couplets, put up window decorations and dance the yangko."

Spring Festival couplets are parallel couplets celebrating the Spring Festival. They are usually written on red paper and attached to the door or doorframe. They usually express warm wishes for the New Year. The window decorations are red paper cuttings of various auspicious animals or plants, pasted on windows during the Spring Festival.

🎧14　（上）

远亲不如近邻

今年春天，我们在郊区农村盖了一个四合院。一个星期六，我们装了满满一卡车的木头和水泥，准备送过去装修我们的新房子。我们到村子里的时候，家家都开始做晚饭了。邻居们听到汽车的声音都走了出来，远远地站着，好奇地看着我们。

我和丈夫跳下车来就忙着搬木头，想快点儿把东西卸完，好让司机回城去。我们在城市生活久了，已经不太习惯干重活儿了。刚搬了两趟，我俩就累得走不动了。

邻居们不但没有笑话我们，反而围了过来想帮助我们，可是又不知道我们会怎么想，他们好像有些犹豫。一个小伙子开玩笑地说："怎么了？难道你们俩打算干到明天吗？你们这么干，即使干到明天早上，恐怕也干不完！"大家听了都笑起来了。我靠在车上，也跟着他们一起笑。

那个小伙子看我们俩也跟着笑，就接着说："你们检查一下，有什么重要的东西没有。要是有，就先把它收好。"然后又对大家说："别站着看了，大

家都帮帮忙吧！"邻居们马上推出了自己的小车，就帮我们干起来。他们干得又快又好，不到一个小时，就把一车的东西卸完了，整整齐齐地摆在院子里。

司机把汽车开走了，邻居们也拍拍衣服，准备回去。我连忙跟丈夫商量，应该给每个人多少报酬。邻居们听说要给钱，都急着推车往外走，不管我们怎么说，他们都不听。尤其是那个小伙子，他一边走还一边说："你们城里人，什么事儿都讲钱！家里饭都凉了，我们该回家吃饭了。以后咱们都是邻居了，要是你们有什么事儿，就说一声，⑤别客气……"

他们都走了，我们俩坐在院子里休息。我对丈夫说："在城里的大楼里，邻居们谁也不认识谁；可是今天在村里我又感觉到了'远亲不如近邻'。"

生词 New Words

1. 远亲不如近邻	yuǎnqīn bùrú jìnlín	IE	a close neighbour means more than a distant relative
2. 四合院	sìhéyuàn	N	quadrangle, traditional residential compound with houses built around a square courtyard
			盖了四合院，住在四合院里，北京的四合院
院（子）	yuàn (zi)	N	courtyard 坐在院子里休息，院子里放着花儿和盆景

3. 装	zhuāng	V	to load, to pack　装车，装了满满一车，装了很多书
4. 卡车	kǎchē	N	lorry, truck　装了满满一卡车，卡车司机，开卡车
5. 木头	mùtou	N	wood, log　搬木头，抬木头，一卡车木头
6. 水泥	shuǐní	N	cement　搬水泥，一卡车水泥
7. 装修	zhuāngxiū	V	to fit up (a house, etc.), to renovate　装修新房子，装修商店
8. 邻居	línjū	N	neighbour　好邻居，有邻居
9. 卸	xiè	V	to unload, to discharge　卸车，卸木头，从车上卸水泥，从船上卸鱼和虾
10. 干活儿	gàn huór	V O	to work　不习惯干重活儿，干轻活儿，干了一天活儿，干什么活儿
11. 趟	tàng	M	*measure word for trips*　搬了两趟，去王府井一趟，来北京一趟
12. 笑话	xiàohua	V/N	to laugh at sb.; joke　没有笑话我们，别让人笑话；说笑话，讲一个笑话
13. 犹豫	yóuyù	A	hesitant　好像有些犹豫，很犹豫
14. 推	tuī	V	to push　推自行车，推门
15. 小车	xiǎochē	N	wheelbarrow　推小车，推出了自己的小车，装上小车
16. 拍	pāi	V	to pat　拍拍衣服，拍拍孩子，拍身上的雪
17. 连忙	liánmáng	Adv	promptly, at once　连忙跟丈夫商量，连忙说对不起
18. 声	shēng	M	*measure word for sounds*　说一声，叫一声，问一声，告诉一声，通知一声

补充生词 Supplementary Words

1. 拜年	bàinián	VO	to pay a New Year's call
2. 花生	huāshēng	N	peanut
3. 梨	lí	N	pear
4. 杏儿	xìngr	N	apricot
5. 压岁钱	yāsuìqián	N	money given to children as a Lunar New Year gift
6. 年底	niándǐ	N	end of the year
7. 富	fù	A	rich, wealthy
8. 小康	xiǎokāng	A	relatively well-off
9. 山沟	shāngōu	N	remote mountainous area
10. 彩电	cǎidiàn	N	colour television
11. 农业	nóngyè	N	agriculture, farming
12. 养蜂	yǎng fēng	V O	to raise or keep bees
13. 蜂蜜	fēngmì	N	honey
14. 缺	quē	V	to be short of (sth.), to lack (sth.)

注释　Notes

⑤ 要是你们有什么事儿，就说一声。

"If you need anything, just let us know."

In this case, "声" is a verbal measure word for sounds, for example, "叫了两声", "唱了几声".

In the construction "V +一声", "一声" is generally used after a verb of inquiry, informing, etc., to express an informal and brief tone. "说一声" means "告诉我们一下". For example,

我想问一声，明天你有空儿吗？

这件事决定以后，你通知一声。

二、练习　Exercises

练习 与运用　**Drills and Practice** 🎧15

核心句 KEY SENTENCES

1. 我们想快点儿把东西卸完，好让司机回城去。
2. 怪不得很多城里人不是到外地去旅游，就是到农村来过节。
3. 看看我们村是不是也可以发展旅游事业，尤其是文化旅游。
4. 都吃完饭了，为什么还包饺子？难道还有客人要来吗？
5. 我连忙跟丈夫商量，应该给每个人多少报酬。
6. 邻居们不但没有笑话我们，反而围了过来想帮助我们。
7. 那他太高兴了。
8. 要是你们有什么事儿，就说一声。

1. 熟读下列词组 Read the following phrases until you learn them by heart

（1）好准备吃住　好早点儿休息　好通过面试　好解决这个问题　好给他回信
好了解情况　好多干点儿活儿　好参加实习　好发挥你们的作用

（2）怪不得就业这么难　　怪不得条件这么差　　怪不得风格不一样
怪不得赢不了他们　　怪不得这么冷　　怪不得没人卖鞭炮

怪不得他很生气　　　怪不得他不愿意参加

（3）反而出名了　　　　　反而不习惯了　　　　　反而没有成功

反而受到了批评　　　反而得到了夸奖　　　　反而发展得更慢了

反而没有了竞争　　　反而担负很重的工作　　反而她买单了

（4）尤其要注意发音　　　尤其喜欢古典音乐　　　尤其是老人和孩子

尤其是《红楼梦》　　尤其没想到他会不高兴　尤其爱好下象棋

尤其可爱　　　　　　尤其安静　　　　　　　尤其熟悉这儿的环境

（5）连忙打电话　　　　　连忙站起来　　　　　　连忙把他送到医院

连忙告诉经理　　　　连忙去火车站买票

（6）随便谈谈　　　请随便坐　　　　随便吃点儿什么　　　随便什么都行

随你的便　　　挺随便　　　　不能太随便

2. 句子练习　Sentence drills

A. 用所给词语完成句子

Complete the following sentences with the given words and expressions

好

（1）你马上把公司贷款的情况告诉经理，他＿＿＿＿＿＿＿＿＿＿。（研究）

（2）你还有什么要跟他说，现在告诉我，我＿＿＿＿＿＿＿＿＿＿。（回信）

（3）明天要来多少人，我们＿＿＿＿＿＿＿＿。（准备）

（4）他们跟你很熟悉，你＿＿＿＿＿＿＿。（了解）

（5）让他做他最喜欢干的工作，这样＿＿＿＿＿＿＿＿＿。（发挥）

尤其

（1）你的发音还有些问题，＿＿＿＿＿＿＿＿＿＿。（s 和 sh 的发音）

（2）他姐姐特别喜欢音乐，＿＿＿＿＿＿＿＿＿＿。（古典音乐）

（3）今天来的人很多，要照顾好他们，＿＿＿＿＿＿＿＿。（老人和孩子）

（4）这些盆景很好看，＿＿＿＿＿＿＿＿＿＿。（小松树）

（5）我没想到大家会不高兴，＿＿＿＿＿＿＿＿。（他会不高兴）

怪不得

（1）门没关好，_____。（冷）

（2）北京城里除春节以外禁止放鞭炮，_____。（卖）

（3）这么晚了，你们还唱歌跳舞，_____。（生气）

（4）北京烤鸭这么好吃，_____。（尝一尝）

（5）你们足球队不经常活动，也不参加比赛，_____。（人家赢了）

连忙

（1）他知道自己的考试成绩不错，_____。（打电话）

（2）丁力波看了妈妈的来信以后，他_____。（回信）

（3）爷爷突然病了，爸爸_____。（送到医院）

（4）她听说弟弟还没有吃饭，就_____。（做好吃的）

（5）陈老师去宿舍看林娜，_____。（站起来）

难道

（1）你来北京快一年了，_____还没_____？（游览过长城）

（2）他们都能学好汉语，_____我就_____？（学不好）

（3）他很喜欢中国古诗，_____不知道_____？（大诗人李白）

（4）你在中国过了好几次春节，_____不知道_____？

（年夜饭要吃鱼）

（5）他父母都老了，健康情况又不太好，他_____不_____？

（该照顾老人）

B. 用"不但不／没……，反而……"回答问题

Answer the following questions, using "不但不／没……，反而……"

（1）她和丈夫干不了卸车的活儿，邻居们笑话他们了吗？

邻居们不但没有笑话他们，_____。（热情地帮助）

（2）雨是不是小了点儿？

雨不但没有小，_____。（越下越大）

（3）杰克第一次见到玉兰父母的时候，他叫他们爸妈了吗？

他不但没叫他们爸妈，＿＿＿＿＿＿＿＿＿＿＿＿＿＿＿＿。（先生、太太）

C. 用"难道……吗"改写句子

Rewrite the following sentences, using "难道……吗"

例：男人做得到的事，女人也能做到。→

男人做得到的事，难道女人就不能做到吗？

（1）不按时还贷款的人没有信用，一辈子不借贷款的人也没有信用。

＿＿＿＿＿＿＿＿＿＿＿＿＿＿＿＿＿＿＿＿

（2）他们的工作很重要，你们的工作也很重要。

＿＿＿＿＿＿＿＿＿＿＿＿＿＿＿＿＿＿＿＿

（3）小王知道陈老师是林娜他们的汉语老师。

＿＿＿＿＿＿＿＿＿＿＿＿＿＿＿＿＿＿＿＿

（4）马大为很想去黄山旅游。

＿＿＿＿＿＿＿＿＿＿＿＿＿＿＿＿＿＿＿＿

（5）他介绍的情况是真的，我介绍的也是真的。

＿＿＿＿＿＿＿＿＿＿＿＿＿＿＿＿＿＿＿＿

D. 用"不是……，就是……"回答问题

Answer the following questions, using "不是……，就是……"

（1）中国一年放两次长假，年轻人是怎么过的？

年轻人几乎都去旅游，＿＿＿＿＿＿＿，＿＿＿＿＿＿＿。（国外，外地）

（2）中国男人做家务吗？

中国男人也做家务，他们＿＿＿＿＿＿＿，＿＿＿＿＿＿＿。

（买菜，打扫房间）

（3）这儿七月的天气怎么样？

这儿七月的天气很不好，＿＿＿＿＿＿＿，＿＿＿＿＿＿。（刮风，下雨）

3. 根据课文回答问题　Answer the following questions according to the texts

（1）玉兰和杰克为什么又回到农村来了？

（2）这次杰克是怎样称呼他岳父岳母的？这样称呼合适吗？

（3）对称呼的问题，现在玉兰爸妈有什么看法？

（4）中国人吃年夜饭的时候为什么总是有"鱼"这个菜？

（5）为什么很多中国人喜欢带"8"的号码？

（6）为什么吃过年夜饭以后还包饺子？

（7）除了吃年夜饭以外，农村过春节还有什么活动？

（8）今年春天，他们在郊区农村盖了一个什么样的房子？

（9）他们装了一卡车的木头和水泥准备去做什么？

（10）他们还习惯干重活儿吗？

（11）是谁帮助他们卸完木头和水泥的？

（12）他们打算付给邻居们报酬，邻居们是怎么想的？

（13）最后，妻子跟丈夫说什么了？

4. 会话练习　Conversation practice

会话常用语　IDIOMATIC EXPRESSIONS IN CONVERSATION

恭喜发财！ (May you be prosperous!)

怎么（叫）都行。(Whatever you call it is fine.)

这没什么。(It doesn't matter. / It's not important.)

我随便。(Anything will do for me. / Anything is okay with me.)

【春节祝愿　Spring Festival greetings】

（1）A：新年好，恭喜恭喜！

　　B：恭喜恭喜！

（2）A：恭喜发财！

　　　B：祝你万事如意！

（3）A：祝你新春快乐！

　　　B：祝你健康幸福！

【反诘　Asking a rhetorical question】

（1）A：这件事儿我好像今天才第一次听到。

　　　B：不是早就打电话通知你了吗？难道你还不知道吗？

（2）A：真对不起，我最近确实工作很多，这件事情又太急，恐怕……

　　　B：你再想想，有一个月的时间呢，难道还做不完吗？

（3）A：王总现在很忙，没有时间见你们。

　　　B：你们怎么能突然改变主意呢？难道跟他只谈十分钟都不行吗？

【不在乎　Expressing not taking something to heart】

（1）A：你想吃点儿什么？

　　　B：我随便，什么都可以。

（2）A：这次游览的路线有一些变化，想跟你商量一下。

　　　B：你们决定吧，怎么玩儿都行。

（3）A：很抱歉，我们来晚了。

　　　B：这没什么，我们也刚来。

5. 交际练习　Communication exercises

(1) Discuss the customs of the Chinese Spring Festival and compare them with those of Christmas or any other important holiday of your own country.

(2) Discuss how to manage the relations with neighbours. Which of the two kinds of relationships is better: the close relationship described in Text 2 or the less intimate relationship common in urban areas?

After discussing the two topics above with your classmates, write a short essay on either one.

阅读 与复述 Reading Comprehension and Paraphrasing

🎧16 舅舅进城拜年（bàinián）

春节快要到了。

我记得在我上小学的时候，每年春节前舅舅都要带着两个孩子来一次北京。他们不是带来点儿花生（huāshēng）、瓜子，就是带来梨（lí）、杏儿（xìngr）什么的，说是来给我们拜早年。回去时，我妈妈也总是把早就准备好了的礼物让他们带回去：大人和孩子每人都换上一套新衣服，带上些点心、水果糖和过年用的东西，还要给每个孩子一两百块压岁钱（yāsuìqián），好帮他们交学校的书费。

"都到年底（niándǐ）了，怎么又不见他们来？"我爸爸问妈妈。我妈妈也觉得有点儿奇怪，她说："他们已经三年没来了，难道是对我们有意见吗？"我说："现在的农村变化可大了，学校组织我们到郊区农村参观过，那儿的农民比城里人富（fù）得多。不少农民家里都有车。舅舅他们也可能正忙着挣钱发财呢吧。"

我爸爸说："没那么简单，你去的是北京郊区农村。我看，全国都过上小康（xiǎokāng）生活了，他们那山沟（shāngōu）里也不会有太大的变化……"

我们正说着，舅舅开着一辆新卡车来了。

"舅舅，怎么您一个人来？我表哥、表姐呢？"我问。

"他们在家跟你舅妈忙温室里的活儿呢。我这次来北京，一是给你们拜早年，二是想在北京买一台大彩电（cǎidiàn）。两个孩子说，从电视里可以学到很多农业（nóngyè）技术。去年村里通电了，他们就要我来买。这两年，我确实没空儿，所以也没来给你们拜年。今年不管怎么忙也得来看看你们。"

舅舅开着卡车来买大彩电，我爸爸妈妈都感到很突然。舅舅见他们都没说话，连忙笑着说："你们只知道城里人过好日子，现在我们穷山沟里的农民也开始有钱了，政府派了农业技术员帮助我们种果树，还教我们怎么养蜂 (yǎng fēng)、养羊。果树的收入不用说，卖蜂蜜 (fēngmì) 这一项，一年少说也要收入一两万块钱。"

这次，舅舅只在北京住了一天，需要买的东西他都买了。除了大彩电以外，还买了不少农业技术方面的书。他说："这些书是你表哥要我买的。我们那儿就缺 (quē) 这个。"他走的时候，还给了我五百块压岁钱，对我说："等今年把房子盖好了，我再来接你们全家到我那儿过春节。"

三、语法　Grammar

词语 例解　Word Usage and Examples

1 好

"好" (so that) is often used as an optative verb with the connotation of "可以". Placed before the verb in the second clause, it explains the purpose of the action in the first clause, for example,

他们想快点儿把东西卸完，好让司机回城去。

明天别忘了带词典，做翻译练习的时候好用。

今天大家早点儿睡觉，明天好早点儿起来。

你把手机号告诉我，有事儿的时候我好给你打电话。

2 怪不得

The adverb " 怪不得 " is used to indicate that one has realized the cause of a certain situation and therefore is no longer confused. It is often used as an adverbial in front of a subject-predicate construction, preceded or followed by a sentence or phrase that indicates the cause, for example,

下大雪了，怪不得这么冷。

丁力波的妈妈是北京人，怪不得他的普通话说得这么好。

城里过春节没有农村热闹，怪不得很多城里人不是到外地旅游，就是到农村来过节。

怪不得他今天九点还没起床，昨天晚上十二点他才从网吧回来。

3 尤其

The adverb " 尤其 " is usually used in the latter part of a sentence. It indicates that the object of discussion stands out in its group or in comparison to other objects, for example,

他家有很多珍贵的中国画，齐白石画的虾尤其珍贵。

张教授爱好养花儿，尤其喜欢养君子兰。

邻居们对他们都很热情，尤其是那个小伙子。

很多人每天都在街心花园打太极拳，尤其是退了休的老年人。

4 连忙

The adverb " 连忙 " is usually used in declarative and descriptive sentences. It indicates a rapid action performed in an urgent situation, for example,

客人都坐下了，她连忙送上茶。

快七点了，他连忙从床上爬起来。

他连忙跑过来，扶住了老人。

东西卸完了，她连忙跟丈夫商量，应该给每个人多少报酬。

句子 结构　Sentence Structure

1 反问句（2）　The rhetorical question (2)

The adverb "难道" is often placed before the subject or the verb of an interrogative sentence to stress the rhetorical tone. It emphasizes the meaning contrary to that of the sentence. "难道说" is also often placed in front of the subject to denote the same meaning. For example,

都吃完晚饭了，为什么还包饺子？难道还有客人要来吗？

（不应该有）

大家都知道明天要考口语，难道你不知道吗？（应该知道）

这么点儿小问题，难道我们就解决不了吗？（一定能解决）

难道说马大为不打算去黄山旅游吗？（应该去）

> The rhetorical questions we have learned previously:
>
> 你不是去过香港吗？（Lesson 28）
>
> 他哪开得了口叫"爸爸"？
>
> 你怎么会不知道呢？

2 不但不／没……，反而……
The construction "不但不／没……，反而……"

The adverb "反而" implies a meaning that is opposite to the preceding context, and serves as the turning point of the sentence, for example,

他这次病好以后，身体反而比以前更好了。

我本来想劝劝他的，没想到他反而更生气了。

In a compound sentence with the construction "不但不／没……，反而……", "不但" is placed in the negative clause, and "反而" is placed in front of the predicate of the positive clause to indicate that the condition in the context has brought about a result contrary to one's expectation, for example,

风不但没停，反而越刮越大了。

这样不但不能解决问题，反而会带来更多的矛盾。

听了大家的批评，他不但没生气，反而很高兴。

邻居们不但没有笑话我们，反而围了过来想帮助我们。

3 不是……，就是……　The construction "不是……，就是……"

The construction "不是……，就是……" means "either ... or ...". "不是" and "就是" can be followed by nouns, verbs, phrases or clauses in this construction, implying that either statement is true, for example,

她穿衣服只喜欢两种颜色，不是黑色，就是白色。

他从早到晚都很忙，不是工作，就是学习。

他每次去上海，不是坐特快火车，就是坐飞机。

放长假的时候，年轻人不是去外地旅行，就是去国外旅游。

四、字与词　Chinese Characters and Words

1 集中识字　Learn the characters of the same radicals

火：炒　炎　烤　烧　炮

口：可　右　叶　号　只　叫　另　吃　吗　员　听　吧　告　君　味
　　呢　咖　啡　虽　品　咱　哪　啊　唱　啤　喝　嘴　响

又：叉　友　双　发　圣　对　戏　观　欢　鸡　变　艰　难

2 词语联想　Learn the following groups of associated words

四合院　院子　楼房　平方　厨房　客厅　餐厅　卧室　书房　宿舍

新房　旧房　客房　花园　装修　木头　水泥　居民　房客　邻居

买房　租房　房子　房东　房屋　房租　房间　房钱　房产

年	今年	去年	明年	前年	后年	本年	当年		
月	上月	下月	本月	一月	二月	三月	四月	五月	六月
	七月	八月	九月	十月	十一月	十二月			
天	今天	明天	昨天	前天	后天				
星期	星期一	星期二	星期三	星期四	星期五	星期六	星期日		
	星期天								
日期	初一	初二	初三	初四	初五	初六	初七	初八	初九
	初十								
时间	早上	上午	中午	下午	晚上	夜里	半夜	深夜	

Spring Festival and the Travel Rush

Spring Festival, also called the Chinese New Year, is the most important traditional festival in China.

Spring Festival is the most lively and bustling day in a year. A variety of preparations need to be done before it, including cleaning the house, steaming rice cakes, frying meatballs and buying new clothes, Spring Festival couplets, New Year pictures, firecrackers and all kinds of other stuff. During the Spring Festival, people paste Spring Festival couplets and New Year pictures, set off firecrackers, have *jiaozi* (Chinese dumplings)

together, stay up late waiting for the New Year to come and extend New Year greetings to each other. For Chinese people, Spring Festival is a day of family reunion, so all the people, no matter where they are, would try their best to get home and spend the day with their family.

China is a country with a vast area and huge population. To have a better life, many people have left their hometown to work in other places. Every year when the Spring Festival comes, these migrant workers, together with the college students going back home for vacation and people paying visits to relatives and friends, crowd into a massive population movement, resulting in the unique Chinese phenomenon of the "Spring Festival Travel Rush".

This travel rush brings about enormous pressure to the transport industry in China. During this period, which lasts 40 days or so, the number of passenger trips reaches more than three billion, which is half the world's population. Put in other words, it's like the whole Chinese population moving twice. Therefore, the "Spring Festival Travel Rush" is tagged as the largest seasonal human migration in human history. It has even been recognized as a candidate for the world's biggest seasonal transport peak by the World Record Association and created several Chinese and world records.

第四十三课
Lesson 43

读《孔乙己》

Reading "Kong Yiji"

Do you know Lu Xun, one of the most famous writers in the history of modern Chinese literature? Ding Libo is reading Lu Xun's short story, "Kong Yiji". He doesn't understand some parts of it, so Wang Xiaoyun is trying to explain it to him.

一、课文 Texts

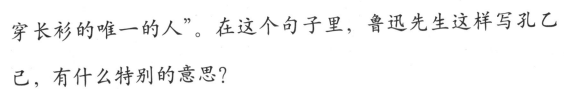

17 （一）

读《孔乙己》

王小云： 力波，你在读什么呢？

丁力波： 《孔乙己》。①

王小云： 你现在读《孔乙己》这样的小说，觉得难不难？

丁力波： 难死了。有些句子虽然没有生词，但是我仍然读不懂它的意思。

王小云： 什么句子？

丁力波： 比如说，"孔乙己是站着喝酒而穿长衫的唯一的人"。在这个句子里，鲁迅先生这样写孔乙己，有什么特别的意思？

王小云： 有啊。当时"穿长衫"的，不是读书人就是有钱人，他们去咸亨酒店，都是坐着喝酒、吃菜的。在酒店里，站着喝酒的人都是做工的穷人，都穿着短衣。只有孔乙己跟别人不同，他认为自己是读书人，总是要穿着长衫；可是他现在已经很穷了，不可能坐下来跟有钱人一样地吃、喝，只能和穿短衣的穷人一起"站着喝酒"。这句话表示他虽然很穷，可是仍然要摆读书人的架子。② 不了解当时的社会情况，就很难理解这句话的意思。

丁力波：那么，这句话的意思是讽刺孔乙己吧？

王小云：是讽刺孔乙己。鲁迅先生在这篇小说里也揭露了封建社会。

丁力波：你说得很对。小云，谢谢你，没有你的解释，我就搞不清楚这句话的意思。

王小云：别那么客气。听说昨天下午你们系举行汉语节目比赛了？

丁力波：是啊，我们班演的相声，大家都笑死了。你知道吗？有个节目就是表演孔乙己在咸亨酒店喝酒。

王小云：谁演孔乙己？

丁力波：高年级的一个留学生演孔乙己。他个子高高的，头发长长的，穿着一件又脏又破的长衫，站在柜台前问店里的小伙计：你读过书吗？你知道"回"字有几种写法？他演得有意思极了。

王小云：怪不得你今天就在这儿看《孔乙己》了。可惜我昨天下午出去了，没有来看你们的节目。要是早点儿知道就好了。③

丁力波：没关系，明年这个时候我们系还有汉语节目表演，我想明年该演《阿Q正传》了。

生词 New Words

1. 仍然	réngrán	Adv	still, yet　仍然读不懂，仍然犹豫
2. 而	ér	Conj	*used to connect two elements in a sentence to indicate transition*
3. 长衫	chángshān	N	long gown　穿长衫，一件长衫，站着喝酒而穿长衫
4. 唯一	wéiyī	A	only, sole　唯一的人，唯一的机会，唯一的要求
5. 当时	dāngshí	N	then, at that time　当时穿长衫的人，当时的技术水平，当时很满意
6. 读书人	dúshūrén	N	scholar, intellectual　一般都是读书人，认为自己是读书人
7. 做工	zuògōng	VO	to do manual work, to work　在外边做工，在城里做工
8. 穷人	qióngrén	N	poor person, the poor　做工的穷人，帮助穷人
穷	qióng	A	poor, impoverished　穷山沟，穷地方
9. 摆架子	bǎi jiàzi	V O	to put on airs　又穷又要摆架子，仍然要摆读书人的架子，不摆架子
架子	jiàzi	N	airs, haughty manner　摆架子，没有架子，架子大
10. 理解	lǐjiě	V	to understand, to comprehend　理解这句话的意思，理解作家的作品，理解他，互相理解，对这件事很不理解
11. 那么	nàme	Conj	then, in that case
12. 讽刺	fěngcì	V	to satirize　讽刺社会，讽刺孔乙己
13. 揭露	jiēlù	V	to expose, to disclose　揭露封建社会，揭露他的老板，揭露矛盾

14.	解释	jiěshì	V	to explain 解释这句话的意思，解释这件事情，解释这个生词
15.	节目	jiémù	N	programme 汉语节目比赛，表演汉语节目，电视节目，一个节目
16.	相声	xiàngsheng	N	comic dialogue, crosstalk 表演相声，说相声
17.	个子	gèzi	N	height, stature 个子很高，个子有多高，高个子，大个子，小个子
18.	头发	tóufa	N	(human) hair 头发很长，长头发，短头发，黑头发
19.	破	pò	A/V	broken, worn-out; to break, to damage 破衣服；盘子破了，打破了酒杯
20.	柜台	guìtái	N	counter 站在柜台前，在柜台前排队，银行的柜台，商店的柜台
21.	伙计	huǒji	N	(old-fashioned) shop assistant
22.	写法	xiěfǎ	N	style of handwriting, way of writing "回"字的写法，文章的写法，诗的写法
23.	可惜	kěxī	A	pitiful, it's a pity 可惜我有课，觉得很可惜，有点儿可惜，真可惜
24.	孔乙己	Kǒng Yǐjǐ	PN	Kong Yiji (name of the protagonist in one of Lu Xun's short stories)
25.	鲁迅	Lǔ Xùn .	PN	Lu Xun (a well-known modern Chinese writer)
26.	咸亨酒店	Xiánhēng Jiǔdiàn	PN	Xianheng Restaurant
	酒店	jiǔdiàn	N	bar, restaurant, hotel
27.	《阿Q正传》	Ā Q Zhèngzhuàn	PN	"The True Story of Ah Q" (a short story by Lu Xun)

注释　Notes

① 《孔乙己》。

This is a sentence of a simple word/phrase. Under certain circumstances, a single word or a phrase that is equivalent to a single word may form a sentence, for example,

（1）A：你在看什么？

　　　B：《孔乙己》。

（2）A：谁？

　　　B：我。

（3）好冷！

（4）啊！真美！

Lu Xun's short story "Kong Yiji" was published in 1919. Kong Yiji, the hero of the story, was a poor and frustrated scholar living in the feudal society. Although he had to make a living by doing manual labour, he was unwilling to take off his worn-out, dirty scholar's gown. He eventually became a thief. Through the story of this tragic character, the writer criticizes the feudal system at that time.

② 这句话表示他虽然很穷，可是仍然要摆读书人的架子。

"This indicates that although he was poor, he still put on the airs of a scholar."

Scholars had a high status in traditional Chinese society and could become officials by passing the civil service examinations.

③ 要是早点儿知道就好了。

"If only I had known this earlier."

The structure "要是……就好了" (if only...) is often used to express regret about things that were not realized in the past, for example,

要是我多问问别人就好了。

要是你告诉我一声就好了。

🎧18 （二）

跟巴金先生握手

——马大为的日记

3 月 20 日　晴

我对中国现代文学很感兴趣，尤其喜欢鲁迅、巴金和老舍这些著名的作家。④ 来北京以前我读过巴金的小说《家》，是翻译成英文的，也看过《家》这部电影。我来北京以后，看过话剧《茶馆》和电视剧《阿Q正传》。我很想多了解一些这几位作家的情况。上星期力波对我说："你还是去参观一下中国现代文学馆吧。中国现代有名作家的资料那儿都有。我那天参观了一上午，也没有看完，可把我累坏了。不过我还想再去几次。我们在北京的时候不去参观参观，以后一定会觉得很遗憾。"力波还非常认真地对我说："你去参观文学馆的时候，别忘了跟巴金先生握手。"我觉得很奇怪，巴金先生已经去世了，怎么会每天在那儿跟参观的人握手呢？这当然是不可能的，那么，力波是什么意思呢？

今天上午学院组织我们去参观现代文学馆。那是一座很普通的新楼，从外边看，平平常常的，简简单单的。但是进了大楼以后，我们就觉得来到了一座文学宝库。一位讲解员给我们介绍了很多著名作家的情况和他们的作品。她讲解得很认真，也很清楚。我一边看，一边听，一边记，有时候还向她提些问题。我觉得这样的参观很有意思，不但可以了解作家的情况，而且还可以了解他们生活的时代，这对理解作家的作品是很有帮助的。我们从楼下看到楼上，把文学馆看了一遍，已经快十一点了。那位讲解员热情地对大家说："你们走的时候，别忘了跟巴金先生握手。"

大家都觉得很奇怪，那位讲解员笑着把我们送到文学馆门口。她指着门上的铜把手说："你们看，这是什么？"这时候我们才注意到这个门的把手做得很特别，像一只真手似的。讲解员接着说："这是巴金先生95岁的时候，按他右手的模型做的。有了这个铜把手，表示巴金先生每天都在这里跟参观的人握手！"

我握着"巴金先生的手"，心里想：尊敬的巴金先生，您好！我很喜欢您的作品，您是中国青年的朋友，也是我们的朋友。

生词 New Words

| 1. 日记 | rìjì | N | diary | 马大为的日记，写日记，一本日记，记日记 |

2.	话剧	huàjù	N	stage play, modern drama 上演话剧《茶馆》，看话剧，演话剧
3.	电视剧	diànshìjù	N	television show, television series 看电视剧，拍电视剧，演电视剧
4.	还是	háishi	Adv	had better 还是去参观一下吧
5.	作家	zuòjiā	N	writer 中国现代著名的作家，这几位作家的情况
6.	资料	zīliào	N	data, material 作家的资料，学习资料，研究资料，历史资料
7.	遗憾	yíhàn	A	regretful 觉得很遗憾，有点儿遗憾，真遗憾，遗憾的是
8.	组织	zǔzhī	V	to organize 组织我们去参观，组织大家学打太极拳
9.	宝库	bǎokù	N	treasure house 像一座文学宝库似的，艺术宝库，文化宝库，知识宝库
10.	讲解员	jiǎngjiěyuán	N	guide, narrator, commentator 博物馆的讲解员，展览会的讲解员
	讲解	jiǎngjiě	V	to explain, to interpret 讲解课文，讲解生词，讲解语法，讲解得很认真，清楚地讲解
11.	时代	shídài	N	times, era, epoch 他们生活的时代，旧时代过去了，开始了新时代，封建时代，大学时代
12.	铜把手	tóng bǎshou		bronze handle 用铜把手，握铜把手
	铜	tóng	N	copper
	把手	bǎshou	N	handle, knob (of a door, window, suitcase, etc.) 门把手，把手坏了
13.	……似的	……shìde	Pt	*a particle indicating similarity* 像一只真手似的
14.	模型	móxíng	N	model, mould 右手的模型，大楼的模型，学院的模型
15.	巴金	Bā Jīn	PN	Ba Jin (a well-known modern Chinese writer)

补充生词　Supplementary Words

1. 眼镜	yǎnjìng	N	glasses, spectacles
2. 伯父	bófù	N	uncle (father's elder brother)
3. 在世	zàishì	V	to be living
4. 鼻子	bízi	N	nose
5. 胡子	húzi	N	beard, moustache, whiskers
6. 直	zhí	A	straight
7. 扁	biǎn	A	flat
8. 碰壁	pèngbì	VO	to run up against a stone wall, to meet with a major setback
碰	pèng	V	to touch, to bump
壁	bì		wall
9. 小心	xiǎoxīn	A/V	careful; to take care, to be careful
10. 硬	yìng	A	hard, solid
11. 拉车	lā chē	V O	to pull a cart or rickshaw
12. 呻吟	shēnyín	V	to groan, to moan
13. 玻璃	bōli	N	glass
14. 扎	zhā	V	to prick, to needle into
15. 脚心	jiǎoxīn	N	the underside of the arch (of the foot), centre of the sole
16. 纱布	shābù	N	bandage, gauze
17. 剩	shèng	V	to be left over, to remain

注释　Notes

④ 我对中国现代文学很感兴趣，尤其喜欢鲁迅、巴金和老舍这些著名的作家。

　　"I am very interested in modern Chinese literature. I especially like such famous writers as Lu Xun, Ba Jin and Lao She."

Lu Xun (1881—1936), Ba Jin (1904—2005) and Lao She (1899—1966) are the most famous writers of modern Chinese literature. Lu Xun's representative works include "The True Story of Ah Q" and "Kong Yiji." Ba Jin's major works include *The Family*, *Spring*, and *Autumn*. Lao She's representative works include the novel *Camel Xiangzi* and the stage play *Teahouse*.

二、练习　Exercises

练习与运用　Drills and Practice　 19

核心句 KEY SENTENCES

1. 有些句子虽然没有生词，但是我仍然读不懂它的意思。
2. 你还是去参观一下中国现代文学馆吧。
3. 那么，这句话的意思是讽刺孔乙己吧?
4. 这个门的把手做得很特别，像一只真手似的。
5. 他个子高高的，头发长长的。
6. 大家都笑死了。
7. 不了解当时的社会情况，就很难理解这句话的意思。
8. 要是早点儿知道就好了。

1. 熟读下列词组　Read the following phrases until you learn them by heart

（1）仍然在生气　　　仍然不会开车　　　　仍然跑得那么快

　　　仍然放在院子里　仍然没有寄钱

（2）还是这本词典新　　还是上海的东西便宜

　　　还是从小路走近　　还是看电视有意思

（3）当时的社会 　　　　当时没看清楚 　　　　当时不同意办

　　　当时都还年轻 　　　　当时没有这么贵

（4）过年似的 　　　　　不高兴似的 　　　　疯了似的 　　　　孩子似的

　　　得了大病似的 　　　像有急事似的 　　像用水洗过似的

　　　像艺术宝库似的 　　　像照顾自己的父母似的

（5）笑死了 　冷死了 　想死了 　忙死了 　担心死了 　别扭死了

　　　急坏了 　怕坏了 　饿坏了 　累坏了 　热坏了 　　高兴坏了 　辣坏了

（6）组织一次讨论 　　　组织普通话比赛 　　组织生日聚会 　组织休闲活动

　　　组织大家学英语 　　组织同学去参观 　　组织他们打太极拳

　　　再组织一些人来

（7）高高兴兴的 　　　平平安安的 　　　　健健康康的 　　　安安静静的

　　　干干净净的 　　　舒舒服服的 　　　　马马虎虎的 　　　辛辛苦苦的

　　　热热闹闹的 　　　清清楚楚的 　　　　远远的 　　　　　瘦瘦的

（8）对我们是很有帮助的 　　　　　　对工作是很有帮助的

　　　对理解作家的作品是很有帮助的

2. 句子练习 Sentence drills

A. 用所给词语完成句子

Complete the following sentences with the given words and expressions

仍然

（1）他学开车学了好几次，可是＿＿＿＿＿＿＿＿＿＿＿＿＿＿＿＿＿。（不会）

（2）杰克第二次见到岳父岳母了，＿＿＿＿＿＿＿＿＿＿＿＿＿。（开不了口叫）

（3）已经是夏天了，天气＿＿＿＿＿＿＿＿＿＿＿＿＿＿。（冷）

（4）下班以后，他＿＿＿＿＿＿＿＿＿＿＿＿＿＿＿＿。（工作）

还是

（1）怎样装修客厅呢？我们决定＿＿＿＿＿＿＿＿＿＿＿＿＿。（中国传统的风格）

（2）这件事比较复杂，＿＿＿＿＿＿＿＿＿＿＿＿＿＿＿。（自己去解释）

（3）大家讨论以后，觉得＿＿＿＿＿＿＿＿＿＿＿比较合适。（这套课本）

（4）这个星期大家都很忙，＿＿＿＿＿＿＿＿＿＿比较好。（下星期）

那么

（1）大家都愿意到东郊去植树，＿＿＿＿＿＿＿＿＿＿。（决定）

（2）男女不能在各个方面享受同样的权利，＿＿＿＿＿＿。（男女平等）

（3）他对这家饭店的服务不满意，＿＿＿＿＿＿＿＿？（为什么）

（4）你们的风俗跟我们的不一样，＿＿＿＿＿＿＿＿？（婚礼）

B. 用"像……似的"改写画线的部分

Rewrite the underlined parts, using "像……似的"

（1）他虽然快六十岁了，但干起活儿来，跟年轻小伙子一样。

＿＿＿＿＿＿＿＿＿＿＿＿＿＿＿＿。

（2）打完电话他就出去了，好像有什么急事。

＿＿＿＿＿＿＿＿＿＿＿＿＿＿＿＿。

（3）这孩子说起话来，跟大人一样。

＿＿＿＿＿＿＿＿＿＿＿＿＿＿＿＿。

（4）最近这个孩子又黄又瘦，好像有什么病。

＿＿＿＿＿＿＿＿＿＿＿＿＿＿＿＿。

C. 用形容词重叠做谓语改写句子

Rewrite the following sentences, using reduplicated adjectives as predicates

（1）他个子很高。

他个子＿＿＿＿＿＿＿＿＿＿。

（2）姑娘的头发很长。

姑娘的头发＿＿＿＿＿＿＿＿＿。

（3）他每天都很高兴。

他每天都＿＿＿＿＿＿＿＿＿。

（4）书架上的书很整齐。

书架上的书＿＿＿＿＿＿＿＿＿。

（5）图书馆里非常安静。

图书馆里_____。

D. 选择适当的词填空

Fill in the blanks with the appropriate words

（1）女儿三年没有回家了，可把妈妈_____坏了。

（2）参加比赛的人这么多，准备的时间又这么少，他们真_____死了。

（3）今天气温有39度，大家都觉得_____死了。

（4）他从下午两点工作到夜里一点半，真是_____坏了。

（5）我早上起床到现在还没有吃东西呢，_____死了。

（累 热 饿 想 担心）

E. 用"不/没（有）……，就……"改写下列句子

Rewrite the following sentences, using "不/没（有）……，就……"

（1）要解释清楚这个问题，必须会用这些生词和句子。

_____。

（2）只有参观过长城、兵马俑、颐和园这些地方，才能很好地理解中国的
古代文化。

_____。

（3）只有农村发展起来，中国社会才能有更大的进步。

_____。

（4）只有贷款后按时还钱，才能建立起自己的信用。

_____。

3. 根据课文回答问题 Answer the following questions according to the texts

（1）《孔乙己》是哪位作家的作品？

（2）孔乙己是一个什么样的人？

（3）作者为什么要写这篇小说？

（4）丁力波他们系里昨天下午举行了什么活动？

（5）丁力波对哪个节目最感兴趣？

（6）马大为喜欢哪些有名的中国作家？

（7）他知道这些作家的哪些作品？

（8）丁力波建议他去参观什么地方？

（9）为什么要去那儿参观？

（10）马大为怎么去参观的？

（11）马大为是怎么听讲解员讲解的？

（12）马大为跟巴金先生握手是怎么回事？他握着"巴金先生的手"，心里是怎么想的？

4. 会话练习　Conversation practice

会话常用语 IDIOMATIC EXPRESSIONS IN CONVERSATION

他是什么意思呢？　(What does he mean?)

有什么特别的意思？　(Is there any special meaning?)

搞不清楚 (... don't understand)

别那么客气。(Don't mention it.)

可把我累坏了。(It has really tired me out.)

【描写人和物　Describing people or things】

（1）A：您知道海关大楼在哪儿吗？

　　B：就在前边，您看见了吗？那儿有两座楼在一起，高高的，黑黑的，像两个大门似的。

　　A：看见了，谢谢您。

（2）A：请问，你们这儿有一位张小姐吗？

B：哪位张小姐？

A：名字我也不清楚，是那位头发长长的，嘴大大的。

B：哦，是戴眼镜（yǎnjìng）吧？

A：不是，她不戴眼镜。她总是穿得整整齐齐的，个子跟您差不多，可是比您瘦一点儿。

B：我不认识。

A：对不起，我的意思是……

【表示遗憾　Expressing regret】

（1）A：这次长假学校组织大家去泰山，你怎么没有参加？

B：我的一个朋友到中国来，我陪他在北京旅游了。

A：你没去爬泰山，太可惜了。这次玩儿得特别好。

B：我也听说了。要是我朋友晚一个星期来就好了。

（2）A：昨天的球赛你们队赢了吗？

B：别提了。3 比 4，最后两分钟被他们踢进一个球。

A：真遗憾，你们队不比他们差啊。

B：可不是。可惜 3 号没能上场；要是 5 号不受伤，也就好多了。

5. 交际练习　Communication exercises

(1) Talk with your classmates about ancient or modern Chinese writers, poets or literary works that you know.

(2) Talk about a favourite writer or literary work in your country.

After the oral presentation, write a short essay on either of the topics above.

🎧20 我的伯父（bófù）鲁迅先生

　　伯父鲁迅先生在世（zàishì）的时候，我还小，不知道鲁迅是谁，以为伯父就是伯父，跟别人的伯父一样。那时候每到周末，我们姐妹三个常常跟着爸爸妈妈到伯父家团聚。

　　有一次，在伯父家里，大家围着一张桌子吃晚饭。我看看爸爸的鼻子（bízi），又看看伯父的鼻子，对他说："大伯，你跟爸爸哪儿都像，就是有一点不像。"

　　"哪一点不像呢？"伯父回过头来，微笑着问我。他吃东西时，嘴唇上的胡子（húzi）也跟着动。

　　"爸爸的鼻子又高又直（zhí），您的呢？又扁（biǎn）又平。"

　　"你不知道，"伯父笑着说，"我小的时候，鼻子跟你爸爸的一样，也是又高又直的。"

　　"那怎么——"

　　"可是到了后来，碰了几次壁，把鼻子碰扁了。"

　　"碰壁（pèngbì）？"我说，"您怎么会碰壁呢？是不是您走路不小心（xiǎoxīn）？"

　　"你想，四周围黑黑的，还不容易碰壁吗？"

　　"哦！我明白了，墙壁当然比鼻子硬（yìng）得多了，怪不得您把鼻子碰扁了。"

　　在座的人都大笑起来。

　　还有一件事情到现在我仍然记得很清楚。

　　一天傍晚，刮着西北风，街上的人都急急忙忙地赶着回家。爸爸妈妈拉着我的手，到伯父家去。走到离伯父家门口不远的地方，看见一个拉车（lā chē）的坐在地上呻吟（shēnyín）。我们走过去，他抬起头来，好像很痛苦的样子。

"怎么了？"爸爸问他。

"先生，"他小声地说，"玻璃（bōli）片儿扎（zhā）进脚心（jiǎoxīn）了。疼死我了，回不了家，我都急坏了，不知道该怎么办。"

爸爸跑到伯父家里去，一会儿，就和伯父拿了药和纱布（shābù）出来。让拉车的坐在车上，他们俩给他取出玻璃片儿，上了药，包上纱布。那个拉车的感激地说："我真不知道该怎么感谢你们！我家离这儿不远，这就可以慢慢地走回去了。"伯父又拿出一些钱来给他，叫他在家里休息几天，把剩（shèng）下的药和纱布也给了他。

三、语法 Grammar

词语 例解 Word Usage and Examples

1 仍然

The adverbs "仍然" and "仍" express that a certain situation remains unchanged. They are mainly used in written Chinese, for example,

到了夜晚，商店仍然像白天一样，非常热闹。

他六十多了，但干起活儿来，仍然不知道累。

这个问题已经研究了五年多了，仍没有解决。

2 还是

The adverb "还是" indicates a choice made after a comparison, for example,

现在去长城有点儿晚了，故宫比较近，还是去故宫吧。

八点出发太早，还是九点吧。

In the structure " 还是 + V/S-PP + A", the adjective at the end denotes the reason why that particular choice is made, for example,

还是大家在一起讨论好。

看了好几家，还是这家商店的东西比较便宜。

想了很久，还是你去最合适。

3 那么

The conjunction " 那么 " is used to introduce a result or judgement that has been derived from the previous context, for example,

你说这样做不行，那么，你认为该怎么办？

孔乙己又穷又要摆读书人的架子，那么，鲁迅先生这样写是讽刺孔乙己吧？

要是有很多人不同意这个办法，那么，就请经理决定吧。

4 ……似的

The structure "……似的", usually preceded by a phrase with "像" or "跟", is used to draw an analogy with or denote a similarity to a certain thing or situation. When it functions as an adverbial modifier, it is written as "……似地". For example,

她又叫又闹，像疯了似的。

你跟他说了这么多，他像没听见似的。

下过雨以后，树叶很绿，像刚用水洗过似的。

汽车像飞似地开过去了。

句子 结构　Sentence Structure

1 形容词重叠做谓语　Reduplicated adjectives functioning as the predicate

Monosyllabic or disyllabic adjectives may be reduplicated and used as predicates. They are descriptive and should generally be followed by " 的 ", for example,

她个子高高的，头发长长的。

他的笑总是假假的。

餐厅里干干净净的。

今天他过生日，一天都高高兴兴的。

2 V/A＋坏/死＋了 The construction "V/A＋坏/死＋了"

The construction "V/A＋坏/死＋了" expresses degree. The word "坏" or "死" often follows an adjective or a verb that describes a psychological state to indicate high degree, for example,

这个工作可把我累坏了。

这几天，他可忙坏了。

听到这个消息，爸爸高兴坏了。

妻子生气，一天没有说话，他觉得别扭死了。

快给我一点儿吃的，我饿死了。

火车马上就要开了，他刚进站，快急死了。

The complements of degree we have previously learned are as follows:

（1）昨天热极了。（Lesson 17）

上海的东西比这儿便宜多了。（Lesson 17）

大家都笑死了。（Lesson 43）

可把我累坏了。（Lesson 43）

（2）他最近忙得很。（Lesson 38）

这个菜比饭馆做的好得多。（Lesson 39）

3 不/没（有）……，就……

The construction "不/没（有）……，就……"

"不/没（有）……，就……" means "without ..., then ...". In this structure, the word "不" or "没（有）" is used to negate the first clause, which indicates an assumption. The word "就" is used in the second clause to introduce the result of the assumption. This sentence pattern emphasizes the importance of the supposed condition, for example,

> 不了解当时的社会情况，就很难理解这句话的意思。
>
> 没有你们的帮助，我就做不完这些事情。
>
> 不亲自尝尝苹果，就不知道苹果的味道。
>
> 你没有时间，我就去给你买车票。

四、字与词 Chinese Characters and Words

1 集中识字 Learn the characters of the same radicals

子：孔 存 孙 学 孩

土：去 寺 地 场 在 坏 址 块 幸 坡 坐 城 埋 培 填
　　墙 境

辶：边 过 达 迅 进 远 运 还 连 近 迎 这 选 适 迹
　　迷 送 退 造 通 道 遍 追

2 词语联想 Learn the following groups of associated words

人　人口　人力　人才　人类　人们　人民　人生　人情　人品　人心
　　人员　人间　人身　人工　人家　男人　女人　爱人　本人　别人
　　法人　富人　穷人　夫人　个人　工人　古人　华人　好人　坏人
　　老人　病人　商人　主人　友人　游人　客人

头　头发　头顶　头脑　头晕　白头　头巾　头疼　头像

手　手指　手机　手表　手工　手迹　手模　手心　手写　手纸
　　手巾　手工业　握手　双手　左手　右手　助手　举手　副手
　　分手　拍手

时间　小时　钟头　点　刻　分　现在　过去　将来　从前　从来

以前　以后　刚才　已经　刚　正在　当时　古代　现代　当代

文学作品　诗歌　小说　散文　传说　笑话　故事　日记　电影

电视剧　话剧

戏剧　京剧　越剧　地方戏　民歌　民乐　舞蹈　秧歌舞

画　中国画　山水画　油画　书法　字画

The Literary Men Lu Xun, Ba Jin and Lao She

We cannot talk about modern Chinese literature without mentioning Lu Xun, Ba Jin or Lao She.

Lu Xun (1881–1936) was a great writer, thinker and revolutionist. He went to Japan to learn medicine at the beginning of 1904 and later devoted himself to literary writing in the hope of improving the national soul with his pen. He wrote about six million words (characters) in his lifetime, and his works included satirical and literary essays, short stories, criticisms and translations, which had a profound influence on Chinese literature after the May Fourth Movement.

The works of Lu Xun are full of pioneering spirit. They are like daggers, trenchant, satirical and exaggerative, analysing the characters of the Chinese nation, safeguarding justice and fighting against the authorities. His representative works include short stories such as "The True Story of Ah Q", "My Old Home", "New Year Sacrifice" and "Kong Yiji".

Ba Jin (1904–2005) was a modern writer, publisher and translator, lauded as one of the most influential writers since the New Culture Movement on May Fourth, 1919. He was an outstanding master of literature in the 20th-century China as well as a giant in the modern and contemporary Chinese literary world.

The most well-known work of Ba Jin is *The Family*, a book about the collapse of an old-fashioned family and the rebellion of the younger generation. Using concise language in a delicate style, his works display a strong sense of humanism and have a heart-touching artistic power. His representative works are the "Torrents" Trilogy, including *The Family*, *Spring* and *Autumn*.

Lao She (1899–1966) was a famous novelist, man of letters, playwright, artist and master of language in modern China. He was the first writer that won the title of "People's Artist" in the People's Republic of China.

The works of Lao She, mostly based on urban life, are of simple, humorous and satirical style. He was good at depicting the life and destiny of the poor living in the city, full of the special flavours of Beijing. His representative works include the stage plays *Teahouse* and *Dragon Beard Ditch* and the novels *Camel Xiangzi* (or *Rickshaw Boy*) and *Four Generations under One Roof*.

第四十四课

Lesson 44

● 复习　Review

买的没有卖的精

Sellers are smarter than shoppers

Many women enjoy shopping, and they can bargain for good prices in smaller shops, a situation which is common in both Eastern and Western countries. Lin Na and Xiaoyun are very delighted to come across a shop which is having a "buy-one-get-one-free" sale. In the end, however, they discover that the buyer may not always be as shrewd as the seller.

一、课文　Texts

🎧 21　（一）

买的没有卖的精

老　板：快来看啊！睡衣便宜了，绣花儿的睡衣，您买一件，我送一
件！就这几件了。这位外国朋友，您不想来一件吗？你们看，
这两只熊猫绣得多好，眼睛圆圆的，黑黑的，很适合您穿。
您穿上它，一定更漂亮。

王小云：看您说的，像真的似的。①不过，这件睡衣上的花儿绣得真
好看。

林　娜：式样也不错。要是价钱合适，我就买一件。老板，这种睡衣
多少钱一件？

老　板：九十八块钱，买一件，送一件。

王小云：买一件，送一件？有那么好的事儿？我不相信，有些商店也说买一送一，不是送小梳子，就是送小镜子。

老　板：您不相信？我送的东西，可不是梳子，而是跟这件一样的睡衣。您自己随便挑选。

林　娜：老板，能不能便宜点儿？别的商店都没有这么贵啊！

老　板：这您就不知道了，货不一样啊。这是名牌的，质量比一般的牌子好得多。我们是直接从工厂进的货，[②] 不直接进货，价钱就不会这么便宜。我不骗您，即使您跑遍了北京城，也找不着比这儿更便宜的。您就放心买吧。

林　娜：您要是便宜点儿，我就买。

老　板：您给个价吧。

林　娜：七十块钱怎么样？

老　板：七十块钱还送一件？小姐，您砍价砍得太厉害了。这么卖，我不但不能赚钱，反而要赔本儿。我现在卖的价，几乎就是进货价，每件就赚您几块钱。这样吧，您要真想买，九十五块您拿两件。

林　娜：行了，我就要这件蓝的和那件绣着熊猫的。给你钱，请把它包起来。

老　板：您这是一百，找您五块。我给您包好。

王小云：老板，这件衣服上不是还写着四十九块钱一件吗？为什么要

说九十八块钱，买一送一呢？

老　板：一件四十九块，两件不是九十八块吗？不管怎么说，我也没

有多要您一分钱。再说买两件可以换着穿，也可以做礼物送

朋友，这不挺好吗？

王小云：哦，你要是直说，我们会一次就买两件吗？怪不得人们常说，

从南京到北京，买的没有卖的精。老板，你真会做生意啊。③

生词 New Words

1. 精	jīng	A	smart, shrewd 很精，没有他精，买的没有卖的精
2. 睡衣	shuìyī	N	night clothes, night gown, pyjamas 一件睡衣，一套睡衣
3. 绣花儿	xiùhuār	VO	to embroider, to do embroidery 绣花儿睡衣，绣花儿旗袍，绣花儿衬衣
绣	xiù	V	to embroider 绣花儿，绣得很好看
4. 圆	yuán	A	round 圆桌，圆圆的眼睛，圆圆的月亮
5. 适合	shìhé	V	to suit, to fit 适合你穿，适合小学生用，适合双职工家庭，不适合小孩儿看
6. 价钱	jiàqián	N	price 价钱合适，讲价钱，最便宜的价钱
价	jià	N	price 给个价，说个价，要价，还（huán）价
7. 梳子	shūzi	N	comb 小梳子
梳	shū	V	to comb 用梳子梳头
8. 镜子	jìngzi	N	mirror 小镜子，照镜子

9. 相信	xiāngxìn	V	to believe, to trust 相信这件事，相信他说的话， 相信他
10. 挑选	tiāoxuǎn	V	to choose, to select 随便挑选，挑选衣服，挑选 学校，挑选专业，挑选公务员
挑	tiāo	V	to choose, to pick 随便挑，挑衣服，挑学校，挑 专业，挑公务员
选	xuǎn	V	to select, to elect 随便选，选课本，选专业，选 总理，选部长
11. 货	huò	N	goods, commodity 货不一样，货很好，进货， 售货
12. 质量	zhìliàng	N	quality 质量好很多，质量很差，衣服的质量， 学生的质量，学习质量
13. 直接	zhíjiē	A	direct, straight 直接来，直接说，直接进货
直	zhí	Adv	straight 直说，直走
14. 工厂	gōngchǎng	N	factory, mill, plant 服装（工）厂，汽车（工） 厂，葡萄酒（工）厂，从工厂直接进货
15. 遍	biàn	V	all over, everywhere 跑遍，走遍，问遍
16. 砍价	kǎnjià	VO	to bargain 会砍价，不能砍价
砍	kǎn	V	to cut, to chop 砍树，砍木头
17. 厉害	lìhai	A	terrible, formidable, serious 砍价砍得太厉害 了，热得厉害，竞争很厉害
18. 赚	zhuàn	V	to make a profit, to gain, to earn 赚钱，赚你几 块钱
19. 赔本儿	péiběnr	VO	to sustain losses in business 反而要赔本儿
赔	péi	V	to stand a loss, to compensate 赔钱，赔他那本书
本儿	běnr	N	capital, principal
20. 蓝	lán	A	blue 蓝的，蓝色的

注释　Notes

① 看您说的，像真的似的。

"Come on. As if it were true."

"看您说的" is frequently used to express mild disagreement with or disbelief of what the other person has said. Here, Xiaoyun is expressing her disbelief of the shopkeeper's exaggerations about the elegance and suitability of the pyjamas. For example,

看您说的，我哪有那么漂亮。

看你说的，我们这儿可没有这样差的服务态度。

看你说的，像真的似的。他没有忘了，那天他病了，所以没有参加聚会。

② 我们是直接从工厂进的货。

"We get our supply of goods directly from the factory."

In a sentence with the emphatic structure "是……的", if the object of the main verb is not a personal pronoun, then it will often be placed after "的", for example,

我是昨天知道的这件事。（也可以说："我是昨天知道这件事的。"）

他是打的去的宋华家。（也可以说："他是打的去宋华家的。"）

王小云是在王府井看见他的。（不能说："王小云是在王府井看见的他。"）

③ 你真会做生意啊。

"You are extremely good at doing business!"

In this sentence, "真……啊" is not used as praise actually; it is somewhat satirical.

 22　（二）

"胖阿姨" 文具店

1998 年，胖阿姨从上海的一家纺织工厂下岗了。她十九岁进厂，在这个厂干了十六年。现在下岗了，她真不知道自己该怎么办。

丈夫是工人，工资也不高，孩子正在上学，一家三口人的生活一下子就困难多了。胖阿姨去过不少招聘的单位，想找个新工作，可是，这些单位不是说她年龄大了点儿，就是说她文化低了点儿。她总是找不到工作。胖阿姨没有失去信心，她想还是自己招聘自己吧，就先摆个小摊子，卖些小孩儿玩具。

　　一天，有位老先生在买玩具的时候，对胖阿姨说："你要是再卖些文具，那对小学生就更方便了。"那位先生是随便说说的，可是，胖阿姨觉得这是个好主意，她想试一试。她租了一间不到六平方米的房子，开了一个"胖阿姨"文具店。胖阿姨每天都早开门，晚关门，对小学生尤其热情。她卖的文具，从来不多收孩子们一分钱。要是孩子忘了找钱，她就会追上去把钱找给孩子，还要告诉他们，办事情不能这样马虎。小学生有时把书包什么的忘在店里，她会给他们保管好，等他们来取。有个小学生还给晚报写了信，赞扬胖阿姨的服务态度。附近的中小学生都喜欢到这儿买东西，"胖阿姨"文具店的生意一天比一天好。

　　现在，"胖阿姨"文具店已经发展起来了，她开了第一家连锁店，招聘了六位下岗女工。胖阿姨家也比以前富裕多了，可是她仍

然过着勤俭朴素的生活。有人建议她买房子。她说:"现在还不能买房子,我打算开一家'胖阿姨'文具超市,把生意做得更大些。我相信,等事业真正发展起来了,房子会有的,车子也会有的,生活会更加美好。你说对不?"

生词 New Words

1. 胖	pàng	A	fat, stout	人很胖, 胖子, 胖起来了
2. 阿姨	āyí	N	auntie (a term of address for any woman of one's mother's generation)	胖阿姨, 王阿姨
3. 文具店	wénjùdiàn	N	stationery shop	胖阿姨文具店, 开文具店
文具	wénjù	N	stationery	买文具, 卖文具
4. 下岗	xiàgǎng	VO	to be laid off, to lose one's job	她下岗了, 下岗职工
5. 失去	shīqù	V	to lose	失去时间, 失去机会, 失去工作, 失去幸福
6. 信心	xìnxīn	N	confidence	失去信心, (没)有信心
7. 摊子	tānzi	N	vendor's stand, stall, booth	摆摊子, 摆个小摊子, 玩具摊子, 书摊子
8. 玩具	wánjù	N	toy	小孩儿玩具
9. 关门	guānmén	VO	(of a shop, etc.) to close	商店关门, 展览馆关门
关	guān	V	to close, to turn off	关电脑, 关电视
10. 追	zhuī	V	to chase after	追上去, 追过去, 追女孩子, 追男孩子
11. 书包	shūbāo	N	schoolbag	背书包, 用书包
12. 保管	bǎoguǎn	V	to take care of	保管东西, 保管书包, 保管好
13. 晚报	wǎnbào	N	evening paper	北京晚报, 羊城晚报
14. 态度	tàidu	N	manner, attitude	服务态度, 工作态度, 学习态度, 态度好, 态度差

15. 附近	fùjìn	N	nearby, neighbouring 附近的中小学生，附近的商店，学校附近
16. 连锁店	liánsuǒdiàn	N	chain store 第一家连锁店，开了连锁店
17. 女工	nǚgōng	N	female worker 下岗女工，纺织女工
18. 富裕	fùyù	A	prosperous, rich 家庭富裕，生活富裕
富	fù	A	rich, wealthy 富人
19. 超（级）市（场）	chāo (jí)- shì (chǎng)	N	supermarket 文具超市
超级	chāojí	A	super
市场	shìchǎng	N	market 菜市场

补充生词 Supplementary Words

1. 中奖	zhòngjiǎng	VO	to win a prize
2. 奖品	jiǎngpǐn	N	prize, trophy
3. 项链	xiàngliàn	N	necklace
4. 老百姓	lǎobǎixìng	N	ordinary folk, common people
5. 改革	gǎigé	V	to reform
6. 开放	kāifàng	V	to open, to open up
7. 凭	píng	Prep	to go by, to base on
8. 粮票	liángpiào	N	food coupon
9. 进口	jìnkǒu	V	to import
10. 羡慕	xiànmù	V	to admire, to envy
11. 电器	diànqì	N	electrical appliance
12. 发愁	fāchóu	VO	to worry, to be anxious
愁	chóu	V	to worry, to be anxious
13. 打折扣	dǎ zhékòu	V O	to give a discount

14. 抽奖	chōujiǎng	VO	to draw lots (to give out prizes), to draw a winning number (for lottery, sweepstake, etc.)
15. 值得	zhídé	V	to be worthy of, to deserve
16. 秀水街	Xiùshuǐ Jiē	PN	Xiushui Street (a free market in Beijing)

二、练习　Exercises

练习 与运用　Drills and Practice 23

核心句 KEY SENTENCES

1. 每件就赚您几块钱。
2. 即使您跑遍了北京城，也找不着比这儿更便宜的。
3. 一家三口人的生活一下子就困难多了。
4. 她卖的文具，从来不多收孩子们一分钱。
5. 我们是直接从工厂进的货。

1. 熟读下列词组 Read the following phrases until you learn them by heart

（1）就他一个人　　就去过一次　　就读过一遍　　就他相信这个消息

（2）跑遍了全城　　走遍了全国　　问遍了全系的老师
　　　吃遍了大小饭馆　　找遍了每个宿舍

（3）一下子卖完了　　一下子看不见了　　一下子就到家了
　　　一下子来了很多人

（4）从来没去过　从来不喝酒　从来就很爱干净　从来不多收孩子们的钱

（5）直接从工厂进货　　　直接送到医院　　　直接给他打电话

　　　直接去找总经理谈

（6）失去信心　失去机会　失去信用　失去儿子　失去朋友　失去生意

（7）小区附近　公园附近　邮局附近　附近的银行　附近的商店　在附近

2. 句子练习　Sentence drills

A. 用所给词语完成句子

Complete the following sentences with the given words and expressions

就

（1）今年暑假他在一家公司打工，＿＿＿＿＿＿＿＿＿＿＿＿＿＿。（休息）

（2）晚上十点，很多商店都关门了，＿＿＿＿＿＿＿＿＿。（一家咖啡馆）

（3）老师问的那篇文章，他记不起来了，＿＿＿＿＿＿＿＿。（一遍）

（4）别的同学都到大学工作了，＿＿＿＿＿＿＿＿＿＿。（律师事务所）

（5）他已经读完三年级了，＿＿＿＿＿＿，可是他不能继续学习了。（差一年）

从来

（1）你给我一杯可乐吧，我＿＿＿＿＿＿＿＿＿＿＿＿＿＿。（啤酒）

（2）胖阿姨＿＿＿＿＿＿＿＿＿＿＿＿＿。（多收）

（3）他＿＿＿＿＿＿＿＿＿＿＿＿＿。（放鞭炮）

（4）我从小到大＿＿＿＿＿＿＿＿＿＿＿＿。（这么好的风景）

（5）他们俩结婚以后，＿＿＿＿＿＿＿＿＿＿＿＿。（在一起）

遍

（1）我＿＿＿＿＿＿＿＿＿＿＿都没有找到这种自行车。（全城）

（2）为了了解哪家饭馆的菜做得最好，他＿＿＿＿＿＿＿＿。（饭馆）

（3）这件事他＿＿＿＿＿＿＿＿＿＿，大家都说不知道。（全班的人）

（4）张教授把书房都＿＿＿＿＿＿，还是没有找到昨天刚买的那本书。（找）

（5）这次他去外地参观，真的＿＿＿＿＿＿＿＿＿＿＿。（大小城市）

B. 用"一下子"完成对话

Complete the following dialogues, using "一下子"

（1）A：他们卸车用了很长时间吧？

B：邻居们都来帮忙，＿＿＿＿＿＿＿＿＿＿＿＿＿＿＿＿＿＿＿＿。（完）

（2）A：医生们到农村实习，来检查身体的人多不多？

B：医生们进村以后，＿＿＿＿＿＿＿＿＿＿＿＿＿＿＿。（来）

（3）A：现在你回家很方便吧？

B：现在我们那儿也有公共汽车了，我下了火车，坐上公共汽车，

＿＿＿＿＿＿＿＿＿＿＿＿＿＿，方便极了。（到家）

C. 用"直接"完成对话

Complete the following dialogues, using "直接"

（1）A：你们是从哪儿进的货？

B：我们是＿＿＿＿＿＿＿＿＿＿＿＿＿＿＿＿＿。（从工厂）

（2）A：我该给谁打电话？

B：你＿＿＿＿＿＿＿＿＿＿＿＿＿＿＿＿。（他们的厂长）

（3）A：老师突然病了，我们是不是把他送回家？

B：不，我们＿＿＿＿＿＿＿＿＿＿＿＿＿＿。（医院）

3. 根据课文回答问题　Answer the following questions according to the texts

（1）老板介绍的是一种什么样的睡衣？

（2）老板为什么说这种睡衣的价钱不贵？

（3）这家店的老板用什么办法多卖衣服？

（4）王小云是怎么发现这家老板很"精"的？

（5）胖阿姨在纺织厂工作了多少年？

（6）胖阿姨的丈夫是做什么工作的？

（7）胖阿姨下岗以后，家里的生活有什么变化？

（8）胖阿姨为什么没有找到合适的工作？

（9）胖阿姨决定先做什么？

（10）老先生建议她再卖些什么？

（11）胖阿姨的文具店生意怎么样？

（12）胖阿姨的服务态度怎么样？

（13）胖阿姨开了几家连锁店？

（14）胖阿姨是不是打算先买房子？

4. 会话练习 Conversation practice

会话常用语 IDIOMATIC EXPRESSIONS IN CONVERSATION

看你说的 (Come on/Don't say that)

不管怎么说 (No matter what/Anyway ...)

有那么好的事儿？ (Is there really such a great thing?)

我不相信。(I don't believe it.)

您就放心……吧 (Just rest assured)

我不骗你。(I'm not kidding you.)

【怀疑与不相信 Expressing doubt and disbelief】

（1）A：告诉你一个好消息，语法课不考试了。

B：怎么会呢？昨天老师还让我们好好儿复习呢，我不信。

A：我不骗你，好多同学都知道了。

（2）A：什么事儿这么高兴啊？

B：我接到一张通知单，我的手机号中奖（zhòngjiǎng）了。那家公司让我去取奖品（jiǎngpǐn），还是一条项链（xiàngliàn）呢。

A：看你说的，就像真的似的。你跟那家公司一点儿关系都没有，怎么可能中奖呢？

B：我也不相信啊，可是你看看这张通知单。

A："祝贺您成为我们公司第三名中奖者。"有那么好的事儿？这种事儿
我见多了，都是骗人的广告。

【讲价钱　Bargaining for a good price】

（1）A：老板，您这儿的照相机太贵了，能便宜点儿吗？

　　　B：对不起，我们商场的商品，不能讲价。

（2）A：背包便宜了！35 块钱一个！随便挑，随便选！

　　　B：35 块钱一个可不便宜，别的商店 20 块钱一个，比这个大多了。

　　　A：这您就不知道了，质量不一样啊，这是名牌的。

　　　B：能便宜点儿吗？

　　　A：您给个价吧。

　　　B：20 块，怎么样？

　　　A：您砍得太厉害了。您要是真想买，最低价 25 块。

5. 交际练习　Communication exercises

(1) Do you like to go shopping at stores where you can bargain? Talk about one of your experiences in this regard.

(2) Do you agree with the saying that "the buyer may not always be as shrewd as the seller"? After expressing yourself orally, write a short essay on either of the topics above.

阅读与复述 Reading Comprehension and Paraphrasing

24　老百姓（lǎobǎixìng）手里的钱多了

最近 30 年来，中国的市场有了很大的变化。大商店多了，商品

多了，老百姓手里的钱也多了。改革 (gǎigé) 开放 (kāifàng) 以前，北京最大的商店就是王府井百货大楼。那时候，买什么东西，都要排很长的队。不少商品还要凭 (píng) 票买，买衣服要布票，去饭馆吃饭要粮票 (liángpiào)。当时，人们把手表、自行车、收音机叫做"三大件"。特别是从国外进口 (jìnkǒu) 的，普通老百姓买不起，也看不到。只有从国外回来的人，才买得起这些商品。那时候，谁家有一台很小的黑白电视机，邻居们也都羡慕 (xiànmù) 死了。买汽车、买房子、出国旅游、让孩子自费出国留学，那是连做梦也不敢想的事儿。

改革开放以后，国家的经济有了很大的发展。经过 30 年的努力，从日用商品到工业产品，可以说要什么有什么。现在买什么都不要票了，不但有国产的，而且还有进口的。中国加入 WTO 以后，世界有名的大商店也都到中国来做生意了。各种商品什么地方都能买到。现在城里人，家用电器 (diànqì) 一般都有了。人们正在打算的是买房子、买车子、让孩子出国留学。放长假的时候，不是去外地旅游，就是出国旅行。

现在最发愁 (fāchóu) 的不是顾客，而是那些商店的经理和老板们，他们愁的是商品卖不出去。除了大做广告以外，他们还得想些别的办法，像打折扣 (dà zhékòu)、买一送一、买东西抽奖 (chōujiǎng)、买东西送纪念品……想各种办法让顾客多买他们的东西。

来北京旅游，你一定要去王府井大街走走，那是一条有名的步行商业街。那里有很多老字号的名牌产品值得 (zhídé) 你去买，还有很多外国大商店值得你去参观。要是去北京秀水街 (Xiùshuǐ Jiē) 买东西，你一定要学会砍价。因为买的没有卖的精。

三、语法　Grammar

词语 例解　Word Usage and Examples

1　就⑤

The adverb " 就 " is frequently used to define the scope of something, meaning "only", and it can be followed by a noun, a verb phrase, or a subject-predicate phrase, for example,

绣花儿睡衣都卖完了，就这几件了。

她就学过英语，没有学过别的外语。

昨天就他没有来，别的人都来了。

2　遍

When the verb " 遍 " is used as a resultative complement, it means "to extend all over", for example,

为了研究这个历史问题，他走遍了全国。

他是一个旅行家，几乎游遍了全国的名胜古迹。

我找遍了大小书店，还是没有你要买的这本书。

3　一下子

The adverb " 一下子 " indicates a short duration of time or a sudden or abrupt occurrence. As an adverbial modifier, it is generally used in conjunction with an accomplished action. One may also say " 一下 ". For example,

电脑一下子就修好了。

刚过五点，天一下就黑了。

提到这个名字，他一下就想起来了。

4　从来

The adverb " 从来 " expresses the idea that things have always been like this from the past to the present. It is often used in the negative form. In the structure "从来 + 没（有）+ V/A", the word "过" is generally placed after the verb or adjective. For example,

他从来不喝酒。

这种事我从来没听说过。

他们一辈子都生活在这儿，从来没有去外地旅游过。

他跟我下棋从来都是赢的。

语法 复习 Grammar Review

1 动词重叠 形容词重叠 Reduplication of verbs and adjectives

（1）动词重叠 Reduplication of verbs

The reduplication of a verb indicates that an action is either of very short duration or the number of times that an action took place are not many. For an action that has already taken place, "了" is inserted between the verb and its duplicate to express the short duration of the action. This structure is also used to make the tone of a sentence sound relaxed or informal. For example,

邻居们也拍拍衣服准备回去。

他看了看她说："你瘦了。"

她笑了笑，没有回答。

我给他讲了讲这次旅游的情况。

If an action has not yet taken place or takes place frequently, the verb is often reduplicated to imply that the action is casual and informal, rather than serious or done with effort, or that the action is being done just for the purpose of trying something out. When used in connection with a request, command or wish, the reduplication of verbs can soften the tone of one's speech. For example,

我的手机呢？你帮我找找吧。

我马上就来，你让他去外边等一等。

我想跟你随便谈谈。

退休以后，他每天下下棋、跑跑步、练练书法、听听京剧什么的。

Note:

This structure does not apply to actions in progress. Thus, it is incorrect to say "我正在看看书" or "他们听一听音乐呢". Verbs followed by "过" or "着" cannot be repeated either. It is incorrect to say "看看过" or "听听着".

（2）形容词重叠 Reduplication of adjectives

When reduplicated, adjectives often function as adverbial modifiers or complements to indicate higher degree. "地" is generally required after a reduplicated adjective which acts as an adverbial modifier. For example,

他轻轻地敲门。

孩子高高兴兴地走了。

君子兰的叶子长得长长的。

When acting as an attributive modifier or predicate, the reduplicated form of an adjective usually has a descriptive function rather than emphasizes high degree. When used as an attributive modifier, the reduplicated adjective is usually followed by "的"; when used as a predicate, "的" is needed at the end of the sentence. For example,

她高高的鼻子、大大的眼睛，漂亮极了。

姑娘的头发长长的，个子高高的。

书房里干干净净的。

2 表示比较的方法 Ways of expressing comparison

（1）用"比"或"不比"表示比较 By using "比" (or "不比")

这件旗袍比那件（旗袍）漂亮。（Lesson 17）

我们系比他们系多90个学生。

那本书比这本书贵多了。

我外婆不比我妈妈身体差。（Lesson 37）

今天的生活比过去幸福得多。（Lesson 39）

（2）用"有"或"没有"表示比较 By using "有" (or "没有")

妹妹已经有姐姐这么高了。（Lesson 28）

我们没有你们用刀叉用得好。

（3）用"跟……（不）一样"表示比较　By using "跟……（不）一样"

上海话跟普通话不一样。（Lesson 19）

这个中学跟那个（中学）一样有名。

我爸爸跟我妈妈一样喜欢中国画。

（4）用"更"、"最"表示比较　By using "更" or "最"

这位服务员的声音更大。（Lesson 27）

马大为最爱听中国民乐。

（5）用"越来越"表示比较　By using "越来越"

课文越来越有意思了。（Lesson 26）

他汉语说得越来越流利。

（6）用"一天比一天"表示比较　By using "一天比一天"

你做菜的技术一天比一天好。（Lesson 39）

（7）用"还是"表示比较　By using "还是"

还是你去合适。（Lesson 43）

3　复句小结（1）　Summary of complex sentences (1)

联合复句　Combined Complex Sentences

（1）并列复句　Coordinate complex sentences

①一边……，一边……（Lesson 27）

咱们一边散步，一边聊天儿。

②又……又……（Lesson 30）

他们又说又笑，非常快乐。

③既……，又……（Lesson 33）

北京既是中国的首都，又是世界有名的大都市。

④不是……，而是……（Lesson 39）

这不是谁给谁打工，而是咱们俩分工合作。

⑤……，也就是说，……（Lesson 41）

湖南人不怕辣，也就是说，他们总是觉得"不够辣"。

（2）承接复句　Successive complex sentences

①先……，然后（再）……（Lesson 21，37）

下车以后先往右拐，再向前走三分钟，就到八号楼了。

四位姑娘先向陈老师敬酒，然后又给我们每个人敬酒。

②一……，就……（Lesson 36）

北京一到五月，天气就热起来了。

③……，接着……（Lesson 37）

妻子回到家里换了衣服，接着就到厨房做起饭来。.

（3）递进复句　Progressive complex sentences

①不但……，而且……（Lesson 24）

我们不但盖了一座小楼，而且还买了一辆汽车。

②不但不／没……，反而……（Lesson 42）

这样不但不能解决问题，反而会带来更多的矛盾。

邻居们不但没有笑话我们，反而围了过来想帮助我们。

偏正复句　Subordinate Complex Sentences

（1）假设复句　Hypothetical complex sentences

①如果……，就……（Lesson 25）

如果明天天气不好，我们就不去了。

②要是……，就……（Lesson 40）

要是你生活在中国人的家里，就会发现丈夫每天也要下厨房。

（2）目的复句　Complex sentences of purpose

①为了……，……（Lesson 40）

为了练好汉语口语，他到北京以后就住在中国人家里。

②……，好……（Lesson 42）

丁力波打算学古汉语，好更正确地理解唐诗。

四、字与词 Chinese Characters and Words

1 集中识字 Learn the characters of the same radicals

贝：财 贤 账 货 贫 贵 贴 贷 贸 费 贺 资 赚 赔 赞

走：赶 起 越 超 趣 趟

禾：利 和 季 种 秋 科 租 程 秧 积 称 移 稳 穆

2 词语联想 Learn the following groups of associated words

商　商业　商店　商场　商城　商人　商务　商船　商会　商界

　　商贸　商品　商标　商品经济

　　商量　商议　商谈　商定

价　价钱　价目　半价　比价　报价　差价　单价　定价

　　物价　买价　高价　售价　总价　压价　还价　议价　砍价

Changes in Chinese People's Attitudes towards Consumption

"If you suddenly got five million yuan, what would you do with it?" If you ask Chinese people this question, you may get different answers from the middle-aged and the young. Middle-aged people may tell you they would save the money for

future use, some for their children and the rest for their life in old age, while the younger generation probably will tell you they want to buy an apartment or a car or use the money to travel around the world, in other words, to enjoy themselves when they are young.

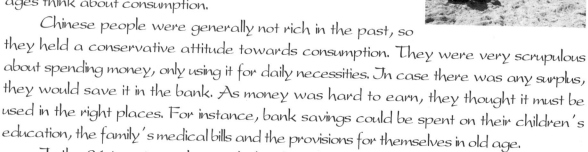

This shows how differently Chinese people at different ages think about consumption.

Chinese people were generally not rich in the past, so they held a conservative attitude towards consumption. They were very scrupulous about spending money, only using it for daily necessities. In case there was any surplus, they would save it in the bank. As money was hard to earn, they thought it must be used in the right places. For instance, bank savings could be spent on their children's education, the family's medical bills and the provisions for themselves in old age.

In the 21st century, along with the deepening of China's reform and opening up, Chinese people's living standards have been significantly improved, and the reform of the health insurance system has made a big progress as well. Gradually, the attitudes towards consumption of more and more people, especially the young, have changed. Young people in the new age are more quick-witted and open-

minded. When they have money, they would make more money with it on

the one hand, by investing in stocks or real estate rather than saving it in the bank like their parents would do, and on the other hand, they would spend the money on cars, beauty treatment, travelling and so on to seek a life of pleasure.

Meanwhile, some young people hold the attitude that one should have fun with or without money, so there've come into being such groups as "The group of young people who live from paycheck to paycheck", "Parent-Dependent Adults" and "Well-Paid Poor People".

第四十五课

Lesson 45

马大为求职

Ma Dawei seeks employment

Ma Dawei sees an Internet message inviting applications for the job of manager of the Market Development Department in a Chinese-Canadian joint venture. He is very interested in the position and applies for it. Let's see how he does in the interview.

一、课文 Texts

🎧25 （一）

马大为求职

马大为：请问，您是钱总经理吗？

钱经理：是的。您是马大为先生吧？

马大为：我是马大为。钱总，您好。 上个月我来贵公司跟张经理谈过

一次，① 后来您的秘书给我打电话，让我今天来公司跟您谈

一谈。

钱经理：是这样。我们请您来，是想再谈一谈您的求职问题。请坐。

您想喝点儿什么？

马大为：不用了，谢谢。

钱经理：您知道本公司市场开发部要招聘经理。市场开发的工作很重要，这个部的经理要常到中国各地出差，参加各种商务活动。这个职务不但要求有工商管理的专业知识，而且要求了解中国的社会和文化，汉语普通话也要说得很流利。我想听听您对这个职务的想法。

马大为：我对这个职务很感兴趣，而且也觉得我本人的条件比较合适。我在美国学的是工商管理，在加拿大当过一家贸易公司的商务代表，有这方面的工作经验，对中加两国的贸易情况也比较熟悉。汉语是我的第一外语，我已经通过了新汉语水平六级考试。② 我喜欢中国文化，为了更多地了解中国，我还在北京语言学院进修了一年多的中国文学。我希望我的知识和经验能很好地用于贵公司的工作，我也相信自己一定能成为贵公司很好的工作人员。

钱经理：很好。我们看了好多人的简历，认为您的条件不错。您是学工商管理的，又会汉语，还有这方面的工作经验。我想您会很快地适应这里的工作环境。

马大为：谢谢，你们对我有这样的看法，我很高兴。工资问题，我上次已经跟张经理提了，不知道贵公司有没有新的考虑？

钱经理：关于您的工资问题，我们还是上次那个意见。在我们公司，经理的工资一般比较高。除了工作要求和工资以外，您还有问题吗？

马大为：现在我没有别的问题。

钱经理：好。如果您同意我们已经谈过的一切条件，那么，我们很快
就可以签订工作合同。

马大为：谢谢您。我想再考虑一下，可以吗？

钱经理：可以。无论同意或者不同意，都希望您在本星期之内把您的
决定告诉我们。

马大为：好的。

钱经理：再见！

马大为：再见！

生词 New Words

1. 求职	qiúzhí	VO	to apply for a job 求职问题，去公司求职
2. 秘书	mìshū	N	secretary 经理秘书，女秘书，秘书小姐
3. 本	běn	Pr	one's own, native, this, present 本公司，本人，我本人，本周之内
4. 市场开发部	shìchǎng kāifābù		Market Development Department 本公司的市场开发部，市场开发部经理
开发	kāifā	V	to develop 开发市场，开发西部
部	bù	N	department, ministry 教育部，文化部，外交部，这个部的经理
5. 出差	chūchāi	VO	to be on an official or business trip 到各地出差，到上海出差，出了一个月的差
6. 商务	shāngwù	N	commercial affairs, business affairs 商务代表，商务工作

7.	职务	zhíwù	N	post, job　经理的职务，对这个职务很感兴趣
8.	要求	yāoqiú	V/N	to demand, to require, to ask; requirement 要求有专业知识，要求普通话说得很好；提出要求
9.	工商	gōngshāng	N	industry and commerce　工商管理，工商业
10.	贸易	màoyì	N	trade　贸易公司，贸易情况，对中国的贸易
11.	代表	dàibiǎo	N/V	deputy, delegate, representative; to represent 商务代表，人民代表，学生代表；代表学校，代表大家
12.	经验	jīngyàn	N	experience　工作经验，生活经验，没有经验
13.	级	jí	N	level, grade　八级，一级，初级，中级，高级
14.	进修	jìnxiū	V	to engage in advanced studies　进修中国文学，进修工商管理，进修班，进修生
15.	于	yú	Prep	in, on, at (indicating time or place)　用于贵公司的工作，毕业于ABC学院
16.	成为	chéngwéi	V	to become, to turn into　成为很好的工作人员，成为公司的经理
17.	简历	jiǎnlì	N	resume, curriculum vitae　个人简历，我的简历，一份（fèn）简历
18.	适应	shìyìng	V	to suit, to adapt to, to adjust to　适应工作环境，适应工作的要求
19.	考虑	kǎolù	V	to think over, to consider　考虑一下，考虑这个问题，考虑考虑
20.	一切	yíqiè	Pr	all, every, everything　一切条件，一切努力，一切机会
21.	签订	qiāndìng	V	to conclude and sign
22.	合同	hétong	N	contract　签订合同，跟公司签合同，讨论合同，一份合同

23.	无论	wúlùn	Conj	regardless of, no matter (what, how, etc.)
				无论同意不同意，无论是谁，无论什么时候
24.	汉语水平	Hànyǔ Shuǐpíng	PN	Chinese Proficiency Test (HSK)　通过了汉语
	考试	Kǎoshì		水平考试，参加汉语水平考试

注释　Notes

① 上个月我来贵公司跟张经理谈过一次。

"I came to your company last month and your manager Mr. Zhang had a talk with me."

The word "贵" is a term of respect. It is often used to refer politely to things related to the other party, for example, "贵姓", "贵国", "贵校", "贵厂", etc.

② 我已经通过了新汉语水平六级考试。

"I have already passed Level 6 Chinese Proficiency Test (HSK)."

Chinese Proficiency Test (HSK) is a standardized Chinese proficiency test to test the communicative skills of non-Chinese speakers all over the world. It consists of six levels of written tests and three levels of oral tests.

 26　（二）

一封求职信

尊敬的总经理先生：③

　　您好！从网上了解到贵公司市场开发部正在招聘经理。贵公司是中加合资企业，现在已发展成为中国大陆有名的高新技术企业，在中国不少城市都有业务。本人对贵公司的业务和市场开发部经理的职务很感兴趣，现在写这封信是向贵公司正式提出求职的申请。

　　我叫马大为，是美国人，毕业于 ABC 商学院。毕业以后，我在加拿大一家贸易公司工作，负责联系亚洲——主要是中国的业务。在工作中，无论有多少困难，我都想办法解决，努力开发市场。在很短的时间里，我们公司对中国的贸易有了很大的发展。我的负责的精神和热情的态度，也多次得到中国方面的称赞。公司对我的工作很满意，认为我熟悉业务，有创新精神。一年以后我当了公司的商务代表。为了更多地了解中国的社会和文化，我辞去了公司的工作，于去年 2 月开始在北京语言学院进修中国文学，现在已经结业。

　　根据贵公司的招聘要求，我认为本人很适合这项工作。我非常想参加贵公司开发中国西北市场的工作，我相信贵公司一定会成功，我自己也会有更大的发展前途。如果贵公司能给我这个机会，那么，我一定会努力为贵公司服务。

　　附上本人的简历。如果有什么问题需要了解，请用电子邮件或打电话跟我联系。谢谢！

　　顺致

诚挚的敬意④

马大为

2012 年 5 月 20 日　于北京⑤

电子信箱：madawei@yahoo.com

手机号码：13521709588

生词 New Words

1. 合资	hézī	V	to enter into partnership, to pool capital 合资企业，合资工厂，合资公司，中加合资
2. 业务	yèwù	N	professional work, business 公司的业务，亚洲的业务，熟悉业务，懂业务
3. 本人	běnrén	Pr	I (me, myself), oneself 本人很感兴趣，本人的简历，他本人，你本人
4. 申请	shēnqǐng	V	to apply for 求职的申请，申请工作，申请职务，申请贷款
5. 负责	fùzé	V	to be responsible for, to be in charge of 负责贸易工作，负责市场开发，负责人
6. 联系	liánxì	V	to contact, to get in touch with 负责联系亚洲的业务，跟他联系，没有联系，以后多联系
7. 精神	jīngshen	N	spirit, mind 负责的精神，勤俭节约的精神，艰苦朴素的精神
8. 创新	chuàngxīn	V	to bring forth new ideas, to be creative 有创新精神，在工作上创新
9. 辞	cí	V	to resign, to dismiss 辞去公司的工作，辞去职务，辞职，老板把他辞了
10. 根据	gēnjù	Prep	according to, in the light of 根据招聘要求，根据现在的情况
11. 附	fù	V	to add, to attach, to enclose 附上本人的简历，附寄照片两张，附表三张
12. 电子邮件	diànzǐ yóujiàn		e-mail 用电子邮件联系，收到电子邮件，发电子邮件
电子	diànzǐ	N	electron 电子钟，电子学
邮件	yóujiàn	N	postal matter, mail 普通邮件，航空邮件，挂号邮件

13.	顺致	shùnzhì	IE	to take the opportunity to express ... (*used at the close of a letter*)
14.	诚挚	chéngzhì	A	sincere, cordial　诚挚的态度，诚挚的友谊，诚挚地关心，诚挚地照顾
15.	敬意	jìngyì	N	respect, tribute　诚挚的致意
16.	信箱	xìnxiāng	N	mailbox, post office box (POB)　电子信箱，203信箱
17.	ABC商学院	ABC Shāng-xuéyuàn	PN	ABC Business College
18.	亚洲	Yàzhōu	PN	Asia
19.	西北	Xīběi		Northwest

补充生词 Supplementary Words

1.	教师	jiàoshī	N	teacher
2.	母语	mǔyǔ	N	native language, mother tongue
3.	教学	jiàoxué	V	to teach
4.	专科学校	zhuānkē xuéxiào		college for vocational training
5.	经历	jīnglì	N	experience
6.	修建	xiūjiàn	V	to build, to construct
7.	高速公路	gāosù gōnglù		expressway
	高速	gāosù	A	high speed
	公路	gōnglù	N	road, highway
8.	维修	wéixiū	V	to keep in (good) repair, to maintain
9.	报名	bàomíng	VO	to sign up for sth., to enter one's name
10.	晒	shài	V	to bask, to dry in the sun
11.	工程师	gōngchéngshī	N	engineer

12.	调	diào	V	to transfer, to move
13.	局长	júzhǎng	N	bureau chief
14.	人才	réncái	N	talented person
15.	侄女	zhínǚ	N	brother's daughter, niece
16.	录取	lùqǔ	V	to enrol, to admit

注释　Notes

③ 尊敬的总经理先生

"Distinguished General Manager"

In China, when writing a letter to the head of an office or institution with whom one is not acquainted, it is polite and appropriate to use "尊敬的" at the beginning of the salutation. If the letter is to an acquaintance, one can use "尊敬的" or "敬爱的" to show politeness, for example, "敬爱的张教授". One may directly address a close acquaintance as "张教授", "陈老师", "王经理", etc. Colleagues and classmates of the same generation may address each other with given names, for example, "小云", "力波" and "雨平". They may also address each other with surnames preceded by "老", "大" or "小", such as "老张", "大宋" and "小王".

④ 顺致

诚挚的敬意

"Let me take the opportunity to express my cordial respect."

This is a polite and relatively formal expression used at the closing of a letter. Other common expressions that are appropriate to use when writing to members of the older generation include "敬祝 健康", "敬祝 安好" and "敬祝 全家安好". Expressions used to address people of the same generation include "此致 敬礼", "顺祝 愉快", "顺祝 进步", "祝你 健康" and "祝 好".

⑤ 马大为

2012 年 5 月 20 日　于北京

"Ma Dawei, May 20th, 2012 in Beijing"

In Chinese, one usually closes a letter to a close acquaintance with one's full name or given name, the date, and the location where the letter was written.

二、练习　Exercises

练习 与运用　**Drills and Practice** 27

核心句 KEY SENTENCES

1. 本公司市场开发部要招聘经理。
2. 根据贵公司的招聘要求，我认为本人很适合这项工作。
3. 我也相信自己一定能成为贵公司很好的工作人员。
4. 我希望我的知识和经验能很好地用于贵公司的工作。
5. 我于去年 2 月开始在北京语言学院进修中国文学。
6. 我毕业于 ABC 商学院。
7. 我们请您来，是想再谈一谈您的求职问题。
8. 无论有多少困难，我都想办法解决。

---

1. 熟读下列词组 Read the following phrases until you learn them by heart

（1）本国　本校　本厂　本公司　　本商店　本系　本班　本单位
　　　本年　本世纪　本月　本月五号　本星期　本星期四　本地

（2）一切活动　一切问题　一切困难　一切业务　一切工作　一切职务
　　　这一切　这儿的一切　我知道的一切　过去的一切　记住这一切

（3）毕业于北大　死于上海　用于学习　写于北京　产于中国　于今年生产
　　　于昨天收到　于星期六上午见面　于去年二月开始工作

（4）成为北大的研究生　　成为著名的作家　　成为京剧爱好者

　　　成为高明的医生　　　成为小偷　　　发展成为　　开发成为

　　　修整成为　　　　　　装修成为　　　进修成为　　绿化成为

（5）根据现在的情况　　根据大家的意见　　根据个人的条件

　　　根据本人的经验　　根据我们的了解　　根据讲解员的介绍

　　　根据双方签订的合同　根据公司的要求

（6）代表老师们　代表公司　代表中文系　代表总经理　代表我们足球队

　　　大家的代表　农民代表　妇女代表　　商务代表　　学生代表

（7）适应要求　适应环境　很不适应　适应得很　对气候不适应

（8）无论工作或学习　无论谁有困难　无论什么事　无论去还是不去

2. 句子练习　Sentence drills

A. 用所给词语完成句子

Complete the following sentences with the given words and expressions

本

（1）_____要招聘女服务员一名。(our store)

（2）经理_____要对这件事负责。(himself)

（3）银行贷款必须由_____提出申请。(oneself)

（4）_____的前十年，高新技术有了更快的发展。(this century)

一切

（1）妇女在_____都应该和男子平等。（方面）

（2）玉兰他们认为婚礼应当_____。（简单）

（3）对_____我都感兴趣。（这儿）

（4）这是他们结婚的新房，_____都是新的。（东西）

成为

（1）张教授把这棵小松树_____美丽的盆景。

（2）这间屋子已经_____电脑室了。

（3）他通过自己的艰苦学习，＿＿＿＿＿＿＿＿＿＿＿一个有名的小学教师了。

（4）经过十年的努力，这个学校已经＿＿＿＿＿＿＿＿有5000多名学生

的中学了。

（成为　发展成为　装修成为　修整成为）

根据

（1）＿＿＿＿＿＿＿＿＿＿＿＿＿＿＿＿，我们决定去黄山旅游。（建议）

（2）＿＿＿＿＿＿＿＿＿＿＿＿＿＿，他现在去当翻译还有点儿困难。（口语水平）

（3）＿＿＿＿＿＿＿＿＿＿＿＿＿＿，明天很不适合爬山。（天气情况）

（4）＿＿＿＿＿＿＿＿＿＿＿＿＿＿，秋天去北京旅游最好。（了解）

于

（1）她＿＿＿＿＿＿＿＿＿＿＿＿＿＿＿大学。（毕业）

（2）这种小汽车＿＿＿＿＿＿＿＿＿＿＿＿＿＿＿，样子很好看，价钱也不算

太贵。（产）

（3）他吃完饭以后＿＿＿＿＿＿＿＿＿＿＿＿＿＿＿＿＿。（习惯）

（4）他爷爷＿＿＿＿＿＿＿＿＿＿＿＿＿＿＿年。（死）

B. 用动词"代表"改写句子

Rewrite the following sentences, using "代表" as a verb

（1）他是我们学校的代表。

＿＿＿＿＿＿＿＿＿＿＿＿＿＿＿＿＿＿＿＿＿＿＿＿＿。

（2）丁秘书是总经理的代表。

＿＿＿＿＿＿＿＿＿＿＿＿＿＿＿＿＿＿＿＿＿＿＿＿＿。

（3）她是我们工厂的妇女代表。

＿＿＿＿＿＿＿＿＿＿＿＿＿＿＿＿＿＿＿＿＿＿＿＿＿。

（4）他是本市公共汽车司机的代表。

＿＿＿＿＿＿＿＿＿＿＿＿＿＿＿＿＿＿＿＿＿＿＿＿＿。

C. 用"是"字句（3）改写下面的句子
Rewrite the following sentences into sentences with "是" (3)

（1）我想了解一下这儿的情况，所以来了。

_____。

（2）他怕大家走错了路，所以开车送大家去。

_____。

（3）张教授教书非常认真，所以大家都很尊敬他。

_____。

（4）由于他非常努力，所以学习成绩很好。

_____。

（5）他身体不太好，决定不去旅行。

_____。

D. 用"无论……，都／也……"完成句子
Complete the following sentences, using "无论……，都／也……"

（1）_____，他都非常认真。（工作或学习）

（2）_____，老王都愿意热情地帮助。（谁有困难）

（3）_____，小张都不想做，不知为什么。（什么事）

（4）_____，你们都应该告诉老师一声。（去还是不去）

3. 根据课文回答问题 Answer the following questions according to the texts

（1）钱总经理的秘书为什么让马大为到公司来？

（2）马大为是怎么知道这家中加合资企业要招聘经理的？

（3）当市场开发部经理这个职务需要什么条件？

（4）马大为毕业于什么学校？

（5）马大为毕业以后在哪儿工作过？

（6）他的工作情况怎么样？

（7）那家贸易公司对马大为的工作满意不满意？

（8）马大为为什么辞去了贸易公司的工作？

（9）马大为有没有信心做好市场开发部的工作？为什么？

（10）钱总经理觉得马大为这个人怎么样？

（11）他们还谈到了什么问题？

（12）他们签合同了没有？为什么？

4. 会话练习　Conversation practice

> ### 会话常用语 IDIOMATIC EXPRESSIONS IN CONVERSATION
>
> 您知道…… (As you know ...)
>
> 对这个职务很感兴趣 (to be very interested in this position)
>
> 本人的条件比较合适。(My background is very suitable for ...)
>
> 有这方面的工作经验 (to have work experience in this field)
>
> 多次得到公司的称赞
>
> (to have won the praise of the company many times)
>
> 对我的工作很满意 (to be pleased with my work)
>
> 一定会努力为贵公司服务
>
> ((I) will certainly work hard to serve your company)
>
> 我想再考虑一下。(I would like to think it over.)

【表示满意　Expressing satisfaction】

（1）A：这儿住的条件差一点儿，您还习惯吗？

　　　B：您说到哪儿去了？我觉得挺好啊！房间很大，也很干净，我很满意。

（2）A：西餐做得还可以吗？

　　　B：做得不错。我有的时候也吃中餐。对他们的服务态度我非常满意。

【求职　Applying for a job】

A：您好！我是来求职的。我从报上了解到贵校英语系要招聘英语教师（jiàoshī），我对这个工作很感兴趣，而且我觉得本人的条件也很适合贵校的要求。

B：您是学什么专业的？以前当过英语教师吗？

A：我是英国人，英语是我的母语（mǔyǔ）；我又是学英语教学（jiàoxué）的，毕业于伦敦大学。我还在台湾教过两年英语，有一定的教中国学生的经验。我希望能有机会在贵校这样有名的学校工作，我愿意把自己的知识和经验用于这儿的英语教学。

B：很好。您对英语教学有什么想法？

A：我认为在二十一世纪的今天，无论在哪儿教英语，都应当培养学生用英语的能力，首先是听、说的能力。在这方面，英语为母语的教师可能有更好的条件。

B：您的想法很好。如果有可能，我们希望本星期之内您能来试讲一次，我们还要听听同学们的意见。对了，您的汉语也说得很好，您本人一定也有学习外语的好经验。

A：谢谢。关于试讲的时间我等您的通知。

5. 交际练习　Communication exercises

(1) Practise with your classmates how you would introduce yourself when applying for a job.

(2) Write a job application letter. Explain your understanding of the job and how your background fits the requirements of the position.

阅读与复述 Reading Comprehension and Paraphrasing

28 怎样才能找到理想的工作

现在求职很难，要想找个理想的工作更难。可是，邻居老王就帮两个孩子找到了理想的工作。老王是根据自己的生活经验，给孩子们提了好的建议。

老王的儿子上世纪80年代从专科学校（zhuānkē xuéxiào）毕业以后，没找到合适的工作。老王发现用人单位在招聘员工时，越来越注意专业水平和工作经历（jīnglì）了。

当时正在修建（xiūjiàn）从上海到南京的高速公路（gāosù gōnglù）。老王听说高速公路管理办公室要招聘维修（wéixiū）人员，他认为这是个好机会，立刻给儿子报了名（bàomíng）。他儿子不太愿意去，说他是学电脑的，去维修公路，专业不合适。老王听了很生气，他说："你懂什么！先好好儿地去维修公路，你现在还年轻，多学点儿技术，有什么不好？你想想，哪有高速公路不用电脑管理的？恐怕不是专业不合适，而是专业知识不够用。"儿子觉得爸爸的话是对的，就同意去干维修高速公路的活儿。他干了几年，脸虽然晒（shài）得黑黑的，但确实学到了不少东西。在工作中，小伙子不怕苦，不怕累，重活儿、脏活儿抢着干；下班以后，他不是看书，就是在电脑上进修专业课。很快地，他就成为工程师（gōngchéngshī）了，不久，又被调（diào）到高速公路管理办公室工作。有一次局长（júzhǎng）去检查工作时，发现小伙子对业务很熟悉，而且也很有工作经验，是个人才（réncái），就把他调到局里。现在他已经是局长秘书了。

老王最得意的事儿还是帮侄女（zhínü）找工作。他侄女没考上大学，想找个合适的工作。老王每天都注意看招聘广告。一天，他发现人民银行和工商银行同时招聘工作人员。工商银行要招四十人，人民银行只招十人。老王心里想，这可是人人都希望得到的工作啊！他打算给侄女报工商银行，一看招聘人数，老王就改变了主意：决定报人民银行。

他侄女问他："工商银行招得多，录取的机会也就多，咱们为什么报人民银行？"老王笑了笑说："人民银行是国家银行，要求高，招的人数又少，我认为报名的人不会太多。"报名情况与老王想的差不多。大部分人都报工商银行，竞争非常厉害；而报人民银行的人很少。经过考试，老王的侄女最后被录取（lùqǔ）了。接到录取通知以后，老王笑着对侄女说："咱们为什么报人民银行，现在你该明白了吧？根据你这次的考试成绩，要是报工商银行，谁知道结果会怎么样呢？"

三、语法 Grammar

词语 例解 Word Usage and Examples

1 本

The demonstrative pronoun "本" is used before a noun. The phrase "本 + N" refers to the speaker or his workplace, organization or location, for example,

本人已经向贵系提出了申请。

本校定于九月一日开学。

本公司招聘营业部经理一名。

他要找一位本地人。

In the construction "Pr/N + 本 + N", "本 + N" refers to the pronoun or noun before it instead of the speaker or his workplace or organization, for example,

他本人已经跟工厂签合同了。

住房问题应该由你们本单位解决。

这好像不是上海本地的货。

Sometimes "本" is equivalent to "这", and is often used before a time word, for example,

　　本月一共开了两次讨论会。

　　定于本星期三下午二时举行职工大会。

2　一切

The word "一切" means "all" or "all kinds of", and is often used with the adverb "都". It may be used as an attributive, subject or object, for example,

　　这儿的一切活动大家都可以参加。

　　这两年我跟他失去了一切联系。

　　一切都可以解决，你不用担心。

　　我不会忘了这一切。

3　成为

The word "成为" means "to become", and it must take an object, for example,

　　他已经成为有名的书法家了。

　　我们才认识两个多月，已经成为好朋友了。

　　"团结、创新"已经成为这家公司的企业精神。

The structure "V + 成为" indicates a new state or situation resulting from the action, for example,

　　他们的电脑公司已经发展成为一家中外合资的大企业了。

　　这儿的几条小胡同已经开发成为"电子一条街"了。

　　这所学校已经绿化成为一个美丽的公园了。

In spoken language, "成为" is often replaced by "成了", for example,

　　他已经成了有名的书法家了。

　　我们才认识两个多月，已经成了好朋友了。

4　根据

The preposition "根据" indicates a prerequisite or basis for a certain affair or action. The construction " 根据 + NP / VP " is usually placed at the beginning of a sentence, functioning as an adverbial modifier, for example,

你们根据那儿的情况，自己解决吧。

根据检查的结果，他的病好多了，再过一个星期就可以出院了。

根据贵公司的招聘要求，我认为本人是比较合适的。

根据了解，他们又发现了一些新的情况。

● 句子 结构 Sentence Structure

1 介词短语补语（1） The prepositional phrase used as a complement (1)

The preposition " 于 " is often used in written language. It means "in", "on" or "at". The prepositional phrase " 于 + TW" is used before a verb as an adverbial modifier indicating time, for example,

王教授于九月十号到北京。

他的信于昨天收到。

When the prepositional phrase " 于 + TW/PW" is used after a verb or an adjective, it functions as a complement indicating time, location or a certain aspect. This kind of complement is mostly used in written language. For example,

鲁迅生于 1881 年。

这种水果产于海南岛。

马大为毕业于 ABC 商学院。

他从早到晚忙于工作，家务事一点儿也不管。

2 "是" 字句（3） Sentences with "是" (3)

In a sentence with "是", the object may be a verbal phrase, or an adjectival phrase or a prepositional phrase. It expounds on the subject, indicating the purpose or reason, or explains a certain situation. Sometimes both the affirmative and negative situations are stated for contrast. For example,

我们请您来是想再谈一谈您的求职问题。

他们最后一次聚会是在小张家。

你这样决定是根据什么？

他头晕是太累了，不是病了。

他这次来北京是进修汉语，不是旅游。

> The sentences with "是" that we have already learned include:
>
> （1）她是我外婆。（Lesson 3）
>
> 　　我不是加拿大人。（Lesson 4）
>
> 　　图书馆的东边是宿舍楼。（Lesson 21）
>
> （2）王老师是教汉语的。（Lesson 18）
>
> （3）对不起，我没有来是不知道这件事。（Lesson 45）

3 无论……，都 / 也……　The construction "无论……，都 / 也……"

The construction "无论……，都 / 也……" means "no matter what/how ...". The conjunction "无论" is generally used in the first clause. In a clause with an interrogative pronoun of general denotation like "多少" or "什么", it expresses the notion "no matter what/how ...". In a clause with the conjunction "还是", it indicates an alternative. In the second clause, the adverb "都" or "也" is usually employed to echo the first clause. This kind of sentence expresses the idea that the result or conclusion will never change under any circumstance. For example,

无论有多少困难，他都会想办法解决。

大家无论有什么事，都愿意找他帮忙。

无论去哪儿，我都参加。

无论你怎么说，他都不听。

无论你去还是不去，你都要通知他们。

四、字与词　Chinese Characters and Words

1 集中识字　Learn the characters of the same radicals

人：个　介　从　今　以　令　全　会　企　余　舍　命　拿　盒

阝：队　阳　阴　际　陆　阿　陈　附　除　院　陪　随　隐　防

　　邦　那　邮　邻　郎　郊　都　部

刂：刚　创　别　判　刻　剑　剧　副　到　制

2 词语联想　Learn the following groups of associated words

贵　贵姓　贵客　贵人　贵重　宝贵　富贵　名贵　珍贵　尊贵
　　高贵　可贵

重　重大　重地　重点　重读　重活儿　重量　重视　重心　重要
　　重音　重用　重工业

　　敬重　保重　超重　尊重　看重　体重　严重　稳重　轻重

轻　轻便　轻活儿　轻快　轻声　轻视　轻松　轻舟　轻工业
　　轻音乐　年轻　看轻　轻手轻脚

简　简便　简称　简单　简短　简化　简历　简练　简明　简朴
　　简要　简易　简写　简装　简章　简体字

Chinese College Students' Job Hunting

Chinese college students' job hunting in the past and present is an epitome of the development of Chinese economy.

In the early days of China's reform and opening-up, the economy of China was at its very beginning of development. College students were few in number. The education they got in the universities was "elite education" and then they were assigned jobs by the government after they graduated. There were more employers than job-hunters at that time, so college students never had to worry about finding a job. When students got into a college, the only thing they needed to bear in mind was to "study hard in order to serve the country in the future".

The situation has long since changed into a "two-way choice", mostly with one employer choosing from a number of job seekers. The employment situation is much severer than before. The major reason for this change is the rapid increase in the number of college students. Today, there are nearly 30 million college students in China, and the number increases by 1.3–1.6% each year. The "elite higher education" has turned into "mass higher education"; the government has stopped guaranteeing jobs; the number of employers grows much slower than that of students.

As a result, every year there are large numbers of graduates who cannot find a suitable job. Students have a common feeling that they are facing too much competition and pressure while seeking for employment.

The government has paid great attention to the situation of employment as it would have impact on the economic development and social stability. On the one hand, the country strives to develop its economy and improve its economic structure in order to create more jobs; on the other hand, students are expected to lower their expectations and get a job first before choosing one. Apart from that, they are also encouraged to go to the underdeveloped western part of China, take lower-level positions or start their own businesses if conditions permit.

Facing the severe situation of employment, college students start early to do preparations. They work part-time, doing all kinds of internships during spare time or holidays, so as to train themselves, improve their practical abilities and accumulate work experience, which will make them more competitive in the job market.

现在谁最累

Who is the most tired now?

In China, people often say that elementary school students have to study too much. Why is it so? How do teachers and parents educate their children? What do the children themselves think?

一、课文　Texts

🎧 29　（一）

现在谁最累

陆雨平：陈老师，您好，星期六带着孩子去哪儿玩儿？

陈老师：我哪是去玩儿？我是陪孩子去上电脑辅导班。你这位大记者，
该关心关心小学里的情况了。

陆雨平：是啊，以后我也要当家长啊！您孩子学习怎么样？

陈老师：孩子学习还可以，就是负担太重，全家人都为她着急。

陆雨平：最近我做了一个调查，早上坐头班车的，几乎都是小学生和
送他们上学的家长。家长们真辛苦，除了上班以外，每天早
上晚上还得送孩子、接孩子。

陈老师：孩子们更累了。他们每天都要上六七个小时的课，晚上还要
做很多作业。有些作业本来可以在上课的时候完成，老师也

③ 让学生拿回家来做。家长还嫌孩子不努力，又给他们增加了很多辅导和练习。孩子经常晚上十点半以后才睡觉。他们连看电视的时间都没有啊！

陆雨平：怎么能这样呢？① 他们还都是小学生，玩儿可是他们的权利。

陈老师：可是家长都希望把自己的孩子培养成为优秀的学生，希望他们有一个好的前途；老师也希望自己的学生都能考上好的学校。为了能上名牌大学，孩子就得先考上名牌小学、名牌中学。在这种风气的影响下，孩子们从小学就开始竞争了。

陆雨平：这太不应该了。他们从星期一到星期五都忙于学习，周末应该让他们放松一下了吧？

陈老师：周末无论成绩差的还是好的，都放松不了。成绩差的学生要上补习班，学习好的得培养他们的特长。拿我的孩子来说吧，他算是学习好的，不用补习。② 可是星期六上午，要么我陪他去上电脑辅导班，要么他爸爸带着他去上书法班。

陆雨平：小朋友，你周末学书法，是想当书法家吗？

小朋友：我不知道。我爸爸喜欢书法，是他让我去学的。

陆雨平：星期六这一天是没有了。明天是星期日，你该好好儿地玩儿一玩儿了吧？

小朋友：我很想好好儿地玩儿一玩儿，可是老师不让我玩儿。

陈老师：星期日上午，他还得做英语作业。只有下午才能让他玩儿一会儿。说实在的，我真不愿意让孩子累成这样。

陆雨平: 听说，很多学校的领导和老师们已经注意这个问题了。有的

学校提出"快乐教育"，老师已经不要求学生做家庭作业了。

小朋友: 老师不要求我们做家庭作业，这太好了，我百分之百地赞成。③

陈老师: 可是你知道吗？家长们并不都同意学校这样做。

生词 New Words

1. 辅导	fǔdǎo	V	to give guidance in study or training, to tutor 电脑辅导班，辅导他们口语，老师给我们辅导
2. 就是	jiùshì	Adv	only, merely 就是太爱玩儿，就是发音不好，就是说得太快
3. 负担	fùdān	N/V	load, burden; to bear, to shoulder 负担太重，学习的负担；负担老人的房租，负担父母的生活费
4. 调查	diàochá	N/V	survey; to investigate 做了一个调查；调查公共汽车情况，调查得很清楚
5. 头班车	tóubānchē	N	first bus or train 坐头班车，五点的头班车
头	tóu	A	first 头一个，头一杯，头一辆车
班	bān	M	*measure word for scheduled forms of transportation* 有班车，第二班船，下一班飞机
6. 家长	jiāzhǎng	N	parent or guardian of a child 孩子的家长，学生家长
7. 作业	zuòyè	N	school assignment, homework 做作业，交作业，改作业
8. 本来	běnlái	Adv	originally, at first 本来同意，本来可以在上课的时候做
9. 完成	wánchéng	V	to accomplish, to complete 完成作业，完成调查，完成作品，完成得很好

10. 嫌	xián	V	to dislike, to complain about 嫌孩子不努力，嫌十天时间太长
11. 增加	zēngjiā	V	to increase, to raise 增加了很多辅导，增加知识
12. 经常	jīngcháng	Adv	often, frequently 经常十点半以后才睡觉，经常到各地去，经常辅导，经常调查
13. 培养	péiyǎng	V	to foster, to train, to cultivate 培养成为演员，培养孩子学习英语的兴趣
14. 优秀	yōuxiù	A	outstanding, excellent 优秀的学生，优秀的画家，优秀的作品，优秀的小说
优	yōu	A	excellent 他的考试成绩是"优"
15. 风气	fēngqì	N	general mood, atmosphere 这种风气，好的风气，学校的风气
16. 影响	yǐngxiǎng	V/N	to influence, to affect; effect 影响孩子，影响学习，在这种风气的影响下；造成了很大的影响
17. 周末	zhōumò	N	weekend 周末学书法，本周末
周	zhōu	N	week 本周，一周之内，两周的时间
18. 放松	fàngsōng	V	to relax, to loosen 周末应该放松一下，不能放松学习，放松工作，放松要求
19. 补习	bǔxí	V	to take extra classes after school 上补习班，电脑补习班，补习外语
20. 特长	tècháng	N	what one's skilled in, strong point, speciality 培养他们的特长，发挥他的特长，艺术方面的特长，舞蹈方面的特长
21. 要么	yàome	Conj	or 要么我陪他去，要么你就别去了
22. 领导	lǐngdǎo	N/V	leader; to lead 有能力的领导，学校的领导；领导公司，领导人民，正确地领导
23. 赞成	zànchéng	V	to approve of, to agree with 百分之百地赞成，赞成这种想法，赞成他的意见，赞成多锻炼，赞成他去

| 24. 并 | bìng | Adv | *used before a negative for emphasis, usually as a retort* 并不，并没有 |

注释　Notes

① 怎么能这样呢？

"How can it be like this?"

It is often used to express dissatisfaction or to make a complaint, for example,

怎么能这样呢？他昨天还说今天上午一定来，可是到现在也没有来。

怎么能这样呢？房间里都是他的脏衣服。

② 拿我的孩子来说吧，他算是学习好的，不用补习。

"Take my child as an example. He is one of those who study well and does not need extra classes after school."

The construction "拿……来说" introduces a certain topic or gives an example, for example,

拿服务态度来说，这家饭馆比那家好得多。

拿气候来说，我更喜欢这个城市。

③ 我百分之百地赞成。

"I absolutely agree."

"百分之百" means "one hundred percent".

🎧 30　（二）

女儿今年才八岁

女儿今年才八岁，上小学二年级。她学习还不错，老师称赞她

做作业认真，爷爷奶奶喜欢她聪明。我和她爸爸对她也都满意，就

是觉得她太爱玩儿了。

　　为了培养孩子学习英语的兴趣，今年暑假，我打算让她参加英语夏令营，时间并不长，只去十天。我把自己的想法讲出来，女儿高兴极了，可是家里的人都反对。爷爷奶奶认为孩子太小，从来没有离开过家，让她一个人出去，他们很不放心。孩子的爸爸本来同意让她去，可是听了爷爷奶奶的话，也嫌十天时间太长，觉得孩子没有独立生活的能力，他也改变了主意。听了他们的意见，连我也不想让她去了。女儿看大家都不同意，都急得哭了。她的态度很坚决，她说，英语夏令营是在海边，她想去看大海，他们班的同学都想参加，她一定要去。为了能参加英语夏令营，她向我们保证，她要学会自己洗衣服。在她不断地要求下，我同意了她参加夏令营。她高兴得跳了起来。

　　我对她说："你别高兴得太早，我还有几个条件呢。要么你保证做到这几条，要么你就别去了。"

　　女儿急忙问我："妈妈，什么条件？您快说。"

　　我告诉她：

　　第一，要听老师的话。

　　第二，要跟同学团结。

　　第三，每天要写日记。

　　第四，不要乱花钱。

　　女儿说："你们放心，这四条我保证做到。"她把这四条写在一张纸上，像签订合同似的，我和她都在上边签了字。

　　女儿高高兴兴地去夏令营了。她走了以后，全家人都不放心，总怕她出点儿什么问题。到了第五天，奶奶第一个忍不住了，她说："怎么没有消息呢？都怪你们同意她去。"我急忙给老师家里打了电话，知道一切都很好，爷爷奶奶才放心。

　　十天终于过去了，女儿回来了。她一进门就把手里的一袋水果交给我，她说，这是她带给全家的礼物。这时候，我觉得孩子好像长高了，也长大了。

　　吃晚饭的时候，女儿先向全家介绍夏令营的生活，然后她拿出日记和自己拍的照片给我们看。她特别认真地说，她不但跟班上的同学很团结，而且还认识了几个英国小朋友。英国老师还称赞她英语歌唱得好。她没有乱花钱，去买水果的时候，还学会了砍价。爷爷奶奶听了，满意地说："好，又学会了洗衣服，又学会了唱英语歌，以后这样的活动可以多参加。"

生词 New Words

1. 爷爷	yéye	N	grandfather, father of one's father
2. 奶奶	nǎinai	N	grandmother, mother of one's father

3. 聪明	cōngming	A	intelligent, clever 非常聪明，聪明的小伙子，聪明的办法，聪明的想法，变得聪明，聪明得很
4. 反对	fǎnduì	V	to oppose, to be against 大家都反对，反对他的建议，反对这种做法，反对老板，反对跟他签订合同
5. 离开	líkāi	V	to leave, to depart 离开家，离开广州，离开父母，远远地离开
6. 独立	dúlì	V	to be independent 独立生活的能力，独立工作，独立研究，国家独立，民族独立，经济独立，实现独立，得到独立
7. 哭	kū	V	to weep, to cry 急得哭了，哭了起来，哭得很厉害，不哭了
8. 坚决	jiānjué	A	firm, resolute, determined 态度很坚决，声音很坚决，坚决赞成，坚决要求，坚决保护，坚决禁止，坚决反对
9. 保证	bǎozhèng	V	to pledge, to promise, to guarantee 向我们保证，保证做到，保证完成，保证公平
10. 不断	búduàn	Adv	continuously, constantly 不断地要求，不断地努力，不断地发展，不断地变化，不断地挑战，不断地了解，不断地研究
11. 急忙	jímáng	Adv	hurriedly, hastily 急忙问，急忙回答，急忙离开，急忙停下，急忙站起来
12. 听话	tīnghuà	A	obedient 很听话，不听话，听老师的话
13. 团结	tuánjié	V	to unite, to rally 跟同学团结，团结同学，影响团结，闹不团结
14. 乱	luàn	Adv/A	randomly, arbitrarily; untidy, in disorder 乱花钱，乱吃；房间很乱，写得太乱

15.	签字	qiānzì	VO	to sign one's name 请你签字，在合同上签字，这是他本人的签字，签个字
16.	忍	rěn	V	to endure, to tolerate 忍住头疼，忍不住，忍不住说了
17.	怪	guài	V	to blame 不怪他，就怪你，怪你们同意她去
18.	袋	dài	N/M	bag, sack 洗衣袋，袋子；一袋苹果，一袋米，一袋水泥，一袋糖

补充生词 Supplementary Words

1.	产品	chǎnpǐn	N	product, produce
2.	糊涂	hútu	A	muddled, confused
3.	县官	xiànguān	N	county magistrate
4.	两	liǎng	M	tael (old unit of weight for silver or gold)
5.	银子	yínzi	N	silver, money
6.	鸡蛋	jīdàn	N	chicken egg
	蛋	dàn	N	egg
7.	服	fú	V	to be convinced, to obey
8.	审	shěn	V	to interrogate, to try
9.	迟到	chídào	V	to be late, to arrive late
10.	大人	dàren	N	Your Excellency, His Excellency
11.	麦子	màizi	N	wheat
12.	收成	shōucheng	N	harvest, crop
13.	胡说	húshuō	V	to talk nonsense
14.	脸	liǎn	N	face

二、练习 Exercises

练习与运用 Drills and Practice 🎧31

核心句 KEY SENTENCES

1. 孩子学习还可以，就是负担太重。
2. 有些作业本来可以在上课的时候完成，老师也让学生拿回家来做。
3. 家长还嫌孩子不努力，又给他们增加了很多辅导和练习。
4. 家长们并不都同意学校这样做。
5. 在这种风气的影响下，孩子们从小学就开始竞争了。
6. 拿我的孩子来说吧，他算是学习好的。
7. 要么我陪他去上电脑辅导班，要么他爸爸带着他去上书法班。
8. 爷爷奶奶喜欢她聪明。

1. 熟读下列词组 Read the following phrases until you learn them by heart

（1）本来就很忙　　本来就不赞成　　本来很高兴　　本来打算学工商管理
本来不能参观　　本来身体不好　　本来就应该去　　本来可以完成
本来想先告诉你

（2）嫌辣　嫌太闹　嫌麻烦　嫌工作太忙　嫌环境不好　嫌工资太低
嫌他说话太快　　嫌丈夫不爱干净　　嫌她走得太慢　　嫌妻子乱花钱
嫌孩子做作业不认真

（3）增加收入　　增加工资　　增加人员　　增加负担　　增加报酬　　增加信心

　　增加矛盾　　贸易增加　　学生增加　　机会增加　　挑战增加　　权利增加

　　生意增加　　增加得很多

（4）影响生活　　影响健康　　影响环境　　影响别人休息　　影响孩子的前途

　　没有影响　　影响很大　　坏的影响　　发挥影响　　　对他的身体有影响

（5）在老师的辅导下　　　在同学们的帮助下　　　在这种风气的影响下

　　在大家的努力下　　　在总经理的领导下　　　在这样艰苦的条件下

　　在经济负担很重的情况下

（6）并不容易　　　并不坚决　　　并不同意　　　并不赞成　　　并不反对

　　并不知道　　并没有看到　　并没有完成　　并没有增加　　并没有保证

　　并没有放松　　并没有影响

（7）保证质量　　　保证做到　　　保证顾客满意　　　　保证完成作业

　　保证公平　　　保证节约　　　保证不放松学习　　　保证不影响别人

　　向领导保证过多次　　　坚决保证

2. 句子练习　Sentence drills

A. 用所给词语完成句子

Complete the following sentences with the given words and expressions

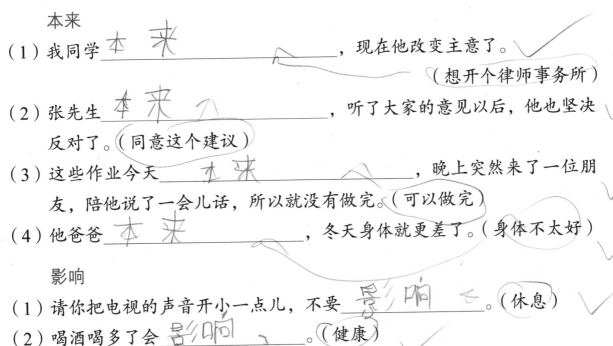

本来

（1）我同学本来_____，现在他改变主意了。

（想开个律师事务所）

（2）张先生本来_____，听了大家的意见以后，他也坚决

反对了。（同意这个建议）

（3）这些作业今天本来_____，晚上突然来了一位朋

友，陪他说了一会儿话，所以就没有做完。（可以做完）

（4）他爸爸本来_____，冬天身体就更差了。（身体不太好）

影响

（1）请你把电视的声音开小一点儿，不要影响_____。（休息）

（2）喝酒喝多了会影响_____。（健康）

（3）城里汽车太多，会不会 ~~影响~~ ？（生活环境）

（4）爸爸妈妈努力工作的精神，对丁力波 ~~影响~~ 。（很大）

保证

（1）我们卖的商品 ~~保证~~ 。（满意）

（2）老师提出的要求，我们 ~~保证~~ 。（做到）

（3）他向 ~~保证~~ ，但每次都没有做到。（很多次）

（4）经理 ~~保证~~ ，下个月给大家增加工资。（公司职工）

在……下

（1）在 下 ，他们很快就把东西从卡车上搬下来了。（帮助）

（2）在 下 ，马大为很快就做完了翻译练习。（辅导）

（3）在 下 ，他们仍然坚持搞科学研究，而且有了很好的成绩。

（困难的条件）

（4）在 下 ，大华贸易公司发展得很快。（领导）

B. 用"就是"改写句子

Rewrite the following sentences, using "就是"

（1）除了历史课以外，他别的课考的成绩都很好。（差一点儿）

~~他别的课考的成绩都很好就历史课。~~

（2）除了住的条件以外，大家对这次旅游很满意。（不太好）

~~大家对这次旅游很满意，就是住的条件不太好。~~

（3）除了眼睛以外，她长得不像她妈妈。（有点儿像）

~~她长得不像她妈妈，就是眼睛有点儿像。~~

（4）除了这件蓝的以外，这几件羽绒服都不太好看。（还可以）

~~这几件羽绒服都不太好看，就是这件蓝的还可以。~~

C. 用"嫌"改写句子

Rewrite the following sentences, using "嫌"

（1）丈夫不爱干净，妻子对他这方面很不满意。

妻子 ~~妻子对他在这方面。~~

~~妻子嫌丈夫不爱干净~~

（2）她走路走得太慢，年轻人有点儿不高兴。

年轻人 ~~生车子人 嫌为世表上各~~ 。

（3）孩子太爱玩儿了，爸爸妈妈经常批评他。

爸爸妈妈 ~~爸爸妈妈女嫌孩子爱玩儿~~ 。

（4）妻子总是乱花钱，丈夫很不满意。

丈夫 ~~丈夫女嫌妻子乱花钱~~

D. 用"并 + 不 / 没有"完成对话

Complete the following dialogues, using "并 + 不 / 没有"

（1）A：家长都同意"快乐教育"吗？

B：家长们 ___并不___ 学校这样做。（都同意）

（2）A：他当时为什么不反对？

B：因为当时他 ~~没有~~ 并不 这些情况。（了解）

（3）A：你知道吗？杰克已经结婚了。

B：不知道，杰克 ~~并不没有~~ 他已经结婚了。（告诉我）

（4）A：这篇文章比较长，学生看得懂吗？

B：这篇文章虽然很长，但生词不多，所以___并不___。（难懂）

E. 用"要么……，要么……"完成对话

Complete the following dialogues, using "要么……，要么……"

（1）A：今天下午我们在哪儿讨论呢？

B：~~今天下午在图书馆我们讨论区~~ 。 要么在图书馆 要么在教室

（2）A：咱们周末去哪儿轻松一下呢？

B：~~咱们周末去在海汉住午子去兑~~ 要么去爬山

（3）A：明天上午咱们几点出发呢？

B：~~明天上午几点出发~~ 。 要么11点出发，要么12点出发

（4）A：第 46 课咱们讨论什么问题呢？

B：~~第四十六之果咱们讨论"现在最累~~

3. 根据课文回答问题　Answer the following questions according to the texts

（1）陈老师的孩子每天的学习情况怎么样？

（2）孩子们周末做什么？

（3）为什么孩子的学习负担这么重？

（4）孩子们自己愿意这样忙吗？

（5）学校领导和老师们打算怎样解决这个问题？

（6）家长们都同意学校和老师这样做吗？

（7）陈老师的女儿是个什么样的女孩儿？

（8）对孩子参加英语夏令营，爷爷奶奶是什么态度？

（9）孩子的爸爸妈妈赞成还是反对她去夏令营？

（10）孩子自己是什么态度？

（11）最后家长为什么同意孩子去参加夏令营了？

（12）孩子在夏令营过得怎么样？

（13）家长对夏令营有什么新的看法？

4. 会话练习　Conversation practice

会话常用语　IDIOMATIC EXPRESSIONS IN CONVERSATION

怎么能这样呢？　(How can it be like this?)

拿我的孩子来说 (Take my child as an example)

百分之百地赞成 (absolutely agree)

就是太爱玩儿了。(only too fond of playing)

时间并不长。(It is not a long time.)

这太不应该了。(This is simply not right.)

【抱怨　Complaining about something】

A：你走得这么快，有什么好事儿？

B：哪是好事儿？我是去找他们的领导。

A：怎么了？

B：真倒霉，我怎么参加了这个辅导班？这儿的老师太不负责了，上课都二十分钟了，他还没有来；来了以后连该讲哪一课都记不清了，你说怎么能这样呢？

A：这太不应该了。

B：都怪你给我介绍了这么个辅导班。要是早知道，我就不会来了。

【承诺　Making a promise】

A：你们能按时交货吗？

B：没问题。不管有什么困难，我们都保证按时交货。

A：希望产品（chǎnpǐn）的质量能得到保证。

B：关于产品的质量，请放心，绝对不会有问题。即使有问题，我们也一定负责解决。

A：既然这些条件都谈好了，咱们很快就可以签订合同了。

B：好，我们一定在三天之内做好一切准备工作。

5. 交际练习　Communication exercises

(1) Is the children's education provided by Chinese teachers and parents similar to that in your own country? Why or why not?

(2) In your opinion, what kind of education should elementary school students receive?

After expressing yourself orally, write a short essay on either of the topics above.

阅读 与复述 Reading Comprehension and Paraphrasing

🎧32 糊涂（hútu）县官（xiànguān）

　　从前有个做工的，在一家饭馆里吃了一只烧鸡。吃完了，他对店老板说："等我去送了货，回来再付钱，可以吗？"店老板说："可以，要是你现在不方便，这次就先记上账。"做工的谢了谢店老板就走了。

　　过了十几天，做工的来付烧鸡的钱了。店老板看了看账本，又算了算，抬起头来对他说："你该付给我十两（liǎng）银子（yínzi）。"做工的以为自己没有听清，就问："什么？您说十两银子。您是不是记错了？您的鸡怎么这么贵？"店老板解释说："没记错。你吃的是一只母鸡，你想想，要是你不吃它，这十几天它该生多少鸡蛋（jīdàn）？那些鸡蛋能变成多少小鸡？小鸡长大了又能生蛋。这样鸡生蛋，蛋变鸡，只收你十两银子，这是最便宜的价钱了……"做工的听了，很生气，大声地对他说："你这样的糊涂账，我是不会付钱的。"

　　店老板说："你不付钱，我就跟你打官司。"

　　第二天，他们就去见县官。

　　县官听了他们两个人说的情况，想了想，就对做工的说："店老板说得很对。母鸡生蛋，蛋变小鸡，小鸡长大又生蛋，这些难道你都不知道吗？你应该付给店老板十两银子，这事就这样决定了。"做工的听了，当然不服（fú），要求再审（shěn）。县官虽然嫌麻烦不想再审，但为了让做工的心服口服，就同意了他的要求。他对做工的说："你要求再审，也可以。但是我要把话说在前头，你再打不赢官司可要加倍还钱。"

　　再审的那天，来了很多人。县官、店老板都来了，可是做工的还没有来。县官很不高兴地等着。过了好一会儿，做工的才来。县官问他："你怎么这么晚才来？"做工的说："因为我有一件非常重要的事要做，所以迟到（chídào）了，真对不起。"县官又问："什么事情比你打官司还重要？"做工的说："县官大人（dàren），明天得种麦子（màizi）了，如果种晚了，就会影响明年的收成（shōucheng）。可是，我还没有炒麦种。刚才我在家把麦种都炒熟了，所以我迟到了。"

听完他的话，大家都笑起来了。有些人还大声地说："炒熟的麦种还能种吗？"县官拍了拍桌子，问做工的："你说你在家炒麦子了，炒熟的麦种还能长吗？"

做工的很认真地说："大家说的很对。炒熟的麦种不能种，也不能长，这是连孩子都知道的事情，可是县官大人却不知道。"

县官非常生气："胡说（húshuō），我怎么会不知道？炒熟的麦种当然不能长。"

做工的说："县官大人，您既然知道炒熟的麦种不能长，为什么又认为烧鸡还能生蛋呢？"

县官低着头，红着脸（liǎn），半天说不出话来。

三、语法　Grammar

词语 例解 Word Usage and Examples

1 就是

The adverb "就是", meaning "just, simply", specifies a certain aspect and excludes others, for example,

桌上就是几本书。

孩子学习还可以，就是负担太重。

这些菜她就是喜欢红烧鱼。

这件事别人都不知道，就是你知道。

我一切都好，就是嗓子有点儿疼。

2　本来

The adverb "本来", meaning "originally" or "previously", functions as an adverbial modifier, for example,

孩子爸爸本来同意让她去，现在也改变主意了。

她本来身体不太好，后来天天打太极拳，现在好多了。

他们三个人本来就不是一个学校的。

她本来就不瘦，现在更胖了。

3　嫌

The verb "嫌" means "to dislike" or "to complain". It is often used before a noun, a pronoun, an adjective or a verb. It can also be used to form a pivotal sentence. For example,

他的东西放得很乱，宿舍里的人都嫌他。

这位服务员态度很好，一点儿也不嫌麻烦。

她嫌太闹，想换个地方。

爸爸嫌十天的时间太长。

4　并

The adverb "并" is usually placed before a negative adverb, such as "不" and "没有", to emphasize that the reality of a situation is not the same as expected, for example,

时间并不长，只去十天。

大家都批评他，但我并不认为这件事是他的错。

你说他已经回国了，可是我发现他并没有离开这儿。

他昨天晚上在宿舍里做作业，并没有参加班上的活动。

句子 结构　Sentence Structure

1 兼语句（3）　Pivotal sentences (3)

In some pivotal sentences, V_1 is a verb denoting love, hate, like or dislike, for example, "喜欢，爱，称赞，夸奖，欣赏，嫌，怪，批评，笑话".

Subject₁	Predicate₁		
	V_1	$O_1(S_2)$	P_2
老师	称赞	她	做作业认真。
爷爷奶奶	喜欢	她	聪明。
家长	嫌	孩子	不努力。
姑娘	爱	小伙子	聪明能干。
领导	批评	小王	工作马虎。

"$S_2 + P_2$" usually explains the reason for V_1, for example,

家长嫌孩子不努力。→

因为孩子不努力，所以家长嫌孩子。

2 在……下　The construction "在……下"

Sometimes, the prepositional phrase "在 + NP/VP + 下" does not indicate a particular location, but a certain condition instead, for example,

在这种情况下，我同意女儿去夏令营。

在老师和同学的帮助下，他的汉语水平提高得很快。

在孩子不断地要求下，我决定送她去夏令营。

在没有家庭作业的情况下，孩子们可以学习他们需要的东西。

3 要么……，要么……　The construction "要么……，要么……"

The construction "要么……，要么……" means "either ... or ...". When "要么" is placed at the beginning of both clauses in a sentence, it denotes two alternatives, for example,

要么我陪他去上电脑辅导班，要么他爸爸带着他去上书法班。

要么你保证做到这几条，要么你就别去了。

要么他来，要么我去，我跟他一定得坐下来谈一谈。

要么把这件衣服买了，要么回家，不能总是在商店里浪费时间。

四、字与词　Chinese Characters and Words

1 集中识字　Learn the characters of the same radicals

钅：金　钉　针　银　钓　钟　钱　铁　锄　错　锣　锻　锁

车：转　轻　轿　辅　辆　输

忄：忙　快　性　怕　怪　情　惊　惯　愉　慢　懂　憾

2 词语联想　Learn the following groups of associated words

特　特别　特产　特长　特点　特定　特级　特价　特技　特区

　　特色　特性　特种　独特　奇特

不　不便　不安　不比　不必　不错　不但　不断　不对　不够

　　不管　不过　不和　不见　不久　不可　不利　不论　不满

　　不如　不是　不行　不幸　不要　不只　不足　不停　不在

忙　忙于　忙乱　帮忙　急忙　连忙　农忙　手忙脚乱

Chinese Kids—The Busiest People

If you ask who are the busiest and most tired people in China today, young people may tell you they are, since they are busy with working, making money, getting married and having kids. If I'm asked the question, however, I would tell you that kids are definitely the busiest people. That's because young people today are busy with basically the same things, compared with those in the old times, while kids nowadays are much busier and more tired than those in the past.

As early as in kindergarten, some children are compelled by their  parents to learn various kinds of specialties and skills, such as painting, English, musical instruments, mathematical Olympiads and calligraphy, which take away most of their time for play.

Once getting into primary school, they become even busier. Classes normally begin at an early hour. Take Beijing for instance. At present, classes in primary schools begin at eight o'clock, but students of many schools are required to arrive at 7:40 or even earlier. Every morning, children are dragged out of their beds early. Some barely have enough time to take a few quick bites of breakfast, and others  have to bring breakfast with them, rushing to school with a heavy schoolbag on their back. Thus begins a school day. When they get home after school, they bring back a lot of homework to do. The weekend is finally here. But all kinds of training lessons and intensive classes are waiting for them. The majority of children never get a whole day off.

Children have been kept busy constantly, which has done much harm to their physical and mental health. According to a comparison study of the results of the sample surveys on children between 6 and 14 done by China Youth & Children Research

Center in 1999 and in 2005, the time children spent doing homework was increasing and the time they spent playing and sleeping was decreasing. In 2005, 45.7% children slept less than the national standard (9 hours). Due to the persistent pressure of study, lack of sleep, fast food and neglect of physical exercises, an increasing number of children are troubled by obesity or myopia, even depression.

This busy life of children is caused by the pressure of competition for getting into higher schools. To make sure their children won't lose at the very beginning, parents, especially parents in cities, send their children to learn this and that no matter whether the children like it or not. Though the children may have acquired more skills, they have sacrificed the most precious happy time of their childhood for that.

第四十七课
Lesson
47

打工的大学生多起来了

More college students are taking part-time jobs

Chinese university students started doing part-time jobs only during the last ten to twenty years. Why is this? Ding Libo asks Song Hua to explain it. Only then does he realize that the problem of working part-time involves the traditional Chinese ideas concerning how parents bring up their children and how children care for their parents.

一、课文 Texts

🎧33 (一)

打工的大学生多起来了

丁力波：中国的大学生打工吗?

王小云：打工。不过，过去的大学生基本上不打工，最近一二十年，打工的学生多起来了。

丁力波：这就奇怪了。我听说在实行改革开放以前，中国人的生活水平比现在低多了，^① 很多大学生的经济条件也不太好。他们既然经济有困难，就应该去打工啊。

宋 华：那时候大学生不打工的原因很多：第一，过去上大学，学生不用交学费。家庭经济困难的学生还可以得到国家的帮助，^② 他们吃、住基本上没有问题。第二，中国的父母一般都希望把自己的孩子培养成为大学生，而且他们认为孩子在正式工作以前，无论岁数多大，生活上都应该由父母来负担。所以大学生在经济上还要靠父母来支持，中国的父母也愿意想办法支持孩子上学。第三，人们认为，对大学生来说，主要的时间都应该用于学习，这个时候，他们不应该自己去挣钱。

丁力波：哦，他们认为打工会影响学习。

宋　华：除了上边我说的那些原因以外，还有一个重要原因是：即使你想去打工，也没有单位用你。

丁力波：是不是因为中国劳动力太多了？

宋　华：不完全是。那时候，无论国营企业，还是集体企业，工作岗位和工资都是由国家来计划的。在这种情况下，你去打工，单位没办法付给你工资。

丁力波：可是我在书上看到过，以前不是也有大学生去工厂和农村劳动吗？

王小云：是有。不过，那时候他们无论去工厂干活儿，还是去农村干活儿，都是义务劳动，没有报酬。

丁力波：那么，现在的大学生都打工吗？

宋　华：这很难说，③可能大部分都打工。拿我来说，我也在打工。

丁力波：你既然也在打工，就给我介绍一下中国大学生打工的情况吧。你们都干些什么工作呢？

宋　华：干什么的都有：有送报纸的，有做家教的，也有在商店或者公司干活儿的。我和几个同学一起搞家教，我们组织了一个家教小组，他们选我当组长。

王小云：大家都开玩笑地称他为"打工头儿"。

丁力波：我想你们打工并不都是为了解决经济问题吧？

宋　华：对。很多学生是为了早点儿到社会上去锻炼自己，得到一些工作经验。有的学生想知道什么工作适合自己。不过，对城市低收入的家庭和很多农民家庭来说，每年拿出那么多的钱来培养一个大学生，确实是一个很重的负担，所以，这些家庭的孩子大部分是靠向银行申请贷款和打工挣钱来完成自己的学习的。

丁力波：有打工经验的学生是不是更容易找到工作？

宋　华：也许是这样。打过工的学生在生活经验上，在工作能力上，一般都比没有打过工的学生强。招聘单位当然要考虑这一点。但是，如果学生因为打工的时间太多，学习成绩差了，招聘单位也不会欢迎。

生词 New Words

1. 基本上	jīběnshang	Adv	basically, essentially	基本上不打工，基本上没问题

基本	jīběn	A/Adv	basic, fundamental; basically, fundamentally 基本条件，基本要求；基本做完了
2. 实行	shíxíng	V	to put into practice, to carry out　实行市场经济，实行AA制
3. 改革	gǎigé	V	to reform　实行改革，改革经济，改革风俗，政治改革
4. 开放	kāifàng	V	to open, to open up　实行开放，对外开放，开放城市，开放农村
5. 既然	jìrán	Conj	since, as, now that　既然经济有困难，既然你也在打工，既然父母在给我寄钱
6. 原因	yuányīn	N	cause, reason　不打工的原因，需要补习的原因，反对的原因，改革的原因，一个原因
7. 学费	xuéfèi	N	tuition fee 交学费，不用交学费，提高学费
8. 支持	zhīchí	V	to support, to hold out　靠父母来支持，支持孩子上学，支持不住
9. 劳动力	láodònglì	N	labour force　劳动力多，主要劳动力，农村劳动力
劳动	láodòng	V/N	to work; work, labour　劳动去；参加劳动，农村劳动，艰苦的劳动
10. 集体	jítǐ	N	collective　集体企业，集体经济，集体精神，我们的集体，集体完成，集体决定，关心集体
11. 岗位	gǎngwèi	N	post, job　工作岗位，劳动岗位，现在的岗位，重要的岗位，离开岗位
12. 计划	jìhuà	V/N	to plan; plan　由国家来计划，计划假期的活动；学习计划
13. 义务	yìwù	A/N	voluntary; duty, obligation　义务劳动，义务教育；律师的义务，有义务，没有义务
14. 难说	nánshuō	V	to be hard to say　这很难说
15. 部分	bùfen	N	part　大部分学生，小部分公务员，这篇文章有三个部分

16. 家教	jiājiào	N	private tutor, private tutoring 搞家教，做家教的工作
17. 小组	xiǎozǔ	N	group, team 家教小组，书画小组，学习小组，舞蹈小组，京剧小组
18. 组长	zǔzhǎng	N	group leader 选他当组长
长	zhǎng	Suf	chief, head 班长，队长，院长，校长，馆长，所长，行长，市长
19. 称	chēng	V	to call 称他"王老"，称他"先生"，怎么称呼
20. 为	wéi	V	to take as, to act as, to serve as 称他为"打工头儿"，选他为代表
21. 头儿	tóur	N	(coll.) head, chief, boss 家教小组的头儿，学院的头儿，选我当头儿，打工头儿
22. 也许	yěxǔ	Adv	perhaps, probably 也许是这样，也许能生活得轻松一点儿
23. 强	qiáng	A	strong, better 能力很强，比他们强，没有他们强

注释 Notes

① 我听说在实行改革开放以前，中国人的生活水平比现在低多了。

"I heard that before China's reform and opening-up policy was adopted, the living standards of the Chinese people were much lower."

After experiencing the disasters of the Cultural Revolution during the 1960s and 1970s, the Chinese Communist Party and the Chinese Government put into practice a policy of reform and opening to the outside world. As a result, China has scored great achievements that have caught the attention of the entire world over the last thirty years.

② 家庭经济困难的学生还可以得到国家的帮助。

"Students from low-income families can get assistance from the state."

In the past, the Chinese Government gave grants to students from low-income families to guarantee their basic livelihood during their school years. Although at present most schools provide opportunities for low-income students to do paid work, for the most part they encourage students to borrow money from banks to solve their financial difficulties. At the same time, they also provide scholarships for students with good marks.

③ 这很难说。

"This is hard to say."

The structure "难 + V", contrary to "好 + V", means "it is difficult to do something", for example,

这一课的作业很难做。

上山的路很难走。

34 （二）

我懂得了挣钱不容易

2007 年，我去新西兰读书。为了减轻父母的负担，我到那儿三个月以后就开始在餐厅打工。

这家餐厅不大，有两层，装修得很漂亮。我每周在这儿打两次工：星期五和星期六从下午四点干到夜里十二点或者更晚。我在家里连自己的饭碗也很少洗，本来不会干活儿，开始的时候，老板总嫌我动作慢。在打工朋友的帮助下，我很快就学会了干活儿。当我第一次拿到打工报酬的时候，我低着头看看两只泡白了的手，揉揉又累又痛的腰，深深地感觉到挣钱不容易。

过节的时候，我一周要打三四天工，主要工作是洗盘子。晚上十点以后，盘子最多，高得像座小山似的。我拼命地洗，这座盘子山却总是不变小，当时我想，人要是多长几只手就好了。我常常干到一点多钟，工作才能完成。

圣诞节快到了，饭馆的生意越来越好，我的工作也就一天比一天重。每天我得干十几个小时，把手上的皮都洗破了，腰也直不起来了。我真有点儿支持不住了。有时候我也想：我为什么要出国吃这么大的苦呢？既然父母在不断地给我寄钱，我就可以不打工了，也许我能生活得轻松一点儿。但是，我很清楚，我父母都是靠工资生活的，我不能跟有钱人家的孩子比。父母是用一辈子的积蓄支持我出国留学的，我怎么能总是靠他们呢？现在我要早点儿独立生活，自己养活自己。毕业以后有了工作，我要让他们生活得更好，过上幸福的老年生活。爸爸妈妈对我说过："出国以后，什么工作最苦最累，你就从什么工作做起。有了那种经验，以后什么苦你也不会怕了。"所以，在最艰苦的时候，我就好像听见妈妈在旁边给我加油："坚持下去！坚持就是胜利。"

2011年我终于读完了大学，而且考上了研究生。父母要我回国过春节。他们看到我长高了、长大了，非常高兴。妈妈指着我的那双穿旧了的旅游鞋，难过地问我："孩子，是不是一点儿钱都没有了？"

我说："妈，我有钱。我把你们寄给我的钱和打工挣的钱都存在银行里了，以后你们不用再给我寄了。我可以靠打工来完成自己的学习。"

爸爸妈妈看着我，满意地笑了。

生词 New Words

1. 懂得	dǒngdé	V	to understand, to know　懂得挣钱不容易，懂得怎样研究
2. 减轻	jiǎnqīng	V	to lighten, to reduce, to relieve　减轻父母的负担，减轻学习负担，减轻困难，减轻家务
减	jiǎn	V	to reduce, to decrease, to subtract　五减三得二，减肥（féi, fat）
3. 当	dāng	Prep	just at (a time), when　当我拿到打工报酬的时候，当我看见他的时候
4. 只	zhī	M	measure word for one of a pair or for certain animals or utensils　两只手，三只鸡，一只烤鸭，一只羊
5. 泡	pào	V	to steep, to soak　泡白了手，泡在水里，泡茶
6. 揉	róu	V	to rub, to knead　揉揉胳膊，揉揉腿，不要揉眼睛
7. 腰	yāo	N	waist　揉揉腰，又累又痛的腰，弯腰
8. 深	shēn	Adv/A	deeply, profoundly; deep, difficult　深深地感觉到；河很深，这篇课文很深

9. 拼命	pīnmìng	Adv	desperately, exerting one's utmost 拼命地 洗，拼命地工作，拼命地干活儿
10. 却	què	Adv	but, yet, however 这座山却总不变小
11. 皮	pí	N	skin, leather 手上的皮，洗破了手上的皮， 一块皮，羊皮，苹果皮，树皮，皮衣服，皮鞋
12. 出国	chūguó	VO	to go abroad 出国留学，出国旅游，出了两 次国
13. 吃苦	chīkǔ	VO	to bear hardship 吃这么大的苦，不怕吃 苦，能吃苦
14. 轻松	qīngsōng	A	easy, relaxed 生活得轻松一点儿，轻松的工 作，轻松地赢了比赛
15. 坚持	jiānchí	V	to persist in, to insist on 坚持下去，坚持 打工，坚持学习，坚持自己的想法，坚持上 班，坚持买单
16. 胜利	shènglì	V	to win a victory 坚持就是胜利，得到胜利， 胜利完成，比赛胜利了
17. 旅游鞋	lǚyóuxié	N	walking shoes, sneakers 穿旅游鞋，一双旅 游鞋
鞋	xié	N	shoe(s) 一只鞋，一双鞋
18. 难过	nánguò	A	(to feel) sorry, (to feel) bad/sad 难过地问， 心里很难过，感到难过
19. 存	cún	V	to deposit 存在银行里，存钱
20. 新西兰	Xīnxīlán	PN	New Zealand

补充生词 Supplementary Words

1. 难忘	nánwàng	A	unforgettable
2. 克林	Kèlín	PN	Collin (name of a person)

3. 争取	zhēngqǔ	V	to strive for
4. 奥运	Àoyùn	PN	the Olympic Games
5. 大爷	dàye	N	uncle (a respectful form of address for an elderly man)
6. 大妈	dàmā	N	aunt (a respectful form of address for an elderly woman)
7. 业余	yèyú	A	spare, leisure
8. 耐心	nàixīn	A/N	patient; patience
9.《雪绒花》	Xuěrónghuā	PN	"Edelweiss" (a song from the film *Sound of Music*)
10. 起名字	qǐ míngzi	V O	to give a name
11. 早退	zǎotuì	V	to leave early
12. 请假	qǐngjià	VO	to ask for leave of absence

二、练习　Exercises

练习与运用　**Drills and Practice** 35

核心句 KEY SENTENCES

1. 他们吃、住基本上没有问题。

2. 当我第一次拿到打工报酬的时候，我深深地感觉到挣钱不容易。

3. 也许我能生活得轻松一点儿。

4. 我拼命地洗，这座盘子山却总是不变小。

5. 他们选我当组长。

6. 大家都开玩笑地称他为"打工头儿"。

7. 大学生在经济上还要靠父母来支持。

8. 他们既然经济有困难，就应该去打工啊。

1. 熟读下列词组　Read the following phrases until you learn them by heart

（1）基本上都打工　　　基本上没有困难　　　基本上听懂了

　　基本上做完了　　　基本上调查清楚了

　　基本看法　基本矛盾　基本特点　基本完成　基本同意　基本实现

（2）当他打算回国的时候　　　　　当他第一次拿到工资的时候

　　当演员走下舞台的时候　　　　当他准备参加考试的时候

　　当老师称赞他的时候　　　　　当他拿到出国护照的时候

（3）也许不上课　　也许会下雨　　也许明天来　　　也许更熟悉

　　也许是对的　　也许更便宜　　也许开得太快　　也许非常别扭

　　也许就不疼了　也许稳定得多　也许他不想参加

（4）在经济上　在学习上　在生活上　在工作上　在书法上

　　在文学上　在武术上　在家教上　在爱情上　在食物上

（5）实行绿化　实行法律　实行合作　实行分工　实行自己的权利

　　实行竞争　实行管理　实行创新　实行计划　实行改革开放

　　实行得早　基本实行

（6）支持他的工作　支持他的想法　用一辈子的积蓄支持我出国留学

　　坚决支持　　　支持不了

（7）计划这件事　　　计划经济　　　计划用钱　　　计划下个月的工作

　　计划得不错　　　认真地计划　　　旅游计划　　　研究计划

（8）非常难过　难过得很　为他难过　难过地说　难过得说不出话来

2. 句子练习　Sentence drills

A. 用所给词语完成句子
Complete the following sentences with the given words and expressions

基本上（basically）

（1）现在大学生 基本上都打工 。（打工）

（2）他的看法我 基本上同意 。（同意）

（3）这件事情＿＿＿＿＿＿＿＿＿＿＿了。（调查清楚）

（4）他说的上海话，我＿＿＿＿＿＿＿＿＿。（懂）

（5）今天的作业我＿＿＿＿＿＿＿＿＿。（做完）

当……的时候

（1）当决定回家（旅游）的时候，机票已经买不到了。（决定）

（2）当拿到钱的时候，他才感觉到现在自己在生活上真正独立了。
（拿到工资）get paid

（3）当称赞的时候，她还有点儿不好意思。（称赞）praise

（4）当"收到"的时候，小伙子高兴得像疯了一样。
（姑娘的第一封信）

（5）当回家过春节的时候，杰克还是觉得开不了口叫爸爸、妈妈。
（回家过春节）

也许　Maybe

（1）现在快九点了，大家都来了，他怎么还没来？也许参加。（参加）

（2）你再到别的商店看看，便宜也许。（便宜）

（3）天气怎么一下子变得这么热？也许要下雨。（下雨）

（4）我对你的看法想了很久，看来，你的看法也许对。（对）

（5）他今天是不会来了，也许明天来。（明天）

却

（1）他本来说一定要来的，＿＿＿＿＿＿＿＿＿＿。

（2）在咸亨酒店，穿长衫的都坐着喝酒，孔乙己＿＿＿＿＿＿＿＿。

（3）他前两次考试都考第一，这次＿＿＿＿＿＿＿＿。

（4）小王说他非常喜欢这个工作，可是半年以后＿＿＿＿＿＿。

（5）他说他一定坚持自己的看法，可是讨论的时候＿＿＿＿＿＿。

拼命 Desperately

（1）为了更好地提高画画儿的水平，他每天都＿＿＿＿＿＿。
（练习中国画和书法）

（2）小伙子今年要结婚，所以他＿＿＿＿＿＿。（挣钱）

（3）他在一家餐厅打工，一上班就＿＿＿＿＿＿，老板还嫌他动作慢。
（干活儿）

（4）要想考上名牌大学，就得＿＿＿＿＿＿。（参加辅导班和补习）

（5）他＿＿＿＿＿＿，终于追上了那个小偷。（跑）

B. 替换练习
Substitution drills

（1）他们选我当组长。

王小云	学生代表
丁力波	班长
宋 华	足球队队长

（2）大家称他为打工头儿。

经理	老板
黄河	母亲河
黄山	中国第一山

C. 用"在……上"改写句子

Rewrite the following sentences, using "在……上"

（1）我每月花了不少钱买书。

在买书上 我每月花了不少钱。

（2）他一周最少要用五个小时练书法。

在 练书法 上 ，他一周最少要用五个小时

（3）我觉得自己在文学方面有很大的发展前途。

在文学 上

（4）他在国外留学的主要困难不是学习差，而是生活不习惯。

他在国外留学 在 生活习惯上 有困难.

（5）这位女企业家不但工作能力很强，家务也管理得很好。

在 上

D. 用"既然……，就……"完成句子

Complete the following sentences, using "既然……，就……"

（1）你既然去过那儿，就给旅游

（2）你既然不喜欢搞家教，就 你 去 现又.

（3）既然没有人反对，就 我们 可以分享果

（4）既然你同意一切合作的条件，就 我将感力

（5）既然孩子一定要去夏令营，就 你 必须得去.

3. 根据课文回答问题 Answer the following questions according to the texts

（1）为什么以前的中国大学生基本上不打工？

（2）那时候为什么没有打工的地方？

（3）现在大学生们打工主要干些什么？

（4）为什么大家称宋华为"打工头儿"？

（5）宋华他们打工是为了什么？

（6）现在打工与毕业以后找工作有没有关系？

（7）课文（二）中的"我"去了哪个国家留学？他为什么要去餐厅打工？

（8）他每周打几次工？他每次干多长时间？

（9）当他第一次拿到打工报酬的时候，有什么感觉？为什么？

（10）过节的时候，他是怎样打工的？

（11）他是怎样考虑他和父母的关系的？

（12）他爸爸妈妈春节看到他的时候，为什么满意地笑了？

4. 会话练习　Conversation practice

会话常用语 IDIOMATIC EXPRESSIONS IN CONVERSATION

这就奇怪了。(This is strange.)

不完全是。(It is not entirely ...)

也许是这样。(Perhaps so.)

这很难说。(This is hard to say.)

干什么的都有。(They do all sorts of things.)

【不能确定　Expressing uncertainty】

A：中国的年轻人，比如说上大学的时候或者在找到工作以前，都靠父母生活吗？

B：一般是这样，但也不完全是，还要看家庭经济情况。经济困难的家庭，孩子很早就要帮父母挣钱。当然，他们常常也上不了大学。

A：那么，一般家庭的年轻人什么时候在经济上独立呢？

B：这很难说。有的人结婚以后还需要得到父母的帮助，当然，也有的人工作以后却把工资都交给父母，他们在有自己的小家庭以前，常常跟父母生活在一起。

A：我听说中国的父母不但要想办法培养自己的孩子，而且还要帮助培养第三代，也就是孩子的孩子。是不是因为中国人的家庭观念比较重？

B：也许是这样。中国的传统观念是：父母要培养自己的孩子；父母老了以后，孩子要照顾自己的父母。

【说明原因　Explaining the reason】

A：听说像北京这样的地方，做家教的机会非常多。有的家长还请外国人教孩子外语。为什么家长这么喜欢请家教？难道学校对学生的学习都不负责吗？

B：完全不是。学校给学生的学习负担已经很重了。

A：既然学生的负担已经很重了，家长就不该再请家教了。

B：家长还要请家教，原因也很复杂。有的是孩子学习成绩不好，需要给他们补习；更多的家长是为了让孩子学得再好一些。

A：像北京这样的大都市，学生的竞争一定很厉害。

B：这当然是一个原因，但更主要的原因是中国家长太关心孩子的前途了，他们愿意把自己一辈子的积蓄用于孩子的教育。

5. 交际练习　Communication exercises

(1) What is special about the relationship between Chinese parents and their children according to the texts of this lesson and those of the last one?

(2) Compare and contrast the relationship between Chinese parents and their children to that between parents and children in your country.

After expressing yourself orally, write a short essay on either of the topics above.

阅读 与复述 Reading Comprehension and Paraphrasing

🎧 36 难忘（nánwàng）的经历

克林（Kèlín）是美国人。2004 年他在语言学院进修了一年汉语。回国以后，他又争取（zhēngqǔ）到一个来北京工作的机会。现在他已经在北京生活六年多了，能说一口流利的普通话，而且还带北京味儿。

2008 年，北京成功举办奥运（Àoyùn）。北京市民对学习英语因此越来越感兴趣，不但年轻人坚持学，而且老年人也在认真地学。团结湖小区的大爷（dàye）大妈（dàmā）就组织了一个英语学习班。他们还请来了一位外国老师，他就是克林。克林是用业余（yèyú）时间来给大爷大妈们上英语课的。每次上完课，这些白头发的学生都要问他不少问题，他总是耐心（nàixīn）地回答。他喜欢这些又认真又热情的学生。

在上课以前，班长 Summer 大爷总要让大家唱英文歌曲《雪绒花》（Xuěrónghuā）。这是克林教他们的，他们唱得还真不错。班长姓夏，"夏"有夏天的意思，所以大家称他为"Summer 大爷"。在课堂上，克林也叫他 Summer 大爷。克林根据每个学生的姓或者名字的意思，给他们都起了英文名字（qǐ míngzi）。在上课的时候，克林总是用英语跟大爷大妈们作简单的会话。他了解到这个班的学生大部分是退休职工，有的是公务员，有的是教师，有的是医生，有的还是单位的领导。他们的文化水平有高有低，但学习态度却都很认真。这些白头发学生很尊重这位年轻老师，从来不迟到、不早退（zǎotuì），有事不能来上课还要向克林请假（qǐngjià）。克林也很尊敬自己的学生，叫他们的英文名字时，按北京人的习惯，总要加上"大爷"或"大妈"。

克林的父母要来北京看儿子。他们也很想看看儿子教的学生。大爷大妈们知道这个消息以后，就为他们准备了一个欢迎会。当克林的父母来到这个班的时候，班长 Summer 大爷用英语表示欢迎，同学们也用英语加汉语跟克林父母交谈。有听不懂的地方，克林就当翻译。大家又说又笑，欢迎会开得很热闹。克林的父母看到儿子这么受尊重，他们非常高兴。

克林常说，给北京大爷大妈们当英语老师，这是他在中国最难忘的经历。

三、语法 Grammar

词语 例解 Word Usage and Examples

1 基本上

When used as an adverbial modifier, the adverb "基本上" or "基本" expresses the idea of "principally" or "for the most part", for example,

过去的大学生基本上不打工。

这部电影我们基本上看懂了。

经理基本同意我们的看法。

2 当……的时候

Usually placed before the subject, "当 + S-PP/VP + 的时候" is used as an adverbial modifier that indicates the time at which another motion or action takes place, and expresses the idea of "when ...", for example,

当我第一次拿到打工报酬的时候，我深深地感觉到挣钱不容易。

当水在 0 度或 100 度的时候，就会有变化。

当她见到爸爸妈妈的时候，她高兴得哭起来了。

当发现问题的时候，我们一定要想办法解决。

③ 也许

When the adverb "也许" is used as an adverbial modifier, it expresses the idea that one is uncertain about something and is only making a guess. It can be placed at the beginning of a sentence or used as an independent sentence. For example,

今天阴天，很冷，明天也许会更冷。

你也许认识这个人。

许多年以后，也许你还记得他，也许你早已经忘记。

A：你能参加吗？

B：也许吧。

④ 却

When the adverb "却" is used as an adverbial modifier, it frequently occurs in the second clause to indicate a turn in the event, i.e., the condition is not the same as mentioned earlier. This expression is more commonly used in writing. For example,

盘子高得像座小山似的，我拼命地洗，这座盘子山却总是不变小。

风停了，雪却越下越大。

该来的人没来，不该来的人却来了。

"却" is frequently used with the conjunction "但是" or "可是" for emphasis, for example,

课文虽然不长，但生词却不少。

别人都很忙，可是他却觉得没有事儿干。

● 句子 结构 Sentence Structure

① 兼语句（4） Pivotal sentences (4)

In this type of sentence, the first verb expresses an appellation or belief, such as "称，叫，认为，选". The verb after the pivotal element is usually "为，做，当" or "是".

Subject₁	Predicate₁		
	V₁	O₁(S₂)	P₂
大家	称	他	为打工头儿。
同学们	都　认为	他	是园艺师。
他们	选	他	当组长。

2 在……上　The construction "在……上"

Sometimes when "在 + NP + 上" is used as an adverbial modifier, it does not indicate a concrete location, but expresses the idea of "in a certain way or aspect", for example,

　　大学生在经济上还要靠父母来支持。

　　同学们在学习上都有很大的进步。

　　他在工作上是非常认真负责的。

3 既然……，就……　The construction "既然……，就……"

The construction "既然……，就……" means "since ..., then ...". The first clause uses "既然" to indicate the reason for something, while "就" is added afterwards to show the conclusion inferred from this situation, for example,

　　你既然也在打工，就给我介绍一下大学生打工的情况吧。

　　大家既然同意，我就不必再说什么了。

　　既然大家都想去游览兵马俑，假期我们就组织一次吧。

四、字与词　Chinese Characters and Words

1 集中识字　Learn the characters of the same radicals

　　囗：四　团　因　园　围　困　国　固　图

月：肚 朋 肥 服 胜 胞 胖 脑 朗 脚 腰 腿 胳 膊

厂：厅 历 厉 厕 厨 厢 厚 原

2 词语联想 Learn the following groups of associated words

在 在于 在先 在家 存在 实在 正在 现在 在……上
在……以上 在……下 在……以下 在……以前 在……以后
在……之内

减 减产 减低 减肥 减价 减轻 减少 减退

增 增产 增大 增多 增高 增加 增强 增收 增长

坚 坚持 坚定 坚决 坚强 坚信 坚实 坚硬

Changes in Chinese People's Opinions about Education

Chinese people's opinions about education have changed a lot with the times.

The traditional mode of education was teacher-centered, with students following their teacher step by step. The criterion for deciding whether a student was good or not was the student's academic scores; a student with high scores was considered a good one and a role model. The fact that "one exam determines one's whole life" made academic scores even more vital. This mode was apt to be divorced from social development. Focusing all their attention on scores, students were more likely to lack creativity, flexibility and comprehensive abilities, which made it difficult for them to meet the needs of the modern society.

Nowadays, China is trying to turn its education from being "exam-oriented" into being "quality-oriented". Apart from scores, more attention is now paid to practical skills and comprehensive abilities of students. Aiming to be "student-centered", schools are devoted to the cultivation of each individual student's creativity and practical abilities according to his/her own characteristics. Students' interests and specialties are developed based on their curiosity and desire for knowledge. There have been many celebrities who have achieved professional success in ways other than through "academic education", such as the famous pianist Lang Lang and the snooker player Ding Junhui.

There is a Chinese saying "活到老，学到老", which means "to live and learn". More people are joining the team of lifelong learning and further education. For one thing, with fast social development and knowledge and techniques being updated constantly, some successful people need further education to improve themselves; for the other, these people have a heated passion for self-fulfillment.

The changes in Chinese people's opinions about education are the inexorable results of the social development.

第四十八课
Lesson
48

我是独生子女

I'm the only child in the family

Ma Dawei has discovered that many of his Chinese classmates are the only child in their families, so he discusses the topic of China's family planning program with Song Hua. They talk about the traditional Chinese ideas about having children and their relationship with the control of the nation's population growth and the development of China's economy. They also discuss the relationship between Chinese family planning and global development.

一、课文　Texts

37　（一）

我是独生子女

只生一个好

宋　华：大为，你的信。

马大为：哦，是我姐姐寄来的。宋华，你是不是独生子女？

宋　华：是啊，我是独生子女。

马大为：我发现你们好像个个都是独生子女。

宋　华：没错。我们国家实行计划生育，① 鼓励一对夫妇只生一个孩
　　　　子。所以，像我这么大的人，基本上都是独生子女。

马大为：听说中国实行计划生育是从上个世纪七十年代开始的。

宋　华：对啊！你知道中国为什么要实行计划生育吗？五六十年代，
　　　　中国的人口增长得太快。1949 年全中国的人口是 5.4 亿，到
　　　　1969 年就达到 8 亿多了。中国的人口确实太多了！尽管经

济在不断地发展，还是不能很快地提高人民的生活水平。从七十年代以来，计划生育成了中国的基本政策。最近三十年，中国成功地控制了人口的增长，现在中国人口的增长率已经低于世界人口的平均增长率。

马大为：这可是很大的成绩啊！如果中国不控制人口的增长，每年经济要保持百分之七八的增长速度，那是不可能做到的。人口增长速度太快，其实也会影响到家庭生活水平的提高，对不对？

宋　华：那还用说？② 穿衣、吃饭、住房、交通、看病、教育等等，③ 哪件事儿跟家庭的经济情况没有关系？中国是发展中国家，④ 大部分家庭还不很富裕，家庭人口越多，经济负担就越重。所以，计划生育也是关系到每个家庭生活水平提高的大问题。

马大为：中国这么大，农村人口又特别多，一直坚持实行这个政策真不容易。

宋　华：可不。控制人口增长是一个很复杂的问题。计划生育工作在城市做得比较好，农村还有不少问题。传统的"重男轻女"的生育观念影响还很深。特别是一些比较穷的地方，有的夫妇尽管已经有了两个女孩儿了，他们还是希望再生一个男孩儿。如果第三个又是女孩儿，他们也许还要生第四个。这样生下去，当然会影响到农村经济的发展和农民生活水平的提高。

马大为：有不少外国人对你们国家的计划生育政策是有看法的，⑤他们

　　　　不太理解这个政策。

宋　华：其实只要客观地分析一下，就不难理解了。就拿你们国家来

　　　　说，它的面积比中国稍微小一点儿，可是人口却只有中国的

　　　　五分之一。要是你们国家的人口跟中国一样多，恐怕你们也

　　　　得实行计划生育。中国是世界人口最多的国家，全世界百分

　　　　之二十二的人口在中国。如果中国不控制人口的增长，你算

　　　　得出现在全世界会有多少人吗？

马大为：中国的计划生育政策不但关系到中国的发展，也关系到世界

　　　　的发展。人们应该好好儿地研究一下这个问题。

生词 New Words

1. 独生子女	dúshēngzǐnǚ	N	only child	我是独生子女
独	dú	Adv	only, alone	独立，独唱，独舞，独奏，独身
生	shēng	V	to give birth to	生孩子，生一个男孩儿
子女	zǐnǚ	N	sons and daughters, children	培养子女，教育子女，靠子女照顾
2. 生育	shēngyù	V	to give birth to, to bear, to beget	计划生育，实行计划生育
3. 鼓励	gǔlì	V	to encourage, to urge	鼓励学生，鼓励只生一个孩子，不鼓励学生打工
4. 对	duì	M	pair	一对大眼睛，一对熊猫
5. 夫妇	fūfù	N	husband and wife, couple	一对夫妇，他们夫妇，杰克夫妇，夫妇俩

6. 年代	niándài	N	decade, age, years　五十年代，上个世纪七十年代
7. 增长	zēngzhǎng	V	to increase, to grow　人口增长得很快，经济增长，能力增长，影响增长，增长知识
8. 达到	dádào	VC	to reach, to attain　人口达到八亿多了，达到很高的水平
9. 尽管	jǐnguǎn	Conj	though, in spite of　尽管经济在不断发展
10. 以来	yǐlái	N	since　五十年代以来，2011年以来，上周以来
11. 政策	zhèngcè	N	policy　基本政策，计划生育政策，实行改革开放政策
12. 控制	kòngzhì	V	to control　控制人口的增长，控制生育，控制感情，控制污染，政府控制，拼命地控制
13. 率	lǜ		rate　增长率，汇率
14. 平均	píngjūn	A	average, mean　平均增长率，平均收入，平均岁数
15. 保持	bǎochí	V	to keep, to maintain　保持增长，保持增长速度
16. 速度	sùdù	N	speed　增长速度，游泳的速度，平均速度，保持速度，达到的速度，提高速度，改变速度，速度太快
17. 其实	qíshí	Adv	in fact, as a matter of fact　其实不难，其实也会有影响
18. 交通	jiāotōng	N	traffic, communications　公共交通，城市交通，发展交通，交通方便，交通困难
19. 等	děng	Pt	and so on, and so forth　穿衣、吃饭、住房、交通等等
20. 一直	yìzhí	Adv	continuously, all along, always　一直坚持实行，一直在学习，一直很努力
21. 传统	chuántǒng	A/N	traditional; tradition　传统观念，传统文化，传统风格；保持传统，社会传统，民族传统

22. 重男轻女	zhòng nán qīng nǔ	IE	to regard men as superior to women, to prefer boys to girls 重男轻女的生育观念
23. 客观	kèguān	A	objective 客观情况，客观的看法，客观条件，客观原因，客观地介绍，讲得很客观
24. 分析	fēnxī	V	to analyse 客观地分析，分析情况，分析问题，分析矛盾，分析小说，分析句子
25. 稍微	shāowēi	Adv	a little, slightly 稍微小一点儿，稍微复杂一点儿，稍微凉快点儿，稍微不注意

注释 Notes

① 我们国家实行计划生育。

"Our country has implemented the family planning policy."

"计划生育" means "family planning".

② 那还用说？

"That goes without saying."

"那" refers to what was mentioned earlier in the text. "还用说" means "不用说" (needless to say), indicating an agreement with the opinion expressed earlier.

③ 穿衣、吃饭、住房、交通、看病、教育等等

"Clothing, food, shelter, transportation, medicine and education, etc."

"等等" is used after two or more parallel words or phrases to indicate that the enumeration is not exhaustive, for example,

昨天我买了很多东西，有梳子、镜子、围巾等等。

涮羊肉、烤鸭等等，都是我喜欢吃的。

"等等" can also take the form of "等", which can be followed by some other words or phrases, for example,

我们访问了北京、上海、西安等城市。

今天参加讨论的有学校、公司、政府等方面的代表。

④ 中国是发展中国家。

　　"China is a developing country."

　　"发展中国家" means "developing country".

⑤ 有不少外国人对你们国家的计划生育政策是有看法的。

　　"Many foreigners are critical of the family planning policy in your country."

　　"有看法" has the same meaning as "有不同的看法" (to have a different opinion). It usually indicates a negative view of something.

🎧38 （二）

"多子多福" 与 "丁克家庭"

　　在中国农村，"重男轻女"和"养儿防老"的生育观念影响是很深的。一对夫妇如果只生女孩儿，即使已经有了两三个，也还要继续生，总希望再生一个男孩儿。这是因为长期以来中国是一个农业社会，劳动力对家庭来说是非常重要的。当父母老了、不能干活儿的时候，就要靠自己的子女来照顾。女儿又要嫁到别人家，所以只能靠儿子，人们也就常说"多子多福"。如果没有儿子，就会担心自己老了以后怎么办。今天社会发展了，情况也不同了。各种社会保险制度已经开始建立，老人也有了退休金，不需要完全靠子女生活了。尽管社会上已经有了这些变化，这种"多子多福"的传统观念在农村还是有很大的影响。

　　但是，城市里的年轻人对生育问题却有了新的想法。根据最新的调查，在北京、上海、广州三个城市的居民中，有21%的居民"赞成"或者"比较赞成"结婚不要孩子。有一部分年轻夫妇选择了"丁克家庭"。"丁克"是什么意思？它就是夫妇俩都工作、没有小孩儿的家庭。这种家庭是上个世纪六十年代在美国出现的，近三十多年以来越来越多了。⑥ 现在，"丁克家庭"在中国也出现了。根据政府的调查，在中国城市里，"丁克夫妇"的总数已达到60多万对，以后大概还会更快地增加。"丁克家庭"实际上已经成为一种新的城市家庭的形式，正从大城市向中小城市发展。

　　中国的"丁克家庭"有两大特点：一是夫妇受过比较好的教育，文化水平都比较高；二是他们的收入也比较高。(对这种"结婚不要孩子"的生育观念，报上已经有不同看法了。不少人批评结婚不生孩子是违反自然规律的，对国家是不利的。) 可是，有些刚从大学毕业的夫妇却认为不要孩子是很实际的考虑，对国家、对个人都是有利的。有些专家认为，生不生孩子，应该让年轻夫妇自由地选择。"丁克家庭"的出现，说明社会对个人的选择更尊重了。对"丁克家庭"，你有什么看法？

生词 New Words

| 1. 丁克家庭 | dīngkè jiātíng | family with double income and no kids |

中国的"丁克家庭"

丁克	dīngkè	IE	double income and no kids (DINK) 丁克夫妇
2. 养儿防老	yǎng ér fáng lǎo	IE	to raise children to provide against old age "养儿防老"的想法
3. 长期	chángqī	N	long-term, long-lasting 长期以来，长期的政策，长期的计划
4. 农业	nóngyè	N	agriculture, farming 农业社会，农业经济，发展农业
5. 保险	bǎoxiǎn	N/A	insurance; safe, secure 参加保险，汽车保险，交通保险，医疗（yīliáo）保险，保险金，保险公司；绝对保险，不保险
6. 制度	zhìdù	N	system, institution 社会保险制度，社会制度，国家制度，经济制度，封建制度，旧制度，建立制度
7. 居民	jūmín	N	resident, inhabitant 城市的居民，小区的居民
8. 出现	chūxiàn	V	to appear, to emerge 出现了新问题，出现了矛盾，出现了麻烦，出现了很多好作品，"丁克家庭"在中国出现了
9. 总数	zǒngshù	N	total, sum "丁克夫妇"的总数，学生总数，熊猫的总数
10. 大概	dàgài	A/Adv	general, rough; probably 大概的意思，大概的情况；大概会来，大概还会增加
11. 实际上	shíjìshang	Adv	practically, actually 实际上可以
实际	shíjì	A	realistic, practical 实际的考虑，实际的情况，实际的水平，实际的作用，了解实际情况
12. 形式	xíngshì	N	form 家庭形式，广告的形式，上课的形式，讨论的形式

13. 违反	wéifǎn	V	to violate, to run counter to, to go against 违反法律，违反科学，违反政策
14. 规律	guīlù	N	law, regular pattern　自然规律，经济规律，语法规律，客观规律，一般规律，基本规律，发现规律，违反自然规律
15. 不利	búlì	A	unfavourable, disadvantageous　对国家不利，对学校不利
16. 有利	yǒulì	A	advantageous, beneficial　对个人有利，对社会有利
17. 专家	zhuānjiā	N	expert, specialist　汉语专家，书法专家，舞蹈专家，盆景专家，蔬菜专家
18. 自由	zìyóu	A/N	free; freedom　自由地选择，自由地决定，自由地讨论，自由地生活；得到自由，保证自由，爱好自由，人民的自由，艺术的自由
19. 说明	shuōmíng	V/N	to explain, to show; explanation　说明情况，说明原因；写一个说明

补充生词 Supplementary Words

1. 负增长	fù zēngzhǎng		negative growth
2. 太爷爷	tàiyéye	N	great-grandfather
3. 清朝	Qīngcháo	PN	Qing Dynasty (1616-1911)
4. 民国	Mínguó	PN	Republic of China (1912-1949)
5. 储存	chǔcún	V	to store
6. 积谷防饥	jī gǔ fáng jī	IE	to store up grain against famine
7. 佩服	pèifu	V	to admire
8. 邓小平	Dèng Xiǎopíng	PN	Deng Xiaoping (1904-1997) (a leader of the Communist Party of China)

9. 小叶子	Xiǎoyèzi	PN	Xiao Yezi (name of a TV programme hostess)
10. 了不起	liǎobuqǐ	A	amazing, outstanding
11. 主持人	zhǔchírén	N	anchorperson, host or hostess
12. 岸	àn	N	bank, shore
13. 歌星	gēxīng	N	star singer, accomplished vocalist
14. 哄	hǒng	V	to coax, to humour
15. 劝	quàn	V	to try to persuade, to try to convince

注释　Notes

⑥ 近三十多年以来越来越多了。

　　"There have been more and more over the last thirty years."

　　"近三十多年" means "the last thirty years". One can also say "近一百年", "近两个月", etc.

二、练习　Exercises

练习与运用　Drills and Practice 39

核心句 KEY SENTENCES

1. 从七十年代以来，计划生育成了中国的基本政策。
2. 其实只要客观地分析一下，就不难理解了。
3. 中国的计划生育政策不但关系到中国的发展，也关系到世界的发展。

4. 一直坚持实行这个政策真不容易。

5. 那是不可能做到的。

6. 你知道中国为什么要实行计划生育吗？

7. 尽管社会上已经有了这些变化，这种"多子多福"的传统观念在农村还是有很大的影响。

1. 熟读下列词组　Read the following phrases until you learn them by heart

（1）上个世纪以来　　改革开放以来　　上大学以来

　　　2011 年以来　　咱们认识以来　　从开始工作以来

（2）其实不简单　　其实很满意　　其实很容易回答　　其实不是这样

　　　其实今天不冷

（3）关系到工作　　关系到人民的健康　　关系到经济的发展

　　　关系到生活水平的提高

　　　跟工作有关系　　跟人民的健康有关系　　跟经济的发展有关系

　　　跟提高生活水平有关系

（4）一直在干活儿　　一直住在学校　　一直学习到夜里

　　　一直往前走　　一直向东开　　一直没有找到他

（5）保持信用　保持健康　保持正常　保持水平　保持收入　保持合作

　　　保持传统　保持特色　保持安静　保持整齐　保持得很久　保持得很好

（6）达到要求　　达到理想　　达到世界的水平　　完全达到

　　　基本达到　　努力达到　　保证达到

（7）对国家不利　对个人不利　对健康不利　对保护环境有利

　　　对发展经济有利

（8）说明经过　　说明问题　　说明自己的看法　　清楚地说明

　　　简简单单地说明　　认真地说明　　电视机的说明　　保险的说明

2. 句子练习 Sentence drills

A. 用所给词语完成句子

Complete the following sentences with the given words and expressions

以来 since

（1） 以来 改革开放 ，中国经济增长的速度一直很快。（改革开放）

（2） 以来上大学 ，他一直利用寒假和暑假打工。（上大学）

（3） 以来 工作 ，他就每个月给父母寄生活费。（工作）

（4） 以来 2011年 ，他就一直在中外合资企业工作。（2011 年）

（5） 以来 认识 ，我就没有看见你批评过他。（认识）

一直

（1）他 一直 用电脑 ，连一分钟也没休息。（用电脑）

（2）我从1982 年 一直 住 ，没有换过地方。（住）

（3）为了准备参加考试，他女儿 一直学习 。（学习）

（4）我在图书馆都找遍了， 一直找到 。（找到）

（5）您 直往东 ，再走 100 多米就到了。（往东）

其实 in fact

（1）外边雪下得很大， 其实不冷 。（不冷）

（2）我以为她不喜欢这件衣服的样子， 其实 。（满意）

（3）他好像不想参加这次活动， 其实 。（参加）

（4）这个问题好像很难， 其实 。（回答）

（5）大家以为是汽车把他撞了， 其实 。（撞上）

B. 用"关系到"改写句子

Rewrite the following sentences, using "关系到"

例：计划生育政策跟中国的发展有关系。→

计划生育政策关系到中国的发展。

（1）这件事跟孩子找工作有关系。

　　这件事 ＿＿关系到跟孩子找工作有＿＿。

（2）环境保护跟人民的健康有关系。

　　环境保护 ＿＿关系到跟人民的健有＿＿。

（3）人口增长跟经济发展有关系。

　　人口增长 ＿＿关系到跟经济发展有＿＿。

（4）计划生育跟每个家庭生活水平的提高有关系。

　　计划生育 ＿＿关系到跟每个家庭活水平的提＿＿。

（5）锻炼身体跟人的健康长寿有关系。

　　锻炼身体 ＿＿关系到跟人的健康长寿有关系＿＿。

C. 用"是……的"句（2）回答问题

　　Answer the following questions, using the sentence pattern "是……的"（2）

（1）你认为这个办法好不好？

　　我 ＿＿认为是有看法为了＿＿。（有看法）

（2）公司提出的计划能实现吗？

　　只要准备工作做得好，＿＿是＿＿的＿＿。（能基本上实现）

（3）这件事他一周之内做得完吗？

　　这件事 ＿＿是做不完的＿＿。（做不完）

（4）你觉得他这个人怎么样？

　　根据他以前工作的情况，＿＿是的很负责＿＿。（很负责）

（5）他们家现在的日子还很困难吗？

　　他们家 ＿＿是比较富裕的＿＿。（比较富裕）

D. 用"尽管……，还是……"完成句子

　　Complete the following sentences, using "尽管……，还是……"

（1）尽管他学习成绩很好，＿＿＿＿＿＿＿＿＿＿。

（2）尽管经济发展得很快，如果不控制人口的增长，＿＿＿＿＿＿＿＿＿＿。

（3）他尽管已经读硕士了，＿＿＿＿＿＿＿＿＿＿。

（4）_____，我还是决定去参加面试。

（5）_____，家长还是不让他打工。

3. 根据课文回答问题 Answer the following questions according to the texts

（1）什么是"计划生育"？

（2）上个世纪七十年代以来，中国为什么一直实行计划生育政策？

（3）计划生育对中国的经济发展有什么影响？

（4）为什么说中国的计划生育政策也关系到世界的发展？

（5）什么生育观念在中国农村影响最深？

（6）根据调查，在中国大城市里，有多少人赞成或比较赞成结婚后不要孩子？

（7）什么叫"丁克家庭"？

（8）中国的"丁克家庭"有什么特点？

（9）对这种"结婚不要孩子"的生育观念，人们有些什么看法？

（10）"结婚不要孩子"是不是违反了自然规律？

4. 会话练习 Conversation practice

会话常用语 IDIOMATIC EXPRESSIONS IN CONVERSATION

实际上 (In fact, ...)

那还用说？ (That goes without saying.)

对……是有看法的。

（to have a different view on .../to be critical of ...）

根据最新的调查 (According to a recent survey, ...)

【表示肯定 Expressing affirmation】

A: 有的地方人们在拼命地多生孩子，人口增长的速度太快，这关系到环境保护和经济发展。

B：没错儿。可是也有的地方人们不愿意生孩子，出现了人口的负增
长（fù zēngzhǎng），这也是对社会发展不利的。

A：那还用说？人口不增长了，社会上老人越来越多，当然会影响到
经济的发展。不过生不生孩子，这是每对夫妇自己的事儿，他们
应该有选择的权利。

B：生孩子确实是每个家庭的事儿，但是也会影响到社会。我认为重
要的是人们对生育问题应该有科学的态度。

A：政府也不应该不管啊！当人口增长速度太快的时候，政府应该适
当地控制；当人口出现负增长的时候，政府就应该鼓励人们生孩
子。所以，计划生育是非常重要的。

【估计　Making an estimate】

A：除了"丁克家庭"外，还有人选择一辈子不结婚。这样的人，在
你们国家多不多？

B：选择不结婚的人过去不多，现在是多起来了，大概以后还会越来
越多。特别是职业妇女中，这种选择"独身"的人真不少。

A：她们决定不结婚，是不是因为自己的条件不好？

B：恐怕不是。这些人大部分都受过很好的教育，也有很不错的工作。
我想可能是因为她们觉得很难找到合适的男人，有的也许不希望
有家庭负担，她们要生活得自由一些。

5. 交际练习　Communication exercises

(1) What do you think of the family planning policy?

(2) What is your view on families with double income and no kids?

After expressing yourself orally, write a short essay on either of the topics above.

阅读 与复述 Reading Comprehension and Paraphrasing

🎧 40 我家太爷爷（tàiyéye）

　　我家人口不多，却有四代人——太爷爷、奶奶、爸爸、妈妈和我。太爷爷今年一百多岁了，经历过清朝（Qīngcháo）、民国（Mínguó），然后过上了新中国的生活，所以他有些看法和想法跟我们不一样。比如，现在他还喜欢储存（chǔcún）粮食。我们告诉他，现在我们国家不缺粮食了，不用把大包小包的粮食放在卧室里。他说："养儿防老，积谷防饥（jī gǔ fáng jī），你们懂吗？"无论爸爸妈妈怎么说，他都不听。没办法，就让他储存吧。不过，妈妈得经常把他储存的粮食拿出来晒晒。

　　特别有意思的是太爷爷对人的看法。他说："我一辈子最佩服（pèifu）两个人，一个是邓小平（Dèng Xiǎopíng），一个是小叶子（Xiǎoyèzi）。邓小平让中国富起来了，老百姓能过上好日子了，他了不起（liǎobuqǐ）。"太爷爷佩服的小叶子是谁？你们恐怕就不知道了。她是我们这儿电视台《每周一歌》的主持人（zhǔchírén），一个二十多岁的年轻姑娘。太爷爷常对我说："小小的人儿多能干，既会唱歌，又会跳舞。对着电视讲话，讲得很有水平，人长得又好看。"

　　我说："这有什么了不起？长得好看是她父母给的，会唱会跳是老师教的。不过，小叶子确实很聪明，我也佩服。"

　　我做完作业以后，常陪太爷爷看《每周一歌》，还跟他比赛唱歌。有一次，我妈听到我跟太爷爷大声地唱："妹妹你坐船头，哥哥在岸（àn）上走……"我妈笑得直不起腰来。太爷爷边唱还边表演，而且他越唱越高兴。我称赞他比歌星（gēxīng）唱得还好，太爷爷就更高兴了。

　　有一天，太爷爷突然说头晕得很，全家人都着急了，陪着他去医院看病。医院让他做脑CT，检查完以后，大夫说行了，太爷爷还躺在检查台上不愿下来。他很生气地对我爸爸妈妈说："交了那么多钱，也不给我好好儿地看病。推进来拉出去，就算看完病了，谁知道他们都干了些什么？"一家人又哄（hǒng）又劝（quàn），才把太爷爷请了下来，医生也偷偷地笑了。

三、语法　Grammar

词语 例解　Word Usage and Examples

1　以来

When placed after expressions of time, "以来" indicates the span of time starting from a certain point in the past until the time of the conversation. Words like "自", "从" and "自从" are frequently used in front of "以来". For example,

改革开放以来，中国旅游业发展得很快。

开学以来，这是第一次口语考试。

进入夏天以来，她的身体一天比一天好。

从结婚以来，他们还没有一起出国旅游过。

2　关系到

The phrase "关系到" means "to affect", "to concern" or "to have to do with". The verb "关系" indicates that something directly influences something else. "到" or "着" is frequently placed after "关系" and linked to an object. The meaning is almost the same as "跟……有关系" (to be related to). For example,

中国的计划生育政策不但关系到中国的发展，也关系到世界的发展。

农业的发展直接关系到农民的生活水平的提高。

口语说得好不好，关系到以后求职的问题。

控制污染是关系着人民身体健康的大事。

3　一直

When the adverb "一直" is used to indicate space, it expresses the idea of going continuously in one direction, for example,

请一直往前走。

你一直往东开，到街心花园再往南拐，然后一直往南就到了。

When "一直" is used to indicate time, it means either that an action continues without interruption or that a state remains unchanged within the period of time previously mentioned, for example,

从上个世纪 70 年代以来，中国一直在实行计划生育政策。

这两个月大家一直很忙。

他一直要学到放暑假。

雨一直下了两天两夜。

4　其实

When placed in front of the subject or the principal word of the predicate, the adverb "其实" indicates that the words following it are true, correcting or supplementing what has been said before, for example,

他普通话说得那么流利，你以为他是中国人，其实他是加拿大人。

古人认为心是管思想的，其实不是。

这件事好像很复杂，其实很简单。

句子 结构　Sentence Structure

1　"是……的"句 (2)　Sentences with "是……的" (2)

Some sentences with a verbal or an adjectival predicate use the expression "是……的". With "是" in front of a verbal or an adjectival phrase and "的" at the end, this kind of sentence indicates the speaker's view on or attitude towards something, implying an affirmative tone to convince the listener to believe what is being said.

Subject	Predicate		
	是	VP / AP	的
那	是	不可能	的。
他	是	不会参加	的。
我	是	来不了	的。
孙女儿	是	很聪明	的。
她的口语	是	很不错	的。
这种病	是	好得了	的。

Notes:

(1) The verbal phrase in the sentence with "是……的" (2) is frequently linked to an optative verb or a potential complement.

(2) Since the sentence with "是……的" (2) is used to express affirmation, it generally does not appear in the negative form "不是……的", nor in affirmative-negative questions.

2　双重疑问句　Double interrogative sentences

Some yes-no questions contain another question, which is signified by an interrogative pronoun. The common verbs that are used to form a double interrogative sentence include "知道, 认识, 了解, 明白, 懂得, 记得" (their objects frequently contain a subject-predicate phrase), or "想, 有, 能" (their objects often contain a verbal phrase).

$$S + V + O \text{ (with QPr)} + 吗?$$

你知道中国为什么要实行计划生育吗？

你明白他说的话是什么意思吗？

你认识他是谁吗？

你算得出现在全世界会有多少人吗？

When answering a double interrogative sentence, one may answer either the yes-no question or the question with an interrogative word. When giving an affirmative answer, one usually answers the question with an interrogative word, which is about the object; when giving a negative answer, one usually answers the yes-no question. For example,

A：你认识他是谁吗？

B：他是小王。

C：我不认识。

> We have already learned ten types of interrogative sentences:
>
> （1）你忙吗？（Lesson 2）
>
> （2）你认识不认识他？（Lesson 7）
>
> （3）昨天的京剧怎么样？（Lesson 6）
>
> （4）他今年多大岁数？（Lesson 9）
>
> 　　从你家到学校有多远？（Lesson 31）
>
> （5）他是英国人还是美国人？（Lesson 12）
>
> （6）晚饭以后我们一起去散步，好吗？（Lesson 9）
>
> 　　您学习汉语，是不是？（Lesson 10）
>
> 　　现在是不是坐电梯上楼去？（Lesson 19）
>
> （7）我学习美术专业，你呢？（Lesson 7）
>
> 　　我的照相机呢？（Lesson 20）
>
> （8）中国大学生队的水平比你们高吧？（Lesson 21）
>
> （9）你知道中国为什么要实行计划生育吗？（Lesson 48）
>
> （10）你想租房子？（Lesson 13）

3 尽管……，还是……　The construction "尽管……，还是……"

The first clause uses the conjunction "尽管" to state a concession, while the second clause indicates an abrupt turn in meaning, frequently using "还是", which means "still", to echo with the first clause. "可" or "却" can also be added before "还是" to reinforce the meaning of the abrupt turn. For example,

尽管国家经济在不断地发展，还是不能很快地提高人民的生活水平。

尽管他已经表示同意，可还是不愿意马上就签合同。

他尽管身体有点儿不舒服，却还是坚持工作。

四、字与词　Chinese Characters and Words

1　集中识字　Learn the characters of the same radicals

竹：笔　笑　笋　第　等　筑　签　简　答　算　筋　管　箱　篇

攵：收　改　放　政　故　教　敢　散　敬　数　整

艹：艺　节　花　苏　苦　苹　英　草　茶　药　菜　葡　萄　蓝　蒙
　　慕　薪　藏

2　词语联想　Learn the following groups of associated words

实	实干	实际	实价	实况	实力	实情	实数	实体
	实物	实习	实现	实行	实验	实用	实在	实证
	坚实	结实	老实	朴实	其实	确实	事实	现实	真实
生	生病	生产	生活	生命	生气			
	生日	生死	生物	生意	生于	生育	生长	生字	生词	生菜
	产生	出生	发生	考生	学生	男生	女生	先生	医生
交	交给	交换	交际	交流	交情			
	交谈	交替	交通	交往	交叉	交班		
	成交	断交	结交	社交	深交	外交	提交	

Changes in the Structure of Chinese Family

Generally speaking, the family structure in China has changed from big families of over five or six people in the early years of the People's Republic of China to nuclear families of three or four people now.

The population of China saw a rapid growth as a result of the improvements in the conditions of production, living and health care soon after the People's Republic of China was founded. A family at that time usually had over five or six people, with parents and children living together. Most families had three or more children. When a daughter got married, she would move out to her husband's home; when a son got married, he would stay. If the son's child didn't move out after he grew up and got married, then there would be three or even four generations living under the same roof. As Chinese people attached much importance to the positions in the family hierarchy and filial piety, a big family of this kind usually had a male of the eldest generation as its head.

In the 1970s, rapid population growth caused a heavy burden to the Chinese economy and society, leading to issues like resource shortage and environmental damage. As of 1980, China has carried out the family planning policy and encouraged late marriage and later, fewer but healthier births, hoping to keep the population under control and coordinate the development of population, economy and society. The policy has been regulated as a long-term fundamental policy of China since then.

After the nationwide implementation of the family planning policy, most families are only allowed to have one child. The family structure has changed from big families of more than five or six people to three-member nuclear families with parents and their only child.

Indeed, the family planning policy has played a significant role in controlling the pace of population growth and promoting economic development. But at the same time, it has caused some new problems and conflicts, such as the increasing percentage of old people. After the "only child" grows up and gets married, the young couple will have to provide for their own child as well as two pairs of parents, which means a lot of pressure on them. To solve this problem, further actions need to be taken, including improving the system of endowment insurance.

第四十九课
Lesson

49

"头痛医脚"

Treat the disease, not the symptoms

Lin Na has a stomachache. Wang Xiaoyun suggests that she go to see a traditional Chinese doctor. Lin Na is very curious about the methods and theories of this time-honoured medicine, and she wants to know how the traditional Chinese medicine treats a disease.

一、课文　Texts

🎧41　（一）

"头痛医脚"

林　娜：我可能得胃病了，这几天我觉得胃有点儿不舒服。

王小云：我劝你去看看中医。你一方面去看病，一方面也可以了解一下中医怎么看病。

林　娜：我在电影里见过。对了，中医看病的时候把手指放在病人的手腕上，你知道那是做什么吗？

王小云：那是在给病人号脉。对中医来说，号脉是很重要的，这跟西医用听诊器检查一样。①

林　娜：号脉怎么跟用听诊器检查一样呢？

王小云：应该说，中医从号脉中得到的信息比西医从听诊器中得到的还多。中医给你号号脉，看看你的气色，听听你的声音，再问你一些问题，你全身的情况怎么样，他基本上就清楚了。

林　娜：看来，学中医很难吧？

王小云：中医有很深的理论，培养中医大夫更重视经验。就拿号脉来说，中医专业的学生要跟老师一起看病，少说也得号几千个病人的脉，一直到他的感觉和看法跟老师的一样，他才算学会了号脉技术。

林　娜：真不容易！可是，现代医学发展得这么快，难道中医就不需要最新的技术吗？

王小云：当然需要。中国的医生一直在研究中西医结合的问题，现在中医看病也做一些检查或者化验。但是，无论用了什么现代医学的新技术，中医还是中医。②

林　娜：为什么？

王小云：因为中医对人的身体健康的理解跟西医不一样。西医一般把人看成一部机器，把人的器官看成是这部机器的零件。比如说，当你得胃病的时候，是胃这个零件坏了。你哪个零件坏了，西医就给你修理哪个零件。简单地说，西医是"头痛医头，脚痛医脚"。③

林　娜：哪个医生不是这样？难道还能"头痛医脚"吗？

王小云：中医的理论就不一样。中医认为，人是一个整体。某个器官有病，不只是那个器官的问题，而是有复杂的原因，可能还关系到其他部分。比如说，眼睛有病，好像是眼睛的问题，其实还可能是肝的问题。所以，中医一方面要治眼睛，一方面也要治肝。在中医那儿，"头痛医脚"是完全可能的。你（相）信不（相）信，按摩脚指头确实能治某种头疼病。

林　娜：真有意思。明天我就去看中医。

生词 New Words

1. 头痛医脚	tóu tòng yī jiǎo	IE	to treat the foot when the head aches　能"头痛医脚"吗
痛	tòng	A	aching, painful　头痛，嗓子痛，全身痛，腰痛，腿痛
医	yī	V/N	to treat, to cure; doctor, medical science　医病，医头痛，医眼睛；学医
脚	jiǎo	N	foot　一只脚，一双脚，医脚
2. 胃病	wèi bìng		stomach trouble, gastric disease　得胃病，有胃病，医胃病，看胃病，胃病好了
胃	wèi	N	stomach　胃痛，胃疼
3. 劝	quàn	V	to advise, to try to persuade　劝她去看病，劝我不要太累
4. 中医	zhōngyī	N	traditional Chinese medical science, doctor of traditional Chinese medicine
5. 病人	bìngrén	N	patient, sick person　关心病人，照顾病人
6. 手腕	shǒuwàn	N	wrist　病人的手腕，放在手腕上
7. 号脉	hàomài	VO	to feel the pulse　给病人号脉，号了两次脉，号了几千个病人的脉

号	hào	V	to examine, to feel
脉	mài	N	pulse
8. 西医	xīyī	N	Western medicine, doctor of Western medicine

看西医，研究西医

9. 听诊器	tīngzhěnqì	N	stethoscope 用听诊器检查
听诊	tīngzhěn	V	to auscultate
器	qì		appliance, implement, utensil 电器，木器
10. 信息	xìnxī	N	information 得到信息，了解信息，经济信息，

学校信息，市场信息

| 11. 气色 | qìsè | N | complexion, colour   看看你的气色，你的气色很好 |
| 12. 理论 | lǐlùn | N | theory   很深的理论，正确的理论，中医理论，文 |

学理论，语言理论

| 13. 大夫 | dàifu | N | doctor   中医大夫，王大夫，给他看病的大夫 |
| 14. 重视 | zhòngshì | V | to attach importance to, to think highly of   重视 |

理论，重视经验，重视计划生育

| 15. 医学 | yīxué | N | medical science   现代医学，医学理论，医学院 |
| 16. 结合 | jiéhé | V | to combine, to integrate   中西医结合，理论跟实 |

际结合

| 17. 化验 | huàyàn | V | to do a laboratory test, to have a chemical or |

physical examination   化验血，化验的结果

18. 机器	jīqì	N	machine 一部机器，纺织机器，生产机器
19. 器官	qìguān	N	organ, apparatus 人的器官，器官移植
20. 零件	língjiàn	N	spare part, component (of a machine) 机器的零

件，汽车零件，飞机零件

| 21. 修理 | xiūlǐ | V | to repair, to mend   修理零件，修理自行车，修理 |

电视机，修理房子

| 22. 整体 | zhěngtǐ | N | whole, entirety   是一个整体，整体的观念，整体 |

的作用，从整体上看

整	zhěng	A	whole 整天，整年，整部，整套，整队
体	tǐ		body
23. 某	mǒu	Pr	certain, some 某个器官，某位大夫，某个病人，某种理论
24. 肝	gān	N	liver 肝的问题，肝病，肝疼
25. 治	zhì	V	to treat (a disease), to cure 治病，治肝，治眼睛，治某种头疼病
26. 按摩	ànmó	V	to massage 按摩头，作按摩
27. 脚指头	jiǎozhǐtou	N	toe 按摩脚指头，脚指头疼
指头	zhǐtou	N	finger, toe 手指头，脚指头

注释　Notes

① 这跟西医用听诊器检查一样。

"This is the same as a doctor of Western medicine examining a patient with a stethoscope."

The Chinese call the medical science imported from the Western countries to China "Western medicine" and the traditional Chinese medical science "Chinese medicine". Doctors practising these two disciplines of medicine are respectively called " 西医 (doctor of Western medicine)" and " 中医 (doctor of traditional Chinese medicine)", for example, "他是一位著名的中医"。

② 无论用了什么现代医学的新技术，中医还是中医。

"No matter what new technology of modern medicine is applied, Chinese medicine will remain Chinese medicine."

This is a type of "是" sentence, in which the element before "是" is the same as that after it, meaning the subject is exactly what the object denotes. "还" indicates there is no change in something.

③ 西医是 "头痛医头，脚痛医脚"。

"Western medicine 'treats the head when the head aches and treats the foot when the foot hurts'."

The idiom "头痛医头，脚痛医脚" means "to treat the symptoms, but not the disease". It is used metaphorically to mean that a problem is only being dealt with superficially, for example,

有的农民孩子上不了学，你可以帮助他。不过，这只是头痛医头，脚痛医脚，还不是解决问题的办法。

🎧 42 （二）

林娜看中医

林娜身体不舒服的时候，总不肯去医院。这回她接受了王小云的建议，去北京同仁堂挂了一个专家号，④ 正好是位老中医给她看病。那位老先生给林娜号了号脉，看了看她的舌头，问了她一些问题，就低头开药方。林娜急忙问："大夫，我得了什么病？得吃点儿什么中药？"

"您没有什么大的病，不要紧的。可能最近学习比较紧张吧？"老中医对她说："您自己到市场上去买两斤山楂，有空儿就吃几个。一方面吃山楂，一方面还得多运动，最好每天锻炼四十分钟。过几天你就会好的。⑤"

他的话，林娜都听懂了，但她却不明白老中医为什么让她吃山楂。尽管她觉得有点儿奇怪，还是到市场上去买了几斤又红又大的山楂，每天都吃几次。从看病的第二天开始，她天天都很早起床，去外边跑跑步、做做操，然后练太极剑。一个星期以后，林娜觉得胃病好了，也想吃东西了。没吃药，病就好了，她简直不敢相信。一天，林娜见到宋华，就把看中医的事儿对他说了。她说："我觉得很奇怪，那位老中医没让我吃中药，只要我吃山楂，还要我多运动。"

　　宋华听了，笑着对林娜说："山楂就是药。因为你的病是消化不好，山楂正好是治这种病的药。是山楂把你的胃病治好了。"

　　林娜又问他："山楂怎么会是药呢？"宋华对她说，中医用的药叫"中药"。很多中药取自植物、动物和矿物，中医利用这些大自然的药来治病。人们平常吃的东西，有些其实就是中药。

　　林娜听了，更觉得奇怪。中医中药治病，就这么简单？宋华告诉她，中医中药已经有几千年的历史。人们在长期的劳动和生活中，发现很多植物、动物和矿物能治病。一些药方都来自民间，经过一代一代有名的医生不断地研究，就成为很好的治病方法。中医有自己独特的理论，这方面的古书很多，现在留下来的就有13000多种；中医也有独特的治病方法，像中药、针灸、按摩、气功等。有些病西医治不好，但用这些中医的方法却能治好。中医中药是中国文化的一个宝库，现在越来越多的西方人对中医中药感兴趣了。

生词 New Words

1. 肯	kěn	OpV	to be willing to	肯努力，肯帮助别人，不肯去医院
2. 正好	zhènghǎo	Adv/A	accidentally, fortunately; just right	正好治这种病，正好没有这种药；你来得正好
3. 舌头	shétou	N	tongue	看了看舌头
4. 开药方	kāi yàofāng	V O	to write a prescription	给她开药方
药方	yàofāng	N	prescription	中药药方
5. 要紧	yàojǐn	A	serious, important	不要紧，要紧的事儿

6.	紧张	jǐnzhāng	A	tense, nervous 学习紧张，紧张的生活，有点儿紧张，别紧张
7.	山楂	shānzhā	N	(Chinese) hawthorn 吃山楂
8.	运动	yùndòng	V/N	to do physical exercises; sports 还得多运动；喜欢什么运动
9.	简直	jiǎnzhí	Adv	simply, just, at all 简直不敢相信，简直忙坏了
10.	消化	xiāohuà	V	to digest 消化不好，不消化，帮助消化
11.	自	zì	Prep	from 来自民间，取自植物
12.	动物	dòngwù	N	animal 各种动物，动物园，珍贵的动物
13.	矿物	kuàngwù	N	mineral 重要的矿物之一
14.	利用	lìyòng	V	to make use of, to utilize 利用这些大自然的药，利用信息，利用市场，被利用
15.	独特	dútè	A	unique, distinctive 独特的理论，独特的方法，独特的想法
16.	针灸	zhēnjiǔ	N	acupuncture and moxibustion 用针灸治病，针灸大夫
17.	气功	qìgōng	N	qigong, a traditional Chinese system of deep breathing exercises 练气功，做气功
18.	同仁堂	Tóngrén Táng	PN	Tongrentang, a famous pharmacy of traditional Chinese medicine

补充生词 Supplementary Words

1.	压倒	yādǎo	VC	to prevail over
2.	艾滋病	àizībìng	N	AIDS
3.	讳疾忌医	huì jí jì yī	IE	to hide one's sickness for fear of treatment, to conceal one's faults for fear of criticism
4.	扁鹊	Biǎn Què	PN	Bian Que (a well-known Chinese doctor of the Warring States Period)

5. 战国	Zhànguó	PN	the Warring States Period (475 B.C.–221 B.C.)
6. 蔡国	Càiguó	PN	the State of Cai
7. 国王	guówáng	N	king
8. 王宫	wánggōng	N	imperial palace
9. 皮肤	pífū	N	skin
10. 医术	yīshù	N	medical skill
11. 大臣	dàchén	N	minister
12. 肌肉	jīròu	N	muscle
13. 肠	cháng	N	intestine
14. 热敷	rè fū		to apply a hot compress
15. 骨髓	gǔsuǐ	N	bone marrow
16. 承认	chéngrèn	V	to recognize, to admit
17. 发作	fāzuò	V	to break out, to show the effect of

注释　Notes

④ 去北京同仁堂挂了一个专家号。

"(She) has made an appointment with a specialist at Tongrentang in Beijing."

Tongrentang in Beijing is a famous pharmacy of traditional Chinese medicine with a long history. It was founded in 1669 and had been the provider of medicine for the Imperial Palace for almost 200 years. Tongrentang has become the number one brand of Chinese medicine, enjoying a good reputation both in china and abroad.

⑤ 过几天你就会好的。

"You will be all right in a few days."

The modal particle " 的 " expresses an affirmative tone when used at the end of a declarative sentence. There may be an optative verb like " 会 " or " 要 " in the predicate sometimes, for example,

别着急，他一定会帮助你的。

他昨天说今天要来的。

 **二、练习 Exercises**

练习 与运用 Drills and Practice 🎧 **43**

核心句 KEY SENTENCES

1. 看来，学中医很难吧？
2. 某个器官有病不只是那个器官的问题。
3. 没吃药，病就好了，她简直不敢相信。
4. 山楂正好是治这种病的药。
5. 正好是位老中医给她看病。
6. 一些药方都来自民间。
7. 你一方面去看病，一方面也可以了解一下中医怎么看病。
8. 过几天你就会好的。

---

1. 熟读下列词组 Read the following phrases until you learn them by heart

（1）有很深的理论 有很深的影响 有很深的关系 有很深的友谊

（2）某人 某地 某事 某工厂 某学校 某年 某月 某日

　　某个单位　　　某个地方　　　某篇文章　　　某些商品

　　某种专业　　　某位记者　　　某家合资企业

（3）接受建议　　　接受批评　　　接受礼物　　　接受考验

　　接受意见　　　接受不了　　　愉快地接受

（4）简直像春天　　简直跟真的一样　　简直站不住

　　简直要把人气死　　简直是骗人

（5）正好开门　　　正好找你　　　正好他来了　　　正好在上课　　　正好回家

　　　正好向他解释一下　　　衣服正好　　　车上的人正好　　　时间正好

　　　来得正好　　　问得正好　　　妆化得正好

（6）来自农村　　　寄自上海　　　选自《鲁迅小说选》　　　出自《红楼梦》

　　　取自深山

（7）东西方文化结合　　　工农业结合　　　学校与工厂结合　　　结合在一起

　　　结合得很紧

2. 句子练习　Sentence drills

A. 用所给词语完成句子

Complete the following sentences with the given words and expressions

（1）你们班的＿＿＿＿＿＿＿＿＿＿＿＿＿，家里经济很困难。（学生）

（2）在＿＿＿＿＿＿＿＿＿＿，人们常常不得不做本来不想做的事情。（情况）

（3）＿＿＿＿＿＿＿＿＿给我来过电话，让我去谈谈工作问题。（单位）

（4）填表的时候，请大家把＿＿＿＿＿＿做什么工作都写清楚。（年，月）

（1）一位多年不见的小学同学突然来看她，她＿＿＿＿＿＿＿＿。（相信）

（2）海南岛的冬天一点儿都不冷，＿＿＿＿＿＿＿＿＿＿。（春天）

（3）那个新西兰学生和非洲学生说的相声＿＿＿＿＿＿＿＿。（棒）

（4）他说的那些骗人的话＿＿＿＿＿＿＿＿。（气）

（5）他从早到晚忙了一天，＿＿＿＿＿＿＿＿＿。（累）

（1）我在门口叫老张，他＿＿＿＿＿出来。

（2）A：你找谁？

　　　B：不找别人，＿＿＿＿＿＿＿＿你。

（3）你们不是要请张老师辅导吗？＿＿＿＿＿＿＿＿＿＿＿＿。

（4）他今天＿＿＿＿＿＿＿＿＿＿了，有事儿的话，可以给他家打电话。

（5）他检查了一下车上的人，发现人数＿＿＿＿＿＿＿＿＿＿。

B. 用 "自" 做补语改写句子

Rewrite the following sentences, using "自" as a complement

（1）现在他们俩在北京工作，其实他们都是从农村来的。

现在他们俩在北京工作，其实＿＿＿＿＿＿＿＿＿＿＿＿＿＿＿。

（2）这封信是从上海寄来的。

这封信＿＿＿＿＿＿＿＿＿＿＿＿＿＿＿。

（3）这篇文章是从《鲁迅小说选》里选来的。

这篇文章＿＿＿＿＿＿＿＿＿＿＿＿。

（4）这些木头是从深山里运出来的。

这些木头都＿＿＿＿＿＿＿＿＿＿＿＿。

（5）"不是东风压倒（yādǎo）西风，就是西风压倒东风"，这是《红楼梦》
里的句子。

"不是东风压倒西风，就是西风压倒东风"＿＿＿＿＿＿＿＿＿＿。

C. 用 "是" 的兼语句作解释说明

Give an explanation to each of the following sentences, using the pivotal
sentence with "是"

例：这张画为什么在地上？ （风，刮）

　　是风把它刮下来了。

（1）今天你课文怎么念得这么好？ （朋友，辅导）

＿＿＿＿＿＿＿＿＿＿＿＿＿＿＿＿＿＿＿。

（2）上周小王打电话通知你了，为什么你昨天没有来？ （我，听）

＿＿＿＿＿＿＿＿＿＿＿＿＿＿＿＿＿＿＿。

（3）你的声音怎么这么小？ （嗓子，痛）

＿＿＿＿＿＿＿＿＿＿＿＿＿＿＿＿＿＿＿。

（4）你们的宿舍怎么这么干净？（小王，打扫）

　　————————————————————————————。

（5）上个月的水电费好像忘了交了。（我，交）

　　————————————————————————————。

D. 用"一方面……，一方面……"改写句子

Rewrite the following sentences, using the construction "一方面……，一方面……"

（1）他在学校里读硕士学位，还教两个班的汉语。

　　————————————————————————————。

（2）这家医院不但用西医的方法，还用中医的方法治艾滋病（àizībìng）。

　　————————————————————————————。

（3）在中国既有"多子多福"的生育观念，也有越来越多的"丁克家庭"。

　　————————————————————————————。

（4）我同学周末在一家公司打工，是为了解决经济上的问题，也是为了得到工作锻炼的机会。

　　————————————————————————————。

（5）职业妇女要在工作上努力竞争，又要在家里担负很重的家务。

　　————————————————————————————。

3. 根据课文回答问题 Answer the following questions according to the texts

（1）林娜觉得哪儿不舒服？

（2）王小云为什么劝林娜看中医？

（3）老中医是怎样给林娜看病的？

（4）中医为什么要号脉？

（5）中医专业的学生怎样跟老师学号脉？

（6）中医为什么要看病人的舌头？

（7）老中医看完病以后，让林娜做什么？

（8）是什么药把林娜的胃病治好了？

（9）为什么说"无论用了什么现代医学的新技术，中医还是中医"？

（10）中医的理论有什么特点？跟西医的理论有什么不同？

（11）中药是用什么做的？

（12）除了吃中药以外，中医还有哪些治病的方法？

（13）中医中药有多长的历史？

（14）在中医方面，现在留下来的古书还有多少种？

4. 会话练习　Conversation practice

> **会话常用语 IDIOMATIC EXPRESSIONS IN CONVERSATION**
>
> 少说也得…… (to say the least, ...)
>
> 不要紧。(It doesn't matter.)
>
> 你信不信…… (Do you believe...)
>
> ……是完全可能的。(... is completely possible.)

【劝告　Persuading or dissuading】

A：我决定暑假回国继续读我的专业。

B：是吗？我劝你再考虑一下，别这么快地决定。在这儿还有半年你就能毕业了，为什么现在要走呢？

A：我朋友希望我早点儿回去。

B：这事儿你最好再跟你朋友商量商量。你得把这儿的情况告诉她，我看你还是再坚持半年吧！

【解释　Giving an explanation】

（1）A：我要的关于市场调查的资料呢？

B：真对不起，现在还没有准备好。

A：我昨天就对你说了，今天我要用。为什么到现在还没有准备好？

B：您听我解释一下，这个资料现在不在公司里，是王总上周拿走了。

（2）A：这是一份新的合同。您看看，有什么意见。

B：这上面说我方完成这个项目的时间是明年 6 月 30 日，可是我记得我们本来说好是 7 月 15 日。为什么又改变了？

A：今天我来是想解释一下这个问题。7 月 15 日已经放假了，我们很难请专家们来讨论，这样，项目最后完成的时间就不是 7 月，而是 9 月，少说也得晚两个月。

B：看来我方恐怕很难达到这个新的要求。

A：其实这也不是新的要求。贵方最早也建议过：希望明年 9 月新项目能开始在学校实行。这就是在放假前完成专家讨论的意思。

5. 交际练习　Communication exercises

(1) Do you agree with the practice of "头痛医头" or "头痛医脚"?

(2) Why do Chinese doctors try to integrate traditional Chinese medicine with Western medicine?

After expressing yourself orally, write a short essay on either of the topics above.

阅读 与复述 Reading Comprehension and Paraphrasing

🎧44 讳疾忌医 (huì jí jì yī)

扁鹊 (Biǎn Què) 是战国 (Zhànguó) 时代一位有名的医生。他走遍各地，去给人治病。

有一次，扁鹊来到蔡国 (Càiguó)。国王 (guówáng) 请他到王宫 (wánggōng) 里做客。会见时，国王向扁鹊问了一些治病的问题，扁鹊都认真地作了回答。他觉得国王的气色不太好，就说："大王，看来您得病了。不过，您的病现在还只在皮肤 (pífū) 里，问题不大，只要快点儿治，就很容易治好。"

国王听了不太高兴，他心里想：我们第一次见面，没说几句话，你就说我有病。你的医术 (yīshù) 也太高明了。所以，他就冷冷地对扁鹊说："谢谢你的关心，我身体很好，没有病。"扁鹊见国王不太高兴，就走了。

扁鹊走后，国王对大臣 (dàchén) 们说："当医生的总想把没有病的人说成有病，好像这样才能表示他的医术高明。大家都说扁鹊是有名的医生，我看，扁鹊也是这种人。他骗得了别人，却骗不了我。"

过了十几天，扁鹊再去看国王，他很担心地说："大王，您的病加重了，已经到肌肉 (jīròu) 里去了。可得马上治疗啊！如果不早治，就会更重了。"

国王连看都不愿意看他，很生气地说："我哪有什么病？你走吧！"扁鹊低着头走了。

又过了十几天，扁鹊第三次见到国王，他非常着急地说："大王，您的气色很不好，病已经到肠 (cháng) 胃里去了，再不治，恐怕就晚了。"国王拍着桌子说："你为什么总说我有病？你简直疯了！"

又过了十几天，国王从王宫出来，正好扁鹊也向王宫走去。他看见国王，一句话也没说就走了。国王觉得很奇怪，马上派一位大臣去问扁鹊。

那位大臣对扁鹊说："先生，您今天看见大王，为什么一句话也没说就走了呢？"扁鹊回答："我该说的都说了。有病不怕，只怕有病说没病，不肯让大夫治疗。其实，只要早点儿治，一般的病都会慢慢地好起来的。病在皮肤里，可以用热敷（rè fū）；病在肌肉里，可以用针灸；病到肠胃里，可以吃药。但是，现在大王的病已经到骨髓（gǔsuǐ）了，是大王自己不承认（chéngrèn）有病，不肯去治病。我也没有办法了。"

五天以后，国王的病突然发作（fāzuò）了。他让人赶快去请扁鹊，但是扁鹊五天以前就到别的国家去了。没过几天，国王就病死了。

怕人知道自己有病，不肯去治，这就叫"讳疾忌医"。

三、语法 Grammar

词语 例解 Word Usage and Examples

1 看来

"看来", meaning "it seems/appears that, it looks as if", is an independent element of a sentence, often used to express one's opinion about a situation, for example,

又阴天了，看来今天要下雨。

看来，学中医很难吧？

您的建议，看来他不会反对。

2 某

The indefinite pronoun "某" is used in front of a noun. It can be followed by the numeral "一" or "几" and a measure word. It is often used in written language to denote an unspecified person or object, for example,

某商店的服务态度太差。

你们公司某一位领导常在这家饭馆请客。

某几件事情现在还没有解决。

某些人总喜欢打听别人的隐私。

Note:

When used to refer to a person or an organization/institution, "某" can be duplicated, but the noun it modifies remains singular. For example，"某某人，某某同学，某某学校，某某单位".

3 正好

The adverb "正好" is used as an adverbial, meaning "just, just in time" or "fortunately, accidentally". It may be placed before the subject. For example,

山楂正好治这种病。

我们刚到公共汽车站，正好来了一辆车。

他送给我的这双旅游鞋正好合适。

这本书正好一百页。

他要找经理，正好经理回来了。

When used as an adjective, "正好" often functions as the predicate or the complement, meaning "just right, just enough, just in time", for example,

您给我的钱正好，不多不少。

你来得正好。

4 简直

The adverb "简直" is used as an adverbial, meaning "simply, virtually". It often stresses the high degree of something in an exaggerated tone, for example,

徐悲鸿画的马简直跟真的一样。

他说广州话，我简直一句都听不懂。

一个八岁的小学生能写出这么好的字，我简直不敢相信。

大家同意女儿去夏令营，女儿高兴得简直睡不着觉。

句子 结构　Sentence Structure

1 兼语句（5）　Pivotal sentences (5)

The verb "是" can be used to form a pivotal sentence with a double-function word in it. This kind of sentence usually has no subject, and the noun or nominal phrase that follows "是", which is its object, also functions as the subject of the second verb in the sentence. We often use this kind of sentence to describe or explain a situation. The verb "是" is used to emphasize the noun or nominal phrase after it, i.e., its object.

Subject$_1$	Predicate$_1$		
	V$_1$	O$_1$(S$_2$)	P$_2$
	正好 是	位　老中医	给她　　看　病。
	是	胃　这个零件	坏　了。
	是	风	把这张画　刮下来　了。
	是	他	帮助了我。
	是	我	没　说清楚。

The following are the pivotal sentences that we have already learned:

（1）宋华让陆雨平来帮助他们。（Lesson 13）

　　我们请你和你朋友吃饭。

（2）有人敲门。（Lesson 31）

　　有几个朋友想去旅游。

（3）老师称赞她做作业认真。（Lesson 46）

　　爷爷奶奶喜欢她聪明。

（4）大家称他为"打工头儿"。（Lesson 47）

　　他们选我当组长。

（5）正好是位老中医给她看病。（Lesson 49）

2 介词短语补语（2）   The prepositional phrase used as a complement (2)

The preposition "自" and its object (usually a noun of place or direction) are used to form a prepositional phrase. "自 + NP" is often used, particularly in written language, as a complement after a verb such as "寄，来，选，出" or "取", for example,

中药大多取自植物、动物和矿物。

他来自中国西北农村。

这封信寄自上海。

"讳疾忌医" 出自《韩非子》(《Hánfēizǐ》)。

The following are the complements that we have already learned:

（1）The complement of state（Lesson 15，30）

他们普通话说得很好。

（2）The complement of degree（Lesson 17，43）

这份工作可把我累坏了。

（3）The directional complement（Lesson 16，23）

他们从外边走进来了。

（4）The resultative complement（Lesson 18，19，25，28，34）

他晚上写汉字常常写到十点。

（5）The complement of quantity（Lesson 17）

这件衣服比那件衣服贵 50 块钱。

（6）The time-measure complement（Lesson 16，19）

他在这儿工作了半年。

（7）The action-measure complement（Lesson 22）

老师让他念了两遍课文。

（8）The potential complement（Lesson 33，36）

他今天做不完这些作业。

（9）The prepositional phrase used as a complement（Lesson 45，49）

我毕业于 ABC 商学院。

3　一方面……，一方面 ……　The construction "一方面……，一方面……"

This construction, meaning "on the one hand ..., on the other hand ...", is used to connect two parallel clauses or to denote two aspects of a state or situation. In the second clause, the word "一方面" is often followed by an adverb such as "又", "也" or "还", for example,

你一方面去看病，一方面也可以了解一下中医怎么看病。

她每天都很辛苦，一方面要去上班，一方面又要照顾老人和孩子。

陆雨平一方面要作些社会调查，一方面还要给报社（newspaper office）写文章。

四、字与词　Chinese Characters and Words

1　集中识字　Learn the characters of the same radicals

疒：疯　　疤　　病　　疾　　疼　　痛　　瘦　　痒

牛：物　　牲　　特

犭：犯　　狗　　猫　　独　　猿　　猴　　猪　　狮

2　词语联想　Learn the following groups of associated words

信　信封　信风　信贷　信服　信号　信件　信念　信物　信心

　　信息　信义　信用　信纸　报信　发信　回信　家信　口信　平信

　　来信　轻信　深信　相信　音信　坚信　自信　明信片

修　修补　修订　修改　修剪　修建　修理　修配　修造　修筑

　　修整　修治　修正　修养

物　物价　物件　物理　物体　物质　物证　物种　物资　物品

　　物业　宝物　财物　产物　动物　植物　矿物　公物　古物

　　怪物　景物　静物　礼物　人物　生物　实物　食物　事物

　　万物　玩物　文物　药物　衣物　化合物　农作物　身外之物

Unique Theories and Therapies in Traditional Chinese Medicine

Theories of traditional Chinese medicine have a long history and are of great extension and profundity. They are closely related to philosophy. Emphasizing the philosophical idea of the "unity of nature and humankind", traditional Chinese medicine takes the theories of yin-yang and "five elements" (metal, wood, water, fire and earth), the theory of "five motions" (respectively of metal, wood, water, fire and earth) and the theory of "six qi" (pathogenic factors, namely wind, heat, fire, dampness, dryness and cold), etc., as its theoretical foundation. Traditional Chinese medicine regards the human body as a systematic whole just like the heaven and earth and applies these theories in explaining the origin of life, physiological phenomena and pathological changes and guiding clinical diagnoses.

There are four common methods of diagnosis in traditional Chinese medicine, which are observation, listening, inquiring and palpation. Observation means to observe the patient's complexion, listening is to listen to the patient's voice or breath, inquiring is to make inquiries about the symptoms, and palpation refers to pulse-taking. Through the connection between different parts of the body, these four methods can help determine which part has gone wrong so as to give corresponding treatment.

Besides medicinal herbs, traditional Chinese medicine also has some distinctive therapies.

Massage is a method of treatment by massaging the channels and acupoints on the human body in various ways.

Acupuncture and moxibustion are often mentioned together. Acupuncture is a method of curing diseases by inserting filiform needles into some acupoints on the body of the patient and manipulating the needles through different hand motions. Moxibustion treats diseases by heating and stimulating the acupoints on the skin with burning moxa.

Based on the theories about skin in traditional Chinese medicine, scraping is a method which dredges channels, invigorates blood circulation and removes blood stasis by scraping the relevant parts of the skin using tools made of ox horns and jade stones and cupping jars.

Cupping is a method to improve and regulate the immunity of the human body by causing broken capillaries and blood stasis on purpose  through physical stimulation and negative pressure so that the healing function of the stem cells and the function of absorbing dead blood cells can be motivated.

Famous practitioners of traditional Chinese medicine in ancient China included Zhang Zhongjing and Hua Tuo in the Eastern Han Dynasty (25–220), Sun Simiao in the Tang Dynasty (618–907) and Li Shizhen in the Ming Dynasty (1368–1644).

第五十课
Lesson
50

● 复习　Review

我有可能坐中国飞船到太空旅行了

I'm likely to take a space trip by a Chinese spacecraft

With the successful launching of the Shenzhou 7 manned spacecraft, China has become the third country in the world to have launched a manned spacecraft into Earth orbit. Ding Libo immediately thinks about the possibility of travelling into space in a Chinese spacecraft.

一、课文 Texts

🎧 45 （一）

我有可能坐中国飞船到太空旅行了

丁力波：喂，宋华，你在网上看什么呢？

宋　华：看今天的新闻。

丁力波：有什么重要的消息吗？

宋　华：听说神舟七号载人飞船又发射成功了。①我刚才恨不得早点儿下课到网上查一下。

丁力波：是吗？咱们快看看。哦，在这儿呢："这次发射成功，说明中国载人航天事业又迈出了一大步。从此，中国航天事业的历史开始了新的一页。"简直太棒了！中国现在已经成为世界上第三个实现载人航天飞行的国家了。

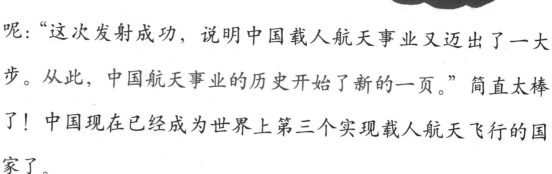

宋　华：其实，中国人是世界上最早想到太空去的民族之一。几千年前，中国就有了"嫦娥奔月"的传说。到了明代，有人想用自己制造的火箭飞到天上去。②一直到二十一世纪的今天，中国完全靠自己的力量实现了中国人的这个千年愿望。

丁力波：看来，现在我也有可能坐中国飞船到太空去旅行了。

宋　华：在理论上，每个人都有这种可能，但不是每个人都能实现这个愿望。尽管神舟七号载人航天成功，我看，离你到太空旅行还是差十万八千里呢。③

丁力波：为什么？

宋　华：你知道航天飞行要有什么条件吗？

丁力波：首先得身体好。

宋　华：那还用说？根据介绍，航天员的标准身高一般是 1.70 米，体重在 65 公斤左右。挑选航天员的时候，要让他们在医院里住一个月的时间，对他们全身的各个器官都进行检查。

丁力波：别的不说，我的身高和体重就不够标准。我身高有 1.80 米，体重 75 公斤。不过我不是想当航天员，而是想去旅游啊！

宋　华：去旅游也得看你的身体条件，而且还得接受严格的训练。

丁力波：这么说，无论我怎么想去太空旅行，都是没有希望了？

宋　华：话也不能说得这么绝对。要是将来去太空旅行跟你现在坐飞机回加拿大一样方便，你不是就有希望了吗？

丁力波：我真希望中国的航天事业发展得更快，这一天早点儿到来就好了。

生词 New Words

1. 飞船	fēichuán	N	spaceship, spacecraft	中国飞船，航天飞船

2. 太空	tàikōng	N	the firmament, outer space	到太空旅行，太空的景色
3. 新闻	xīnwén	N	news	今天的新闻，重要的新闻，新闻照片，新闻记者，一条新闻
4. 载	zài	V	to carry, to be loaded with	载人飞船，载客，载货
5. 发射	fāshè	V	to launch, to project, to discharge	发射飞船，发射成功
射	shè	V	to shoot, to fire, to discharge	
6. 恨不得	hènbude	V	to be dying or itching to	恨不得早点儿下课，恨不得马上飞上太空
恨	hèn	V	to hate	
7. 航天	hángtiān	V	to fly to the outer space	载人航天事业，载人航天成功，载人航天技术
航	háng		to navigate, to sail, to fly	航海，航空，航班
8. 迈	mài	V	to stride, to step (forward or sideways)	迈出一步，迈进大门
9. 从此	cóngcǐ	Adv	from this time on, from now on	
10. 飞行	fēixíng	V	(of an airplane) to fly	载人航天飞行，实现载人航天飞行，飞行了十个小时
11. 嫦娥奔月	Cháng'é bèn yuè	IE	Chang'e flying to the moon	"嫦娥奔月"的传说
12. 制造	zhìzào	V	to manufacture, to make	自己制造，中国制造，制造飞船，制造汽车，飞机制造工厂
13. 火箭	huǒjiàn	N	rocket	发射火箭，中国制造的火箭
箭	jiàn	N	arrow	
14. 力量	lìliàng	N	physical strength, capability, power	靠自己的力量，国家的力量，全身的力量，很强的力量，有力量，发挥力量，增加力量
15. 愿望	yuànwàng	N	desire, wish	有一个愿望，实现这个愿望

16.	航天员	hángtiānyuán	N	astronaut, spaceman	当航天员，第一位航天员
17.	标准	biāozhǔn	N/A	standard, criterion; standard	招聘的标准，达到标准，提高标准；标准的普通话，说得很标准，不够标准
18.	身高	shēngāo	N	height (of a person)	标准身高，身高（有）1.78米
19.	体重	tǐzhòng	N	weight (of a person)	标准体重，体重（有）65公斤
20.	左右	zuǒyòu	N	about, around (indicating an approximate number)	70公斤左右，一百块钱左右，12月5号左右
21.	进行	jìnxíng	V	to conduct, to carry out	进行检查，进行化验，进行讨论
22.	严格	yángé	A	strict, rigorous	严格的标准，严格的要求，严格的制度，考试很严格
23.	训练	xùnliàn	V	to train	接受严格的训练，训练航天员，训练护士
24.	将来	jiānglái	N	future	将来去太空旅行，将来的社会
25.	神舟	Shénzhōu	PN	Shenzhou (name of a Chinese spacecraft)	神舟七号载人飞船
26.	明代	Míngdài	PN	Ming Dynasty (1368-1644)	

注释　Notes

① 听说神舟七号载人飞船又发射成功了。

　　"I heard that the Chinese manned spacecraft Shenzhou 7 has been successfully launched."

　　The Chinese manned spacecraft Shenzhou 7, carrying the Chinese astronauts Zhai Zhigang, Liu Boming and Jing Haipeng, was successfully launched from the Jiuquan Satellite Launch Centre at 9:00 p.m. on September 25th, 2008. It orbited the Earth 45 times as planned, and landed safely on the grasslands of Inner Mongolia at 5:37 p.m. Beijing time on September 28th, 2008.

② 到了明代，有人想用自己制造的火箭飞到天上去。

　　"By the Ming Dynasty, someone had thought about using rockets made by himself to fly up into the heavens."

Wan Hu, a Chinese man of the Ming Dynasty, was the first person in the history of mankind trying to reach outer space by using a rocket constructed by himself. Although he failed and lost his life in the attempt, his actions reflected the inquisitive and exploratory spirit of mankind.

③ 离你到太空旅行还是差十万八千里呢。

"There is still a long way to go before you can enjoy space travel."

"十万八千里" is an idiom from the popular classical novel *The Journey to the West*. In this novel, it is said that the Monkey King (Sun Wukong) could travel one hundred and eight thousand *li* (1 *li* = 0.5 kilometre) in a single somersault. Later, this expression was commonly used to indicate a long distance or great difference.

🎧 46 （二）

公蟹、母蟹和鸡爪

　　我们都知道母蟹比公蟹好吃。在美国，我发现公蟹和母蟹是分开卖的。更让我觉得奇怪的是，这儿公蟹比母蟹受欢迎，公蟹的价钱要比母蟹贵一倍。难道美国人不知道母蟹比公蟹好吃吗？不管他们是怎么想的，我们能用公蟹的一半价钱买母蟹，当然很高兴。每次吃完蟹以后，我和我的中国朋友们都要说："美国人真不会吃！"

　　有一天，一位美国朋友请我们到他家去做客。主人知道中国人爱吃蟹，就买了一大袋。我开玩笑地问他："是公蟹，还是母蟹？"他笑着说："你们中国人最爱吃母蟹，我们美国人却爱吃公蟹。今天我们好好儿地比较一下，看看究竟哪种好吃。"因为他去过中国，所以他知道中国人的爱好。

　　在吃饭的时候，我们一边吃，一边谈。主人吃着公蟹说：好香啊！④"他还解释说，他喜欢公蟹肉又多又嫩，母蟹不但肉少，而且也不香。因为母蟹要生"孩子"，营养都到孩子那儿去了。我们听了，都笑了起来。

主人看了看我们，又接着说："你们觉得我们美国人不会吃，我还觉得你们中国人吃得怪呢！其实这是因为习惯不同。"

听了主人对吃蟹的看法，我觉得他说的很有道理。中国人生活在东半球，美国人生活在西半球，吃的习惯不同，"萝卜青菜，各有所爱"，这是很自然的。地球上有这么多国家和民族，有这么多不同的文化，世界本来就是多样化的。如果我们尊重这种不同，大家就能和平、友好地相处；如果我们能很好地利用这种不同，加强经济合作，大家都有可能生活得更好。比如说，美国人不吃鸡爪，可是在中国，鸡爪的价钱比鸡肉还贵。中国每年都要从美国进口很多的鸡爪，美国人赚了钱很高兴；中国人吃到便宜的鸡爪，也很高兴。既然是大家都高兴的事儿，为什么不多做呢？

生词 New Words

1. 公	gōng	A	male (animal)	公马，公羊，公鸡，公鸭，公狗
2. 蟹	xiè	N	crab	公蟹，喜欢吃蟹，一只蟹
3. 母	mǔ	A	female (animal)	母马，母羊，母鸡，母鸭，母狗，母蟹
4. 爪	zhuǎ	N	claw, talon, paw	鸡爪，猫爪，狗爪，一只鸡爪
5. 分开	fēnkāi	V	to separate	分开卖，分开住，分开付账，把母蟹和公蟹分开
6. 主人	zhǔrén	N	host, master, owner	男主人，女主人，宴席的主人，小狗的主人
7. 香	xiāng	A	aromatic, fragrant, (of food) savoury	香水，菜很香，饭很香
8. 嫩	nèn	A	young and tender, (not overcooked) tender	嫩叶，涮羊肉很嫩，鸡丁炒得很嫩
9. 营养	yíngyǎng	N	nutrition	蔬菜有营养，需要营养，增加营养
10. 道理	dàolǐ	N	reason, sense, truth	很有道理，没有道理，懂道理，讲道理，"入乡随俗"的道理
11. 东半球	dōngbànqiú	N	Eastern Hemisphere	中国人生活在东半球
半球	bànqiú	N	hemisphere	南半球，北半球
12. 西半球	xībànqiú	N	Western Hemisphere	西半球的国家
13. 萝卜青菜，各有所爱	luóbo qīngcài, gè yǒu suǒ ài	IE	no dish suits all tastes, every Jack has his Jill	
萝卜	luóbo	N	radish, turnip	红烧萝卜，一个萝卜
青菜	qīngcài	N	green vegetables	炒青菜，一棵青菜
14. 地球	dìqiú	N	the earth, the globe	保护地球，生活在同一个地球上
15. 多样化	duōyànghuà	V	to be diversified	多样化的世界，多样化的艺术
16. 和平	hépíng	N	peace	世界和平，为了世界和平，和平地生活

17.	相处	xiāngchǔ	V	to get along (with one another)	和平相处，友好相处，相处得很好
18.	加强	jiāqiáng	V	to strengthen, to enhance	加强经济合作，加强友谊
19.	进口	jìnkǒu	VO	to import	进口鸡爪，进口商品，增加进口，减少进口

补充生词 Supplementary Words

1.	模特儿	mótèr	N	model
2.	飞行员	fēixíngyuán	N	pilot, aviator
3.	战争	zhànzhēng	N	war
4.	有趣	yǒuqù	A	interesting
5.	短信	duǎnxìn	N	short text message
6.	同事	tóngshì	N	colleague
7.	问候	wènhòu	V	to send one's regards to sb.
8.	千万	qiānwàn	Adv	to be sure to, must
9.	玩儿游戏	wánr yóuxì	V O	to play a game
10.	分享	fēnxiǎng	V	to share (joy, rights, etc.)
11.	响	xiǎng	V	to make a sound, to ring
12.	冰箱	bīngxiāng	N	refrigerator
13.	老子	lǎozi	N	(coll.) I, me (literally "your father", said in anger or in fun)
14.	猕猴桃	míhóutáo	N	kiwi fruit
15.	讨厌	tǎoyàn	A	disagreeable, disgusting
16.	苍蝇	cāngying	N	fly
17.	误会	wùhuì	V	to misunderstand
18.	丫头	yātou	N	(coll.) girl

| 19. 心情 | xīnqíng | N | frame (or state) of mind, mood |
| 20. 属于 | shǔyú | V | to belong to |

注释　Notes

④ 好香啊！

How dilicious it is!

"好 + A" indicates high degree or great extent with a tone of exclamation. It is more often than not used in an exclamatory sentence. For example,

好热的天气啊！

今天街上好热闹！

他昨天晚上好晚才回家。

二、练习　Exercises

练习与运用　Drills and Practice 47

核心句 KEY SENTENCES

1. 恨不得早点儿下课到网上查一下。
2. 从此，中国航天事业的历史开始了新的一页。
3. 航天员的标准体重在 65 公斤左右。
4. 对他们全身的各个器官都进行检查。
5. 这一天早点儿到来就好了。
6. 好香啊！

1. 熟读下列词组　Read the following phrases until you learn them by heart

（1）50公斤左右　　十个人左右　　40岁左右　　1000块钱左右

　　　九点钟左右　　一周左右　　10号左右　　20米左右

（2）进行调查　进行研究　进行考试　进行分析　进行批评　进行改革

　　　进行培养　进行表演　进行管理　进行生产　进行比较　进行训练

　　　进行计划　进行分工　继续进行　开始进行　要求进行　努力进行

　　　紧张地进行　认真地进行　进行得很快

（3）严格的管理　　　严格的教育　　严格的分工　　严格的控制

　　　严格的选择　　　严格的考试　　严格要求　　严格检查

　　　严格训练　　　管理得很严格　制度很严格

（4）将来的生活　将来的情况　将来的住房　将来的教育　将来的家庭

（5）加强团结　加强管理　加强训练　加强教育　加强锻炼

　　　加强培养　加强研究　加强信心　加强力量　加强竞争观念

　　　努力加强　得到加强

（6）好深　好圆　好嫩　好难　好累　好辛苦　好感人　好紧张

2. 句子练习　Sentence drills

A. 用所给词语完成句子
Complete the following sentences with the given words and expressions

（1）我看这袋米＿＿＿＿＿＿＿＿＿＿＿＿＿。（公斤）

（2）他还很年轻，＿＿＿＿＿＿＿＿＿＿＿。（岁）

（3）学生在校外租房每月要＿＿＿＿＿＿＿＿＿＿＿。（块）

（4）你＿＿＿＿＿＿＿＿＿＿出发正好。（点钟）

（5）一直往南走，再走＿＿＿＿＿＿＿＿＿＿就可以看见那座大楼

　　　了。（米）

进行

（1）这个问题没有解决，他们还要＿＿＿＿＿＿＿＿＿＿＿。（研究）

（2）关于提高工资标准的事儿，现在正在＿＿＿＿＿＿＿＿＿＿。（调查）

（3）对这样复杂的情况，我们应该认真地＿＿＿＿＿＿＿＿＿。（分析）

（4）这件事儿要＿＿＿＿＿＿＿＿＿，大家都同意了，才能办。（讨论）

（5）对年轻人要＿＿＿＿＿＿＿＿，才能提高他们的业务水平。（培养）

B. 用"从此"改写下列句子

Rewrite the following sentences, using "从此"

（1）他是大学毕业那年回的家，后来再也没有回过家。

＿＿＿＿＿＿＿＿＿＿＿＿＿＿＿＿＿＿＿＿＿＿＿＿＿＿＿。

（2）他家在西部农村，现在那儿有了火车，以后回家就方便了。

＿＿＿＿＿＿＿＿＿＿＿＿＿＿＿＿＿＿＿＿＿＿＿＿＿＿＿。

（3）他们毕业以后，一个要去海南岛，一个要去新疆，以后就不容易见面了。

＿＿＿＿＿＿＿＿＿＿＿＿＿＿＿＿＿＿＿＿＿＿＿＿＿＿＿。

C. 用"恨不得"改写下列句子

Rewrite the following sentences, using "恨不得"

（1）妈妈病重了，他真想马上飞回到家里。

＿＿＿＿＿＿＿＿＿＿＿＿＿＿＿＿＿＿＿＿＿＿＿＿＿＿＿。

（2）小学生活真有意思，我能再回到那个年代多好啊！

＿＿＿＿＿＿＿＿＿＿＿＿＿＿＿＿＿＿＿＿＿＿＿＿＿＿＿。

（3）这本小说太好了，真想今天晚上就把它读完。

＿＿＿＿＿＿＿＿＿＿＿＿＿＿＿＿＿＿＿＿＿＿＿＿＿＿＿。

3. 根据课文回答问题 Answer the following questions according to the texts

（1）丁力波和宋华在网上看到了一条什么重要的新闻？

（2）为什么说中国人是世界上最早想到太空去的民族之一？

（3）航天员是怎样挑选出来的？

（4）你认为人们能实现去太空旅行的愿望吗？

（5）在美国卖蟹和在中国卖蟹有什么不同？

（6）中国人和美国人吃蟹的习惯有什么不同？为什么？

（7）对各民族不同的文化和习惯应该有什么样的态度？

（8）什么是大家都高兴的事儿？

4. 会话练习　Conversation practice

会话常用语 IDIOMATIC EXPRESSIONS IN CONVERSATION

这么说 (So/In this way, ...)

别的不说 (Not to mention other things...)

话也不能说得这么绝对。

　　(Don't be so uncompromising./Don't be so sure.)

恨不得

　　(how one wishes one could .../to be dying or itching to ...)

……就好了。(It would be great if ...)

【叙述　Narrating】

A：你是怎么决定学习中医的？

B：我是高中快要毕业的时候才决定学中医的。其实我从小的时候开始，就想当个演员。本来我已经决定学艺术专业了，后来因为我妈妈的病，改变了我的想法。

A：你妈妈得了什么病？

B：我妈妈得了一种很奇怪的病，去了很多医院都看不好。有人告诉我，中医能治好这种病，我就跟爸爸、妈妈一起到了中国，找到了那家中医院。经过半年的时间，我妈妈的病就治好了。我觉得中医太棒了，从此我就决定学习中医。

【希望　Expressing a wish】

A：我希望将来能当一个模特儿（mótèr），穿上世界上最漂亮的衣服表演。我的个子能有 1.80 米就好了。

B：我小时候就有一个愿望：长大了要当飞行员（fēixíngyuán）。我看到飞机在天上飞，恨不得自己马上就长大。

C：我真想做一个高级中文翻译。当我们国家领导人访问中国的时候，我当翻译。我更想把中国那么多有名的文学作品介绍到我们国家去。

D：我希望世界和平，各国人民友好相处，不要有战争（zhànzhēng）。

5. 交际练习　Communication exercises

(1) What is the implication of the story about the male and female crabs?

(2) How can one contribute to world peace and development by mastering a foreign language?

After expressing yourself orally, write a short essay on either of the topics above.

阅读 与复述 Reading Comprehension and Paraphrasing

🎧 48 有趣（yǒuqù）的手机短信（duǎnxìn）

根据调查，中国用手机的人有 7.8 亿，是世界第一。用手机发出的短信也是世界最多的，特别是 15 岁到 25 岁之间的年轻人最喜欢用手机发短信。

　　许小姐是位又年轻又漂亮的女孩儿，在一家外国公司工作。她就是个短信迷，差不多每天都要给我发几条短信，让我轻松、给我快乐。她说："发短信，又方便又经济。给同事（tóngshì）、朋友、亲人发短信，可以让他们知道我在想着他们，也希望我的问候（wènhòu）和那些有趣的笑话能带给他们快乐。"她每个月都要发1000多条短信息，平均每天都有30条左右。今年春节她发给我的短信是："新年到了，想想没什么送给你的，又不打算给你太多，只有给你五千万（qiānwàn）：千万要快乐！千万要健康！千万要平安！千万要有爱心！千万不要忘记我！"我觉得这比收到一张贺年卡更有意思。

　　每天上下班，许小姐都坐公司的班车，路上差不多要花一个多小时。发短信是她坐车时最好的休息方式。她跟朋友聊天儿，向亲人问候，玩儿玩儿游戏（wánr yóuxì），让自己轻松愉快。有时许小姐也让我跟她一起分享（fēnxiǎng）快乐。你看，我的手机响（xiǎng）了，又是许小姐发来的两条信息。

　　第一条是：冰箱（bīngxiāng）里好像放着五个鸡蛋。第一个鸡蛋小声地对第二个说："你看，第五个鸡蛋长毛了，好可怕！"接着第二个对第三个说，第三个又告诉第四个。第五个听见了，它很生气地说："去你的！老子（lǎozi）是猕猴桃（míhóutáo），不是鸡蛋！"

　　第二条是："听着，我要追你，我认定你了，我要找的就是你！你给我一个机会，我还你一个惊喜，我追你要追到底！——讨厌（tǎoyàn）的苍蝇（cāngying），拍死你！"

　　许小姐发的短信有趣吧？别误会（wùhuì），我不是许小姐的男朋友！不信，请看下面这一条短信，她是怎样鼓励我的："胖丫头（yātou），你不能改变天气，但你可以改变心情（xīnqíng）；你不能借来明天，但你可以用好今天。美属于（shǔyú）你，成功属于你，幸福也属于你。"

三、语法　Grammar

词语 例解　Word Usage and Examples

1 恨不得

This phrase expresses a desperate wish to fulfill something (that one most likely cannot achieve). It is usually followed by a verb serving as the object. An adverb such as "马上，都，就" or "全" is often used in front of the verb, for example,

他恨不得马上就能到太空旅行。

我恨不得把词典上的生词都记住了。

他妈妈总觉得自己有病，恨不得把全身都检查一遍。

2 从此

The adverb "从此" is used as an adverbial to indicate a situation taking effect from the present or the mentioned time, for example,

你走吧，我从此再也不想见你。

公路通到山区了，交通从此就方便多了。

儿子出国留学了，从此，就再也没有回过家。

3 左右

The noun of direction "左右" is used after a numeral-measure word phrase to indicate an approximate number, for example,

宋华体重在80公斤左右。

小伙子也就是20岁左右。

她想买一辆10万块钱左右的车。

4 进行

The verb "进行" indicates a continuous action with the meaning of "to carry out, to conduct". The continuous action is often indicated by the verb following "进行" or by the subject of the sentence. This construction denotes formal and serious activities, for example,

大家还在进行讨论。

他们开始进行调查了。

这项工作已经进行了三个月了。

毕业考试正在进行。

Notes:

(1) The verb placed after "进行" cannot be a monosyllabic one. One cannot say "进行看" or "进行谈".

(2) The verb placed after "进行" cannot take an object. The object is usually introduced by "对……".

For example, one cannot say "大家进行讨论训练的时间" or "他们开始进行调查这个问题".

The correct expressions are "大家对训练的时间进行讨论" and "他们开始对这个问题进行调查" respectively.

语法 复习 Grammar Review

1 强调的方法 Methods for expressing emphasis

（1）反问句 By using a rhetorical question（Lesson 28，42）

你不是喜欢中国书法吗？

这哪是小纪念品？

朋友送的礼物怎么会不喜欢呢？

这么点儿小问题，难道我们就解决不了了吗？

难道说马大为不打算去黄山旅游吗？

（2）两次否定　By using double negation（Lesson 40）

她是新娘的好朋友，不能不参加这个婚礼。

一般地说，男人能做的工作没有妇女不能做的。

（3）连……也／都……　By using "连……也／都……"（Lesson 34）

我连他姓什么都不知道。

（4）副词"就"　By using the adverb "就"（Lesson 15，29）

这就是上海话的"我不懂"。

我就来。

（5）动词"是"　By using the verb "是"（Lesson 29）

这种花儿是叫君子兰。

（6）"是……的"句（2）　By using sentences with "是……的"(2)（Lesson 48）

那是不可能达到的。

2 语气助词"吧"、"呢"、"了"　The modal particles "吧"，"呢" and "了"

吧　The modal particle "吧"

　　（1）To relax the tone of a sentence to make a request or to give an order

（Lesson 12）

我问一下吧。

　　（2）To express uncertainty（Lesson 21）

中国大学生队的水平比你们高吧?

呢　The modal particle "呢"

　　（1）To express doubt（Lesson 7，20）

你是加拿大人，他呢?

我的照相机呢?

　　（2）To relax the tone of an interrogative sentence（Lesson 26）

你们在聊什么呢?

（3）To indicate that an action is in progress in a declarative sentence

（Lesson 24）

你舅妈在种温室蔬菜呢。

（4）To express emphasis or exaggeration（Lesson 19，28）

美术馆还没有开门呢。

还是名牌的呢。

了 The modal particle "了"

（1）To confirm the completion or realization of something（Lesson 15）

她去上海了。

（2）To indicate a change of situation（Lesson 24，30，34）

他是大学生了。

我有男朋友了。

天气冷了。

她明天不来了。

现在八点半了。

我妈妈身体好了。

可以进来了。

下雨了。

（3）To indicate an action is going to take place in a short time（Lesson 23）

火车快要开了。

（4）Used at the end of a complement of degree or an exclamatory sentence

（Lesson 6，17，43）

他高兴极了。

这个星期比上星期忙多了。

大家都笑死了。

他今天累坏了。

太好了！

3 复句小结（2） Summary of complex sentences (2)

联合复句　Combined Complex Sentences

（4）选择复句　Alternative complex sentences

① ……，还是……（Lesson 12）

你愿意吃中药，还是愿意吃西药？

② 不是……，就是……（Lesson 42）

她穿衣服只喜欢两种颜色，不是黑色，就是白色。

③ 要么……，要么……（Lesson 46）

要么他来，要么我去，我跟他一定得坐下来谈一谈。

偏正复句　Subordinate Complex Sentences

（3）因果复句　Causal complex sentences

① 因为……，所以……（Lesson 20）

是不是因为现在天气冷，所以北京人常吃火锅？

② 既然……，就……（Lesson 47）

你既然也在打工，就给我介绍一下大学生打工的情况吧。

（4）转折复句　Transitional complex sentences

① 虽然……，但是／可是……（Lesson 22）

我虽然去过南方，但是没有看过越剧。

② ……，不过……（Lesson 28）

他很喜欢运动，不过他可不会打球。

③ 尽管……，还是……（Lesson 48）

他尽管身体有点儿不舒服，却还是坚持工作。

（5）条件复句　Conditional complex sentences

① 只要……，就……（Lesson 31）

只要多练习，就能学好汉语口语。

② 只有……，才……（Lesson 40）

只有在各个方面男女都享受同样的权利，男女才能平等。

③ 不管……，都/也……（Lesson 41）

不管你有什么困难，我都愿意帮助你。

④ 无论……，都……（Lesson 45）

无论你去还是不去，你都要通知他们。

⑤ 越……越……（Lesson 37）

大家越唱越高兴。

（6）让步复句 Concessive complex sentences

① 就是……，也……（Lesson 35）

就是明天下大雨，我也要去参观展览。

② 即使……，也……（Lesson 41）

即使有别人帮助，也得靠自己努力。

四、字与词 Chinese Characters and Words

1 集中识字 Learn the characters of the same radicals

王：主 玛 环 现 玩 珍 班 球 理 望

力：办 加 动 励 努 勤

广：庆 床 应 店 庙 府 度 庭 席 座 唐 康

2 词语联想 Learn the following groups of associated words

发　发表　发病　发财　发出　发达　发挥　发觉　发明　发票　发生
　　发射　发现　发音　发烧　发展　发问　发育　出发　开发　签发
　　自发

进　进步　进餐　进程　进出　进化　进货　进口　进来　进去　进退
　　进行　进修　进展　改进　前进　上进　先进　增进

新　新房　新婚　新郎　新娘　新奇　新人　新生　新式　新手　新闻
　　最新　重新　全新

严　严办　严冬　严防　严父　严格　严寒　严禁　严厉　严重　尊严

文化知识 Cultural Note

Names of China's Space Programs

There is an ancient Chinese legend about "Chang'e flying to the moon", which shows ancient Chinese people's infinite fascination and longing for the beautiful, spacious and mysterious outer space. Today, China's space industry has reached a considerable scale and level, and its achievements have attracted attention from all over the world.

Names of China's space programs are of distinctive features, embodying the characteristics of traditional Chinese culture, Chinese people's dreams over thousands of years and the myths in ancient China. Such names include "Shenzhou" [1] Spacecraft, "Chang'e" [2] Lunar Probe, "Tiangong" [3] Space Station, "Kuafu" [4] Project and so on.

The name of "Shenzhou" means "a magical boat in the Milky Way" literally and sounds the same as the Chinese word for "divine land" (here referring to China). It is characteristic of traditional Chinese culture and symbolizes that the development and manufacture of this spacecraft has received support from the whole Chinese nation. Now, Shenzhou Spacecrafts 1–9 have been launched and completed their missions, among which Shenzhou 5, Shenzhou 6, Shenzhou 7 and Shenzhou 9 are manned. "Shenzhou" Spacecrafts have realized Chinese people's dream of walking in space.

China's lunar probing satellite is named "Chang'e", which bears Chinese people's yearning for the moon and outer space over centuries and has turned the beautiful legend "Chang'e flying to the moon" into reality. Chang'e 1 and Chang'e 2 have both been launched successfully to perform the task of "probing the moon". Moon landing is soon to be realized too.

---

① "Shenzhou" means "divine or magical boat" in Chinese.
② Chang'e is the Chinese goddess who is believed to live in the moon.
③ "Tiangong" means "the palace in Heaven".
④ Kuafu is a man who is believed to chase the sun in an ancient Chinese myth.

"Tiangong" was the way ancient Chinese called the world in Heaven. The Monkey King causing havoc in Heaven and Chang'e flying to the moon are symbols of ancient Chinese people's fantasies concerning the world in Heaven. The year 2011 saw the successful launch of Tiangong  1 and its successful docking with Shenzhou 8, which have laid a foundation for the establishment of China's first space lab.

"Kuafu" Project is a satellite project of solar tracker. Its name came from the mythical story of "Kuafu chasing the sun". Chinese people admire Kuafu's perseverance and hope that the "Kuafu" Project can achieve success regardless of any difficulties.

Congratulations on having completed the study of Book One to Book Four of *New Practical Chinese Reader*. The fifty lessons of the first four volumes of *NPCR* have not only covered every aspect of your daily life, but also touched upon many interesting topics of Chinese culture and society. Along with all these, you have mastered about 2, 400 elementary vocabulary items (of which 1, 900 are required), over 1, 200 Chinese characters, and the basic grammatical items with about 400 key sentences. Now you can communicate more freely in Chinese, and you have laid a very good foundation for your further study of the language.

You will start with a new stage when learning Book Five and Book Six of *NPCR*, which will help you improve your Chinese, and in which you will find a treasure-house of Chinese literature and culture.

语法术语缩略形式一览表
Abbreviations for Grammar Terms

Abbreviation	Grammar Term in English	Grammar Term in Chinese	Grammar Term in *pinyin*
A	Adjective	形容词	xíngróngcí
Adv	Adverb	副词	fùcí
AP	Adjectival Phrase	形容词词组	xíngróngcí cízǔ
AsPt	Aspect Particle	动态助词	dòngtài zhùcí
Coll	Colloquial Expression	口语词语	kǒuyǔ cíyǔ
Conj	Conjunction	连词	liáncí
IE	Idiomatic Expression	习惯用语	xíguàn yòngyǔ
Int	Interjection	叹词	tàncí
M	Measure Word	量词	liàngcí
MdPt	Modal Particle	语气助词	yǔqì zhùcí
N	Noun	名词	míngcí
NP	Nominal Phrase	名词词组	míngcí cízǔ
Nu	Numeral	数词	shùcí
Nu-MP	Numeral-Measure Word Phrase	数量词组	shùliàng cízǔ
O	Object	宾语	bīnyǔ
Ono	Onomatopoeia	象声词	xiàngshēngcí
OpV	Optative Verb	能愿动词	néngyuàn dòngcí
P	Predicate	谓语	wèiyǔ
PN	Proper Noun	专有名词	zhuānyǒu míngcí
Pr	Pronoun	代词	dàicí
Pref	Prefix	词头	cítóu
Prep	Preposition	介词	jiècí
Pt	Particle	助词	zhùcí
PW	Place Word	地点词	dìdiǎncí
QPr	Question Pronoun	疑问代词	yíwèn dàicí
QPt	Question Particle	疑问助词	yíwèn zhùcí
S	Subject	主语	zhǔyǔ
S-PP	Subject-Predicate Phrase	主谓词组	zhǔwèi cízǔ
StPt	Structural Particle	结构助词	jiégòu zhùcí
Suf	Suffix	词尾	cíwěi
TW	Time Word	时间词	shíjiāncí
V	Verb	动词	dòngcí
VC	Verb plus Complement	动补式动词	dòngbǔshì dòngcí
VO	Verb plus Object	动宾式动词	dòngbīnshì dòngcí
V O	Verb-Object Phrase	动宾词组	dòngbīn cízǔ
VP	Verbal Phrase	动词词组	dòngcí cízǔ

生词索引（繁简对照）
Vocabulary Index

(Simplified Chinese Characters vs Traditional Chinese Characters)

词条	繁体	拼音	词性	英译	课号
A					
ABC 商学院	ABC 商學院	ABC Shāng-xuéyuàn	PN	ABC Business College	45
《阿 Q 正传》	《阿 Q 正傳》	Ā Q Zhèngzhuàn	PN	"The True Story of Ah Q" (a short story by Lu Xun)	43
阿姨	阿姨	āyí	N	auntie (a term of address for any woman of one's mother's generation)	44
按摩	按摩	ànmó	V	to massage	49
B					
巴金	巴金	Bā Jīn	PN	Ba Jin (a well-known modern Chinese writer)	43
把手	把手	bǎshou	N	handle, knob (of a door, window, suitcase, etc.)	43
摆架子	擺架子	bǎi jiàzi	V O	to put on airs	43
班	班	bān	M	*measure word for scheduled forms of transportation*	46
半边天	半邊天	bànbiāntiān	N	half the sky, women of the new society	40

半球	半球	bànqiú	N	hemisphere	50
宝库	寶庫	bǎokù	N	treasure house	43
保持	保持	bǎochí	V	to keep, to maintain	48
保管	保管	bǎoguǎn	V	to take care of	44
保险	保險	bǎoxiǎn	N/A	insurance; safe, secure	48
保证	保證	bǎozhèng	V	to pledge, to promise, to guarantee	46
报酬	報酬	bàochou	N	reward, pay	40
本	本	běn	Pr	one's own, native, this, present	45
本儿	本兒	běnr	N	capital, principal	44
本来	本來	běnlái	Adv	originally, at first	46
本人	本人	běnrén	Pr	I (me, myself), oneself	45
必须	必須	bìxū	Adv	must, have to	39
毕业	畢業	bìyè	VO	to graduate	39
鞭炮	鞭炮	biānpào	N	firecrackers	42
遍	遍	biàn	V	all over, everywhere	44
标准	標準	biāozhǔn	N/A	standard, criterion; standard	50
表演	表演	biǎoyǎn	V	to act, to perform	41
别扭	彆扭	bièniu	A	awkward, uncomfortable	39
并	并	bìng	Adv	*used before a negative for emphasis, usually as a retort*	46
病人	病人	bìngrén	N	patient, sick person	49
不断	不斷	búduàn	Adv	continuously, constantly	46
不利	不利	búlì	A	unfavourable, disadvantageous	48
补习	補習	bǔxí	V	to take extra classes after school	46
不管	不管	bùguǎn	Conj	no matter (what, how, etc.)	41
不只	不祇	bùzhǐ	Conj	not only	40
部	部	bù	N	department, ministry	45
部分	部分	bùfen	N	part	47
部长	部長	bùzhǎng	N	minister	40

C ....

财	財	cái	N	wealth, money	42
长期	長期	chángqī	N	long-term, long-lasting	48
长衫	長衫	chángshān	N	long gown	43
尝	嘗	cháng	V	to taste, to try the flavour	42
嫦娥奔月	嫦娥奔月	Cháng'é bèn yuè	IE	Chang'e flying to the moon	50
超级	超級	chāojí	A	super	44
超（级）市（场）	超（级）市（場）	chāo (jí)-shì (chǎng)	N	supermarket	44
炒	炒	chǎo	V	to stir-fry	39
炒鸡丁	炒鷄丁	chǎojīdīng	N	stir-fried chicken cubes	39
称	稱	chēng	V	to call	47
成功	成功	chénggōng	V/A	to succeed; successful	41
成为	成爲	chéngwéi	V	to become, to turn into	45
诚挚	誠挚	chéngzhì	A	sincere, cordial	45
吃苦	吃苦	chīkǔ	VO	to bear hardship	47
出差	出差	chūchāi	VO	to be on an official or business trip	45
出国	出國	chūguó	VO	to go abroad	47
出名	出名	chūmíng	VO/A	to become famous; famous	41
出现	出現	chūxiàn	V	to appear, to emerge	48
初	初	chū	Pref	preliminary, initial, first	39
初中	初中	chūzhōng	N	junior middle school	39
除夕	除夕	chúxī	N	the Spring Festival's Eve, the Lunar New Year's Eve	42
传统	傳統	chuántǒng	A/N	traditional; tradition	48
窗花	窗花	chuānghuā	N	paper-cut for window decoration	42

创新	創新	chuàngxīn	V	to bring forth new ideas, to be creative	45
春联	春聯	chūnlián	N	Spring Festival couplets	42
辞	辭	cí	V	to resign, to dismiss	45
聪明	聰明	cōngming	A	intelligent, clever	46
从此	從此	cóngcǐ	Adv	from this time on, from now on	50
存	存	cún	V	to deposit	47

D

达到	達到	dádào	VC	to reach, to attain	48
打工	打工	dǎgōng	VO	to do odd jobs, to work for others	39
打官司	打官司	dǎ guānsi	V O	to go to court, to engage in a lawsuit	41
打听	打聽	dǎting	V	to inquire, to ask about (sth.)	39
大概	大概	dàgài	A/Adv	general, rough; probably	48
大夫	大夫	dàifu	N	doctor	49
代	代	dài	N	generation	41
代表	代表	dàibiǎo	N/V	deputy, delegate, representative; to represent	45
袋	袋	dài	N/M	bag, sack	46
担	擔	dān	V	to carry	40
担负	擔負	dānfù	V	to bear, to shoulder	40
单位	單位	dānwèi	N	unit (as an organization, a department, a division, a section, etc.)	40
当	當	dāng	Prep	just at (a time), when	47
当时	當時	dāngshí	N	then, at that time	43
导演	導演	dǎoyǎn	N/V	director (of a show, film, etc.); to direct (a show, film, etc.)	41
道理	道理	dàolǐ	N	reason, sense, truth	50
等	等	děng	Pt	and so on, and so forth	48
地球	地球	dìqiú	N	the earth, the globe	50

地位	地位	dìwèi	N	position, status	40
地址	地址	dìzhǐ	N	address	39
电视剧	電視劇	diànshìjù	N	television show, television series	43
电子	電子	diànzǐ	N	electron	45
电子邮件	電子郵件	diànzǐ yóujiàn		e-mail	45
调查	調查	diàochá	N/V	survey; to investigate	46
丁	丁	dīng	N	small cube (dice) of meat or vegetables	39
丁克	丁克	dīngkè	IE	double income and no kids (DINK)	48
丁克家庭	丁克家庭	dīngkè jiātíng		family with double income and no kids	48
东半球	東半球	dōngbànqiú	N	Eastern Hemisphere	50
懂得	懂得	dǒngdé	V	to understand, to know	47
动物	動物	dòngwù	N	animal	49
独	獨	dú	Adv	only, alone	48
独立	獨立	dúlì	V	to be independent	46
独生子女	獨生子女	dúshēngzǐnǚ	N	only child	48
独特	獨特	dútè	A	unique, distinctive	49
读书人	讀書人	dúshūrén	N	scholar, intellectual	43
对	對	duì	M	pair	48
多样化	多樣化	duōyànghuà	V	to be diversified	50

E ··

| 饿 | 餓 | è | A | hungry | 39 |
| 而 | 而 | ér | Conj | *used to connect two elements in a sentence to indicate transition* | 43 |

F ··

| 发 | 發 | fā | V | to make a fortune | 42 |

发财	發財	fācái	VO	to get rich, to make a fortune	42
发挥	發揮	fāhuī	V	to bring into play	40
发射	發射	fāshè	V	to launch, to project, to discharge	50
发音	發音	fāyīn	N/VO	pronunciation; to pronounce	42
法律	法律	fǎlǜ	N	law	41
反对	反對	fǎnduì	V	to oppose, to be against	46
反而	反而	fǎn'ér	Adv	on the contrary	42
方面	方面	fāngmiàn	N	aspect, respect	40
纺织	紡織	fǎngzhī	V	spinning and weaving, textile	40
放	放	fàng	V	to set or let off	42
放鞭炮	放鞭炮	fàng biānpào	V O	to set off firecrackers	42
放松	放鬆	fàngsōng	V	to relax, to loosen	46
飞船	飛船	fēichuán	N	spaceship, spacecraft	50
飞行	飛行	fēixíng	V	(of an airplane) to fly	50
分工	分工	fēngōng	V	to divide work	39
分开	分開	fēnkāi	V	to separate	50
分配	分配	fēnpèi	V	to distribute, to assign	41
分析	分析	fēnxī	V	to analyse	48
风气	風氣	fēngqì	N	general mood, atmosphere	46
封建	封建	fēngjiàn	N	feudal	40
讽刺	諷刺	fěngcì	V	to satirize	43
夫妇	夫婦	fūfù	N	husband and wife, couple	48
服从	服從	fúcóng	V	to obey, to submit to	40
辅导	輔導	fǔdǎo	V	to give guidance in study or training, to tutor	46
负	負	fù	V	to shoulder	40
负担	負擔	fùdān	N/V	load, burden; to bear, to shoulder	46
负责	負責	fùzé	V	to be responsible for, to be in charge of	45
妇女	婦女	fùnǚ	N	woman	40

附	附	fù	V	to add, to attach, to enclose	45
附近	附近	fùjìn	N	nearby, neighbouring	44
副	副	fù	A	deputy, vice	41
富	富	fù	A	rich, wealthy	44
富裕	富裕	fùyù	A	prosperous, rich	44

G ··

改	改	gǎi	V	to alter, to change, to correct	39
改变	改變	gǎibiàn	V	to change	41
改革	改革	gǎigé	V	to reform	47
肝	肝	gān	N	liver	49
敢	敢	gǎn	OpV	dare	39
干	幹	gàn	V	to do, to work	39
干活儿	幹活兒	gàn huór	V O	to work	42
岗位	崗位	gǎngwèi	N	post, job	47
高中	高中	gāozhōng	N	senior middle school	39
个子	個子	gèzi	N	height, stature	43
根据	根據	gēnjù	Prep	according to, in the light of	45
工厂	工廠	gōngchǎng	N	factory, mill, plant	44
工人	工人	gōngrén	N	worker	40
工商	工商	gōngshāng	N	industry and commerce	45
公	公	gōng	A	male (animal)	50
公平	公平	gōngpíng	A	fair, just	40
公务	公務	gōngwù	N	public affairs	41
公务员	公務員	gōngwùyuán	N	public servant	41
鼓励	鼓勵	gǔlì	V	to encourage, to urge	48
怪	怪	guài	V	to blame	46
怪不得	怪不得	guàibude	Adv	no wonder, so that's why	42

关	關	guān	V	to close, to turn off	44
关门	關門	guānmén	VO	(of a shop, etc.) to close	44
关于	關于	guānyú	Prep	about, with regard to	41
官司	官司	guānsi	N	lawsuit	41
广告	廣告	guǎnggào	N	advertisement	41
规律	規律	guīlǜ	N	law, regular pattern	48
柜台	櫃台	guìtái	N	counter	43
国营	國營	guóyíng	A	state-operated	41

H ....

还是	還是	háishi	Adv	had better	43
汉语 水平考试	漢語 水平考試	Hànyǔ Shuǐpíng Kǎoshì	PN	Chinese Proficiency Test (HSK)	45
航	航	háng		to navigate, to sail, to fly	50
航天	航天	hángtiān	V	to fly to the outer space	50
航天员	航天員	hángtiānyuán	N	astronaut, spaceman	50
好吃	好吃	hǎochī	A	tasty, delicious	39
号	號	hào	V	to examine, to feel	49
号码	號碼	hàomǎ	N	number	41
号脉	號脈	hàomài	VO	to feel the pulse	49
合同	合同	hétong	N	contract	45
合资	合資	hézī	V	to enter into partnership, to pool capital	45
合作	合作	hézuò	V	to cooperate, to work together	39
和平	和平	hépíng	N	peace	50
恨	恨	hèn	V	to hate	50
恨不得	恨不得	hènbude	V	to be dying or itching to	50

红烧	紅燒	hóngshāo	V	to braise in soy sauce	42
红烧鱼	紅燒魚	hóngshāoyú	N	fish braised in brown sauce	42
护士	護士	hùshi	N	nurse	40
华人	華人	huárén	N	Chinese people, foreign citizens of Chinese origin	39
化验	化驗	huàyàn	V	to do a laboratory test, to have a chemical or physical examination	49
话剧	話劇	huàjù	N	stage play, modern drama	43
回信	回信	huíxìn	VO/N	to write in reply; letter in reply	39
火箭	火箭	huǒjiàn	N	rocket	50
伙计	夥計	huǒji	N	(old-fashioned) shop assistant	43
货	貨	huò	N	goods, commodity	44

J ....

几乎	幾乎	jīhū	Adv	nearly, almost	40
机会	機會	jīhuì	N	chance, opportunity	40
机器	機器	jīqì	N	machine	49
鸡	鷄	jī	N	chicken	39
基本	基本	jīběn	A/Adv	basic, fundamental; basically, fundamentally	47
基本上	基本上	jīběnshang	Adv	basically, essentially	47
级	級	jí	N	level, grade	45
即使	即使	jíshǐ	Conj	even, even if	41
急	急	jí	A	urgent, pressing, impatient	41
急忙	急忙	jímáng	Adv	hurriedly, hastily	46
集体	集體	jítǐ	N	collective	47
计划	計劃	jìhuà	V/N	to plan; plan	47
既然	既然	jìrán	Conj	since, as, now that	47

加强	加强	jiāqiáng	V	to strengthen, to enhance	50
家教	家教	jiājiào	N	private tutor, private tutoring	47
家庭	家庭	jiātíng	N	family, household	40
家务	家務	jiāwù	N	housework, household chores	40
家长	家長	jiāzhǎng	N	parent or guardian of a child	46
价	價	jià	N	price	44
价钱	價錢	jiàqián	N	price	44
架子	架子	jiàzi	N	airs, haughty manner	43
坚持	堅持	jiānchí	V	to persist in, to insist on	47
坚决	堅決	jiānjué	A	firm, resolute, determined	46
减	減	jiǎn	V	to reduce, to decrease, to subtract	47
减轻	減輕	jiǎnqīng	V	to lighten, to reduce, to relieve	47
简历	簡歷	jiǎnlì	N	resume, curriculum vitae	45
简直	簡直	jiǎnzhí	Adv	simply, just, at all	49
见面	見面	jiànmiàn	VO	to meet, to see	39
健康	健康	jiànkāng	A	healthy	42
箭	箭	jiàn	N	arrow	50
将来	將来	jiānglái	N	future	50
讲解	講解	jiǎngjiě	V	to explain, to interpret	43
讲解员	講解員	jiǎngjiěyuán	N	guide, narrator, commentator	43
奖	獎	jiǎng	V/N	to reward; prize	39
交通	交通	jiāotōng	N	traffic, communications	48
饺子	餃子	jiǎozi	N	Chinese dumpling	42
脚	脚	jiǎo	N	foot	49
脚指头	脚指頭	jiǎozhǐtou	N	toe	49
揭露	揭露	jiēlù	V	to expose, to disclose	43
节目	節目	jiémù	N	programme	43
结合	結合	jiéhé	V	to combine, to integrate	49
结余	結餘	jiéyú	V/N	to remain; surplus	42
解释	解釋	jiěshì	V	to explain	43

尽管	儘管	jǐnguǎn	Conj	though, in spite of	48
紧张	緊張	jǐnzhāng	A	tense, nervous	49
进口	進口	jìnkǒu	VO	to import	50
进行	進行	jìnxíng	V	to conduct, to carry out	50
进修	進修	jìnxiū	V	to engage in advanced studies	45
禁止	禁止	jìnzhǐ	V	to prohibit, to ban	42
经常	經常	jīngcháng	Adv	often, frequently	46
经验	經驗	jīngyàn	N	experience	45
精	精	jīng	A	smart, shrewd	44
精神	精神	jīngshen	N	spirit, mind	45
竞争	競争	jìngzhēng	V	to compete	40
敬意	敬意	jìngyì	N	respect, tribute	45
镜子	鏡子	jìngzi	N	mirror	44
究竟	究竟	jiūjìng	Adv	actually, exactly	39
酒店	酒店	jiǔdiàn	N	bar, restaurant, hotel	43
就是	就是	jiùshì	Adv	only, merely	46
就业	就業	jiùyè	VO	to be employed, to obtain employment	40
居民	居民	jūmín	N	resident, inhabitant	48

K

卡车	卡車	kǎchē	N	lorry, truck	42
开（饭馆）	開（飯館）	kāi (fànguǎn)	V	to operate or run (a restaurant)	39
开发	開發	kāifā	V	to develop	45
开放	開放	kāifàng	V	to open, to open up	47
开药方	開藥方	kāi yàofāng	V O	to write a prescription	49
砍	砍	kǎn	V	to cut, to chop	44
砍价	砍價	kǎnjià	VO	to bargain	44
看不起	看不起	kànbuqǐ	IE	to look down upon	40

考虑	考慮	kǎolǜ	V	to think over, to consider	45
靠	靠	kào	V	to lean on, to depend on	41
可惜	可惜	kěxī	A	pitiful, it's a pity	43
客观	客觀	kèguān	A	objective	48
肯	肯	kěn	OpV	to be willing to	49
孔乙己	孔乙己	Kǒng Yǐjǐ	PN	Kong Yiji (name of the protagonist in one of Lu Xun's short shories)	43
控制	控制	kòngzhì	V	to control	48
哭	哭	kū	V	to weep, to cry	46
苦	苦	kǔ	Adv/A	painstakingly, assiduously; bitter, hard	41
夸	誇	kuā	V	to praise	39
夸奖	誇獎	kuājiǎng	V	to praise, to compliment	39
矿物	礦物	kuàngwù	N	mineral	49

L ....

蓝	藍	lán	A	blue	44
劳动	勞動	láodòng	V/N	to work; work, labour	47
劳动力	勞動力	láodònglì	N	labour force	47
老板	老闆	lǎobǎn	N	boss, shopkeeper	39
离开	離開	líkāi	V	to leave, to depart	46
理解	理解	lǐjiě	V	to understand, to comprehend	43
理论	理論	lǐlùn	N	theory	49
理想	理想	lǐxiǎng	N/A	ideal	39
力量	力量	lìliàng	N	physical strength, capability, power	50
厉害	屬害	lìhai	A	terrible, formidable, serious	44
利用	利用	lìyòng	V	to make use of, to utilize	49
连忙	連忙	liánmáng	Adv	promptly, at once	42
连锁店	連鎖店	liánsuǒdiàn	N	chain store	44

联系	聯繫	liánxì	V	to contact, to get in touch with	45
邻居	鄰居	línjū	N	neighbour	42
零件	零件	língjiàn	N	spare part, component (of a machine)	49
领导	領導	lǐngdǎo	N/V	leader; to lead	46
鲁迅	魯迅	Lǔ Xùn	PN	Lu Xun (a well-known modern Chinese writer)	43
旅游鞋	旅游鞋	lǚyóuxié	N	walking shoes, sneakers	47
律师	律師	lǜshī	N	lawyer	41
率	率	lǜ		rate	48
乱	亂	luàn	Adv/A	randomly, arbitrarily; untidy, in disorder	46
萝卜	蘿蔔	luóbo	N	radish, turnip	50
萝卜青菜，各有所爱	蘿蔔青菜，各有所愛	luóbo qīngcài, gè yǒu suǒ ài	IE	no dish suits all tastes, every Jack has his Jill	50

M

迈	邁	mài	V	to stride, to step (forward or sideways)	50
脉	脉	mài	N	pulse	49
满	滿	mǎn	A	full, filled	39
满意	滿意	mǎnyì	A	satisfied, pleased	41
矛盾	矛盾	máodùn	N	contradiction	40
贸易	貿易	màoyì	N	trade	45
米饭	米飯	mǐfàn	N	(cooked) rice	39
秘书	秘書	mìshū	N	secretary	45
面	面	miàn		face	39
面试	面試	miànshì	V	to interview, to audition	41
明代	明代	Míngdài	PN	Ming Dynasty (1368–1644)	50
模型	模型	móxíng	N	model, mould	43
某	某	mǒu	Pr	certain, some	49

| 母 | 母 | mǔ | A | female (animal) | 50 |
| 木头 | 木頭 | mùtou | N | wood, log | 42 |

N

那么	那麼	nàme	Conj	then, in that case	43
奶奶	奶奶	nǎinai	N	grandmother, mother of one's father	46
男	男	nán	A	man, male	40
男女	男女	nánnǚ	N	men and women	40
男人	男人	nánrén	N	man, male	40
难道	難道	nándào	Adv	*used in a rhetorical question for emphasis*	42
难过	難過	nánguò	A	(to feel) sorry, (to feel) bad/sad	47
难说	難説	nánshuō	V	to be hard to say	47
内	内	nèi	N	inner, within, inside	41
嫩	嫩	nèn	A	young and tender, (not overcooked) tender	50
能干	能幹	nénggàn	A	able, capable	39
能力	能力	nénglì	N	ability, capability	41
年代	年代	niándài	N	decade, age, years	48
年夜	年夜	niányè	N	the Spring Festival's Eve, the Lunar New Year's Eve	42
年夜饭	年夜飯	niányèfàn	N	family reunion dinner on the Spring Festival's Eve	42
农村	農村	nóngcūn	N	rural area, countryside	42
农业	農業	nóngyè	N	agriculture, farming	48
女	女	nǚ	A	woman, female	40
女工	女工	nǚgōng	N	female worker	44

P

拍	拍	pāi	V	to pat	42
胖	胖	pàng	A	fat, stout	44
泡	泡	pào	V	to steep, to soak	47
培养	培養	péiyǎng	V	to foster, to train, to cultivate	46
赔	賠	péi	V	to stand a loss, to compensate	44
赔本儿	賠本兒	péiběnr	VO	to sustain losses in business	44
皮	皮	pí	N	skin, leather	47
骗	騙	piàn	V	to deceive, to fool	41
骗子	騙子	piànzi	N	swindler	41
拼命	拼命	pīnmìng	Adv	desperately, exerting one's utmost	47
聘	聘	pìn	V	to invite sb. to a post (or job)	41
平安	平安	píng'ān	A	safe and sound	41
平常	平常	píngcháng	A	ordinary, common	39
平等	平等	píngděng	A	equal	40
平均	平均	píngjūn	A	average, mean	48
破	破	pò	A/V	broken, worn-out; to break, to damage	43

Q

其实	其實	qíshí	Adv	in fact, as a matter of fact	48
气功	氣功	qìgōng	N	qigong, a traditional Chinese system of deep breathing exercises	49
气色	氣色	qìsè	N	complexion, colour	49
器	器	qì		appliance, implement, utensil	49
器官	器官	qìguān	N	organ, apparatus	49
签订	簽訂	qiāndìng	V	to conclude and sign	45
签字	簽字	qiānzì	VO	to sign one's name	46

前途	前途	qiántú	N	future, prospect	41
强	强	qiáng	A	strong, better	47
敲门	敲門	qiāo mén	V O	to knock at the door	39
亲爱	親愛	qīn'ài	A	dear, beloved	39
青菜	青菜	qīngcài	N	green vegetables	50
轻松	輕鬆	qīngsōng	A	easy, relaxed	47
穷	窮	qióng	A	poor, impoverished	43
穷人	窮人	qióngrén	N	poor person, the poor	43
求职	求職	qiúzhí	VO	to apply for a job	45
全职	全職	quánzhí	A	full-time	40
权利	權利	quánlì	N	right	40
劝	勸	quàn	V	to advise, to try to persuade	49
却	却	què	Adv	but, yet, however	47

R

忍	忍	rěn	V	to endure, to tolerate	46
仍然	仍然	réngrán	Adv	still, yet	43
日记	日記	rìjì	N	diary	43
揉	揉	róu	V	to rub, to knead	47
肉	肉	ròu	N	meat, pork	42

S

山楂	山楂	shānzhā	N	(Chinese) hawthorn	49
商务	商務	shāngwù	N	commercial affairs, business affairs	45
稍微	稍微	shāowēi	Adv	a little, slightly	48
舌头	舌頭	shétou	N	tongue	49
社会	社會	shèhuì	N	society	40

射	射	shè	V	to shoot, to fire, to discharge	50
申请	申請	shēnqǐng	V	to apply for	45
身高	身高	shēngāo	N	height (of a person)	50
深	深	shēn	Adv/A	deeply, profoundly; deep, difficult	47
神舟	神舟	Shénzhōu	PN	Shenzhou (name of a Chinese spacecraft)	50
生	生	shēng	V	to give birth to	48
生意	生意	shēngyi	N	business, trade	41
生育	生育	shēngyù	V	to give birth to, to bear, to beget	48
声	聲	shēng	M	*measure word for sounds*	42
胜利	勝利	shènglì	V	to win a victory	47
失去	失去	shīqù	V	to lose	44
时代	時代	shídài	N	times, era, epoch	43
实际	實際	shíjì	A	realistic, practical	48
实际上	實際上	shíjìshang	Adv	practically, actually	48
实习	實習	shíxí	V	to practise, to do an internship	39
实行	實行	shíxíng	V	to put into practice, to carry out	47
市场	市場	shìchǎng	N	market	44
市场开发部	市場開發部	shìchǎng kāifābù		Market Development Department	45
……似的	……似的	……shìde	Pt	*a particle indicating similarity*	43
事情	事情	shìqing	N	affair, matter, thing	41
事务	事務	shìwù	N	work, affair, routine	41
事务所	事務所	shìwùsuǒ	N	office	41
事业	事業	shìyè	N	cause, undertaking	40
适合	適合	shìhé	V	to suit, to fit	44
适应	適應	shìyìng	V	to suit, to adapt to, to adjust to	45
手机	手機	shǒujī	N	mobile phone	42
手腕	手腕	shǒuwàn	N	wrist	49

守岁	守歲	shǒusuì	VO	to stay up all night on the Spring Festival's Eve	42
瘦	瘦	shòu	A	thin	39
书包	書包	shūbāo	N	schoolbag	44
梳	梳	shū	V	to comb	44
梳子	梳子	shūzi	N	comb	44
熟悉	熟悉	shúxī	V	to be familiar with	41
暑假	暑假	shǔjià	N	summer vacation	39
双	雙	shuāng	A	two, both, double	40
双职工	雙職工	shuāngzhígōng	N	working couple, double-income couple	40
水泥	水泥	shuǐní	N	cement	42
睡衣	睡衣	shuìyī	N	night clothes, night gown, pyjamas	44
顺致	順致	shùnzhì	IE	to take the opportunity to express ... (*used at the close of a letter*)	45
说明	說明	shuōmíng	V/N	to explain, to show; explanation	48
四合院	四合院	sìhéyuàn	N	quadrangle, traditional residential compound with houses built around a square courtyard	42
速度	速度	sùdù	N	speed	48
随便	隨便	suíbiàn	A	any, no matter (what, when, how, etc.)	42
损失	損失	sǔnshī	N/V	loss; to lose	41
所	所	suǒ	N	place, office	41

T ....

太空	太空	tàikōng	N	the firmament, outer space	50
态度	態度	tàidu	N	manner, attitude	44
摊子	攤子	tānzi	N	vendor's stand, stall, booth	44

谈	談	tán	V	to talk, to discuss	39
趟	趟	tàng	M	*measure word for trips*	42
讨论	討論	tǎolùn	V	to discuss	41
特长	特長	tècháng	N	what one's skilled in, strong point, speciality	46
体	體	tǐ		body	49
体重	體重	tǐzhòng	N	weight (of a person)	50
天	天	tiān	N	sky	40
挑	挑	tiāo	V	to choose, to pick	44
挑选	挑選	tiāoxuǎn	V	to choose, to select	44
挑战	挑戰	tiǎozhàn	V	to challenge	41
听话	聽話	tīnghuà	A	obedient	46
听诊	聽診	tīngzhěn	V	to auscultate	49
听诊器	聽診器	tīngzhěnqì	N	stethoscope	49
通过	通過	tōngguò	V	to pass, to pass through	41
同仁堂	同仁堂	Tóngrén Táng	PN	Tongrentang (a famous pharmacy of traditional Chinese medicine)	49
同样	同樣	tóngyàng	A	same, equal	40
同意	同意	tóngyì	V	to agree, to consent	41
铜	銅	tóng	N	copper	43
铜把手	銅把手	tóng bǎshou		bronze handle	43
痛	痛	tòng	A	aching, painful	49
头	頭	tóu	A	first	46
头班车	頭班車	tóubānchē	N	first bus or train	46
头儿	頭兒	tóur	N	(*coll.*) head, chief, boss	47
头发	頭髮	tóufa	N	(human) hair	43
头痛医脚	頭痛醫腳	tóu tòng yī jiǎo	IE	to treat the foot when the head aches	49

突然	突然	tūrán	A	suddenly, unexpectedly	39
团结	團結	tuánjié	V	to unite, to rally	46
推	推	tuī	V	to push	42

W

外地	外地	wàidì	N	parts of the country other than where one is	42
完成	完成	wánchéng	V	to accomplish, to complete	46
完全	完全	wánquán	Adv	completely, wholly	40
玩具	玩具	wánjù	N	toy	44
晚报	晚報	wǎnbào	N	evening paper	44
碗	碗	wǎn	N	bowl	39
万事如意	萬事如意	wàn shì rúyì	IE	to realize all one's wishes	42
为	為	wéi	V	to take as, to act as, to serve as	47
违反	違反	wéifǎn	V	to violate, to run counter to, to go against	48
唯一	唯一	wéiyī	A	only, sole	43
为了	為了	wèile	Prep	for, in order to	40
胃	胃	wèi	N	stomach	49
胃病	胃病	wèi bìng		stomach trouble, gastric disease	49
文具	文具	wénjù	N	stationery	44
文具店	文具店	wénjùdiàn	N	stationery shop	44
握	握	wò	V	to hold, to clasp	39
握手	握手	wòshǒu	VO	to shake hands	39
无论	無論	wúlùn	Conj	regardless of, no matter (what, how, etc.)	45
务	務	wù		affair, business	40

X

西半球	西半球	xībànqiú	N	Western Hemisphere	50
西北	西北	Xīběi	PN	Northwest	45
西医	西醫	xīyī	N	Western medicine, doctor of Western medicine	49
下岗	下崗	xiàgǎng	VO	to be laid off, to lose one's job	44
咸亨酒店	咸亨酒店	Xiánhēng Jiǔdiàn	PN	Xianheng Restaurant	43
嫌	嫌	xián	V	to dislike, to complain about	46
相处	相處	xiāngchǔ	V	to get along (with one another)	50
相信	相信	xiāngxìn	V	to believe, to trust	44
香	香	xiāng	A	aromatic, fragrant, (of food) savoury	50
想法	想法	xiǎngfǎ	N	idea, opinion	41
相声	相聲	xiàngsheng	N	comic dialogue, crosstalk	43
消化	消化	xiāohuà	V	to digest	49
小车	小車	xiǎochē	N	wheelbarrow	42
小组	小組	xiǎozǔ	N	group, team	47
笑话	笑話	xiàohua	V/N	to laugh at sb.; joke	42
鞋	鞋	xié	N	shoe(s)	47
写法	寫法	xiěfǎ	N	style of handwriting, way of writing	43
卸	卸	xiè	V	to unload, to discharge	42
蟹	蟹	xiè	N	crab	50
心	心	xīn	N	heart, mind, feeling	39
心里	心裏	xīnli	N	in the heart, in (the) mind	39
新闻	新聞	xīnwén	N	news	50
新西兰	新西蘭	Xīnxīlán	PN	New Zealand	47
信息	信息	xìnxī	N	information	49

信箱	信箱	xìnxiāng	N	mailbox, post office box (POB)	45
信心	信心	xìnxīn	N	confidence	44
形式	形式	xíngshì	N	form	48
休假	休假	xiūjià	VO	to have/take a vacation	41
修理	修理	xiūlǐ	V	to repair, to mend	49
绣	綉	xiù	V	to embroider	44
绣花儿	綉花兒	xiùhuār	VO	to embroider, to do embroidery	44
需要	需要	xūyào	V	to need, to want, to require	41
选	選	xuǎn	V	to select, to elect	44
学费	學費	xuéfèi	N	tuition fee	47
训练	訓練	xùnliàn	V	to train	50

Y

亚洲	亞洲	Yàzhōu	PN	Asia	45
严格	嚴格	yángé	A	strict, rigorous	50
研究生	研究生	yánjiūshēng	N	graduate student, postgraduate	39
洋	洋	yáng	A	foreign	42
养儿防老	養兒防老	yǎng ér fáng lǎo	IE	to raise children to provide against old age	48
要求	要求	yāoqiú	V/N	to demand, to require, to ask; requirement	45
腰	腰	yāo	N	waist	47
药方	藥方	yàofāng	N	prescription	49
要紧	要緊	yàojǐn	A	serious, important	49
要么	要麼	yàome	Conj	or	46
要是	要是	yàoshi	Conj	if, suppose	40
爷爷	爺爺	yéye	N	grandfather, father of one's father	46

也许	也許	yěxǔ	Adv	perhaps, probably	47
业务	業務	yèwù	N	professional work, business	45
医	醫	yī	V/N	to treat, to cure; doctor, medical science	49
医学	醫學	yīxué	N	medical science	49
一切	一切	yíqiè	Pr	all, every, everything	45
遗憾	遺憾	yíhàn	A	regretful	43
以来	以來	yǐlái	N	since	48
一直	一直	yìzhí	Adv	continuously, all along, always	48
义务	義務	yìwù	A/N	voluntary; duty, obligation	47
营养	營養	yíngyǎng	N	nutrition	50
影响	影響	yǐngxiǎng	V/N	to influence, to affect; effect	46
优	優	yōu	A	excellent	46
优秀	優秀	yōuxiù	A	outstanding, excellent	46
尤其	尤其	yóuqí	Adv	especially	42
邮件	郵件	yóujiàn	N	postal matter, mail	45
犹豫	猶豫	yóuyù	A	hesitant	42
有利	有利	yǒulì	A	advantageous, beneficial	48
于	于	yú	Prep	in, on, at (indicating time or place)	45
余	餘	yú	V	to remain	42
鱼	魚	yú	N	fish	42
原因	原因	yuányīn	N	cause, reason	47
圆	圓	yuán	A	round	44
远亲不如近邻	遠親不如近鄰	yuǎnqīn bù-rú jìnlín	IE	a close neighbour means more than a distant relative	42
院（子）	院（子）	yuàn (zi)	N	courtyard	42
愿望	願望	yuànwàng	N	desire, wish	50
运动	運動	yùndòng	V/N	to do physical exercises; sports	49

Z

载	載	zài	V	to carry, to be loaded with	50
赞成	贊成	zànchéng	V	to approve of, to agree with	46
增加	增加	zēngjiā	V	to increase, to raise	46
增长	增長	zēngzhǎng	V	to increase, to grow	48
占	占	zhàn	V	to make up, to account for	40
长	長	zhǎng	Suf	chief, head	47
招聘	招聘	zhāopìn	V	to invite applications for a job	41
照顾	照顧	zhàogù	V	to look after, to take care of	40
针灸	針灸	zhēnjiǔ	N	acupuncture and moxibustion	49
整	整	zhěng	A	whole	49
整体	整體	zhěngtǐ	N	whole, entirety	49
正好	正好	zhènghǎo	Adv/A	accidentally, fortunately; just right	49
政策	政策	zhèngcè	N	policy	48
之内	之內	zhīnèi	N	within	41
支持	支持	zhīchí	V	to support, to hold out	47
只	隻	zhī	M	*measure word for one of a pair or for certain animals or utensils*	47
直	直	zhí	Adv	straight	44
直接	直接	zhíjiē	A	direct, straight	44
职	職	zhí		post, occupation, profession	40
职工	職工	zhígōng	N	staff members, workers	40
职务	職務	zhíwù	N	post, job	45
只有	祇有	zhǐyǒu	Conj	only	40
指头	指頭	zhǐtou	N	finger, toe	49
制度	制度	zhìdù	N	system, institution	48
制造	製造	zhìzào	V	to manufacture, to make	50
质量	質量	zhìliàng	N	quality	44

治	治	zhì	V	to treat (a disease), to cure	49
中医	中醫	zhōngyī	N	traditional Chinese medical science, doctor of traditional Chinese medicine	49
终于	終于	zhōngyú	Adv	finally, eventually	39
重男轻女	重男輕女	zhòng nán qīng nǚ	IE	to regard men as superior to women, to prefer boys to girls	48
重视	重視	zhòngshì	V	to attach importance to, to think highly of	49
周	周	zhōu	N	week	46
周末	周末	zhōumò	N	weekend	46
主人	主人	zhǔrén	N	host, master, owner	50
爪	爪	zhuǎ	N	claw, talon, paw	50
专家	專家	zhuānjiā	N	expert, specialist	48
赚	賺	zhuàn	V	to make a profit, to gain, to earn	44
装	裝	zhuāng	V	to load, to pack	42
装修	裝修	zhuāngxiū	V	to fit up (a house, etc.), to renovate	42
追	追	zhuī	V	to chase after	44
资料	資料	zīliào	N	data, material	43
子女	子女	zǐnǚ	N	sons and daughters, children	48
自	自	zì	Prep	from	49
自由	自由	zìyóu	A/N	free; freedom	48
总	總	zǒng	A	chief, general	41
总（是）	總（是）	zǒng (shì)	Adv	always	39
总数	總數	zǒngshù	N	total, sum	48
组长	組長	zǔzhǎng	N	group leader	47
组织	組織	zǔzhī	V	to organize	43
左右	左右	zuǒyòu	N	about, around (indicating an approximate number)	50

作家	作家	zuòjiā	N	writer	43
作业	作業	zuòyè	N	school assignment, homework	46
作用	作用	zuòyòng	N	role, effect, function	40
做工	做工	zuògōng	VO	to do manual work, to work	43

补充生词

Supplementary Words

词条	繁体	拼音	词性	英译	课号
A					
艾滋病	艾滋病	àizībìng	N	AIDS	49
岸	岸	àn	N	bank, shore	48
奥运	奥運	Àoyùn	PN	the Olympic Games	47
B					
拜年	拜年	bàinián	VO	to pay a New Year's call	42
报名	報名	bàomíng	VO	to sign up for sth., to enter one's name	45
鼻子	鼻子	bízi	N	nose	43
壁	壁	bì		wall	43
扁	扁	biǎn	A	flat	43
扁鹊	扁鵲	Biǎn Què	PN	Bian Que (a well-known Chinese doctor of the Warring States Period)	49
辫子	辮子	biànzi	N	braid, pigtail	41
冰箱	冰箱	bīngxiāng	N	refrigerator	50
玻璃	玻璃	bōli	N	glass	43
伯父	伯父	bófù	N	uncle (father's elder brother)	43

C

彩电	彩電	cǎidiàn	N	colour television	42
菜谱	菜譜	càipǔ	N	cookbook	39
蔡国	蔡國	Càiguó	PN	the State of Cai	49
苍蝇	蒼蠅	cāngying	N	fly	50
草房	草房	cǎofáng	N	thatched cottage	40
产品	産品	chǎnpǐn	N	product, produce	46
肠	腸	cháng	N	intestine	49
沉思	沉思	chénsī	V	to be lost in thought	39
承认	承認	chéngrèn	V	to recognize, to admit	49
迟到	遲到	chídào	V	to be late, to arrive late	46
抽奖	抽獎	chōujiǎng	VO	to draw lots (to give out prizes), to draw a winning number (for lottery, sweepstake, etc.)	44
愁	愁	chóu	V	to worry, to be anxious	44
储存	儲存	chǔcún	V	to store	48
创作	創作	chuàngzuò	V	to create, to write	41
辞	辭	cí	V	to resign, to quit	39

D

达坂城	達坂城	Dábǎn Chéng	PN	Daban city (name of a town in Xinjiang Uygur Autonomous Region)	41
打折扣	打折扣	dǎ zhékòu	VO	to give a discount	44
大臣	大臣	dàchén	N	minister	49
大妈	大媽	dàmā	N	aunt (a respectful form of address for an elderly woman)	47
大人	大人	dàren	N	Your Excellency, His Excellency	46

大爷	大爺	dàye	N	uncle (a respectful form of address for an elderly man)	47
蛋	蛋	dàn	N	egg	46
邓小平	鄧小平	Dèng Xiǎopíng	PN	Deng Xiaoping (1904–1997) (a leader of the Communist Party of China)	48
电器	電器	diànqì	N	electrical appliance	44
调	調	diào	V	to transfer, to move	45
短信	短信	duǎnxìn	N	short text message	50

F

发愁	發愁	fāchóu	VO	to worry, to be anxious	44
发作	發作	fāzuò	V	to break out, to show the effect of	49
飞行员	飛行員	fēixíngyuán	N	pilot, aviator	50
分享	分享	fēnxiǎng	V	to share (joy, rights, etc.)	50
风衣	風衣	fēngyī	N	trench coat	39
蜂蜜	蜂蜜	fēngmì	N	honey	42
服	服	fú	V	to be convinced, to obey	46
负增长	負增長	fù zēngzhǎng		negative growth	48
副业	副業	fùyè	N	sideline, side occupation	40
富	富	fù	A	rich, wealthy	42

G

改编	改編	gǎibiān	V	to adapt, to revise	41
改革	改革	gǎigé	V	to reform	44
高速	高速	gāosù	A	high speed	45
高速公路	高速公路	gāosù gōnglù		expressway	45
歌王	歌王	gēwáng	N	king of folk songs	41

歌星	歌星	gēxīng	N	star singer, accomplished vocalist	48
工程师	工程師	gōngchéngshī	N	engineer	45
公路	公路	gōnglù	N	road, highway	45
骨髓	骨髓	gǔsuǐ	N	bone marrow	49
国王	國王	guówáng	N	king	49

H

哈萨克族	哈薩克族	Hāsàkèzú	PN	the Kazak ethnic group	41
汉族	漢族	Hànzú	PN	the Han ethnic group	41
哄	哄	hǒng	V	to coax, to humour	48
胡说	胡説	húshuō	V	to talk nonsense	46
胡子	鬍子	húzi	N	beard, moustache, whiskers	43
糊涂	糊塗	hútu	A	muddled, confused	46
花生	花生	huāshēng	N	peanut	42
黄牛	黄牛	huángniú	N	ox, cattle	40
讳疾忌医	諱疾忌醫	huì jí jì yī	IE	to hide one's sickness for fear of treatment, to conceal one's faults for fear of criticism	49
婚姻	婚姻	hūnyīn	N	marriage	40

J

肌肉	肌肉	jīròu	N	muscle	49
鸡蛋	鷄蛋	jīdàn	N	chicken egg	46
积谷防饥	積穀防饑	jī gǔ fáng jī	IE	to store up grain against famine	48
激烈	激烈	jīliè	A	intense, fierce	40
建筑	建築	jiànzhù	N/V	building, architecture; to construct, to build	40
奖品	奬品	jiǎngpǐn	N	prize, trophy	44
脚心	脚心	jiǎoxīn	N	the underside of the arch (of the foot), centre of the sole	43

教师	教師	jiàoshī	N	teacher	45
教学	教學	jiàoxué	V	to teach	45
进口	進口	jìnkǒu	V	to import	44
经历	經歷	jīnglì	N/V	experience; to undergo	45
局长	局長	júzhǎng	N	bureau chief	45

K

开放	開放	kāifàng	V	to open, to open up	44
克林	克林	Kèlín	PN	Collin (name of a person)	47
口袋	口袋	kǒudai	N	pocket	40

L

拉车	拉車	lā chē	V O	to pull a cart or rickshaw	43
蓝色	藍色	lánsè	N	blue (colour)	39
老百姓	老百姓	lǎobǎixìng	N	ordinary folk, common people	44
老子	老子	lǎozi	N	(coll.) I, me (literally "your father", said in anger or in fun)	50
梨	梨	lí	N	pear	42
脸	臉	liǎn	N	face	46
粮票	糧票	liángpiào	N	food coupon	44
粮食	糧食	liángshi	N	grain, cereals, food (provisions)	40
两	兩	liǎng	M	tael (old unit of weight for silver or gold)	46
了不起	了不起	liǎobuqǐ	A	amazing, outstanding	48
留恋	留戀	liúliàn	V	to be reluctant to leave (a place), can't bear to part (from sb.)	41
录取	錄取	lùqǔ	V	to enrol, to admit	45
啰唆	囉唆	luōsuo	A	long-winded, wordy	39

M

麦子	麥子	màizi	N	wheat	46
猕猴桃	獼猴桃	míhóutáo	N	kiwi fruit	50
民国	民國	Mínguó	PN	Republic of China (1912-1949)	48
模特儿	模特兒	mótèr	N	model	50
母语	母語	mǔyǔ	N	native language, mother tongue	45

N

耐心	耐心	nàixīn	A/N	patient; patience	47
难忘	難忘	nánwàng	A	unforgettable	47
年底	年底	niándǐ	N	end of the year	42
宁静	寧静	níngjìng	A	tranquil, peaceful, quiet	39
宁静致远	寧静致遠	níngjìng zhì yuǎn	IE	to accomplish sth. lasting by leading a quiet life	39
农业	農業	nóngyè	N	agriculture, farming	42

P

培训	培训	péixùn	V	to train	40
赔	賠	péi	V	to stand a loss, to lose	40
佩服	佩服	pèifu	V	to admire	48
碰	碰	pèng	V	to touch, to bump	43
碰壁	碰壁	pèngbì	VO	to run up against a stone wall, to meet with a major setback	43
皮肤	皮膚	pífū	N	skin	49
凭	憑	píng	Prep	to go by, to base on	44

Q ··

起名字	起名字	qǐ míngzi	V O	to give a name	47
千万	千萬	qiānwàn	Adv	to be sure to, must	50
欠	欠	qiàn	V	to owe	40
清朝	清朝	Qīngcháo	PN	Qing Dynasty (1616–1911)	48
请假	請假	qǐngjià	VO	to ask for leave of absence	47
劝	勸	quàn	V	to try to persuade, to try to convince	48
缺	缺	quē	V	to be short of (sth.), to lack (sth.)	42

R ··

热敷	熱敷	rè fū		to apply a hot compress	49
人才	人才	réncái	N	talented person	45

S ··

纱布	紗布	shābù	N	bandage, gauze	43
晒	曬	shài	V	to bask, to dry in the sun	45
山沟	山溝	shāngōu	N	remote mountainous area	42
少数民族	少數民族	shǎoshù mínzú		ethnic minority	41
呻吟	呻吟	shēnyín	V	to groan, to moan	43
深	深	shēn	A	deep	41
审	審	shěn	V	to interrogate, to try	46
生产队长	生産隊長	shēngchǎn duìzhǎng		production team leader	40
剩	剩	shèng	V	to be left over, to remain	43

石头	石頭	shítou	N	stone	41
收成	收成	shōucheng	N	harvest, crop	46
属于	屬于	shǔyú	V	to belong to	50

T

太爷爷	太爺爺	tàiyéye	N	great-grandfather	48
讨厌	討厭	tǎoyàn	A	disagreeable, disgusting	50
甜	甜	tián	A	sweet, honeyed	41
同事	同事	tóngshì	N	colleague	50
痛苦	痛苦	tòngkǔ	A	painful, suffering	39

W

玩儿游戏	玩兒游戲	wánr yóuxì	V O	to play a game	50
王宫	王宫	wánggōng	N	imperial palace	49
王洛宾	王洛賓	Wáng Luòbīn	PN	Wang Luobin (name of a Chinese musician)	41
维吾尔族	維吾爾族	Wéiwú'ěrzú	PN	the Uygur ethnic group	41
维修	維修	wéixiū	V	to keep in (good) repair, to maintain	45
温暖	溫暖	wēnnuǎn	A	warm	39
问候	問候	wènhòu	V	to send one's regards to sb.	50
误会	誤會	wùhuì	V	to misunderstand	50

X

西瓜	西瓜	xīguā	N	watermelon	41
县官	縣官	xiànguān	N	county magistrate	46
羡慕	羡慕	xiànmù	V	to admire, to envy	44
响	響	xiǎng	V	to make a sound, to ring	50

项链	項鏈	xiàngliàn	N	necklace	44
小康	小康	xiǎokāng	A	relatively well-off	42
小心	小心	xiǎoxīn	A/V	careful; to take care, to be careful	43
小叶子	小葉子	Xiǎoyèzi	PN	Xiao Yezi (name of a TV programme hostess)	48
心情	心情	xīnqíng	N	frame (or state) of mind, mood	50
杏儿	杏兒	xìngr	N	apricot	42
修建	修建	xiūjiàn	V	to build, to construct	45
秀水街	秀水街	Xiùshuǐ Jiē	PN	Xiushui Street (a free market in Beijing)	44
《雪绒花》	《雪絨花》	Xuěrónghuā	PN	"Edelweiss" (a song from the film *Sound of Music*)	47

Y

丫头	丫頭	yātou	N	(*coll.*) girl	50
压倒	壓倒	yādǎo	VC	to prevail over	49
压岁钱	壓歲錢	yāsuìqián	N	money given to children as a Lunar New Year gift	42
眼镜	眼鏡	yǎnjìng	N	glasses, spectacles	43
养蜂	養蜂	yǎng fēng	V O	to raise or keep bees	42
业余	業餘	yèyú	A	spare, leisure	47
伊斯兰	伊斯蘭	Yīsīlán	PN	Islam	40
医术	醫術	yīshù	N	medical skill	49
银子	銀子	yínzi	N	silver, money	46
引起	引起	yǐnqǐ	V	to give rise to, to cause, to arouse	39
硬	硬	yìng	A	hard, solid	43
勇敢	勇敢	yǒnggǎn	A	brave	40
有趣	有趣	yǒuqù	A	interesting	50
愚人节	愚人節	Yúrén Jié	PN	April Fools' Day	39

圆	圆	yuán	A	round	41
允许	允許	yǔnxǔ	V	to allow, to permit	39

Z

在世	在世	zàishì	V	to be living	43
早退	早退	zǎotuì	V	to leave early	47
扎	紮	zhā	V	to prick, to needle into	43
战国	戰國	Zhànguó	PN	the Warring States Period (475 B.C.-221 B.C.)	49
战争	戰爭	zhànzhēng	N	war	50
张望	張望	zhāngwàng	V	to look around	41
争取	爭取	zhēngqǔ	V	to strive for	47
侄女	侄女	zhínǚ	N	brother's daughter, niece	45
直	直	zhí	A	straight	43
值得	值得	zhídé	V	to be worthy of, to deserve	44
职称	職稱	zhíchēng	N	professional title	40
中奖	中獎	zhòngjiǎng	VO	to win a prize	44
主持人	主持人	zhǔchírén	N	anchorperson, host or hostess	48
煮	煮	zhǔ	V	to boil, to cook	39
专科学校	專科學校	zhuānkē xuéxiào		college for vocational training	45
赚	賺	zhuàn	V	to make a profit, to gain	40
自信	自信	zìxìn	A	self-confident	40

汉字索引

Character Index

Embark on your Chinese learning from the website of
Beijing Language and Culture University Press

北京语言大学出版社网站：www.blcup.com

从这里开始……

International online orders
TEL: +86-10-82303668
     +86-10-82303080
Email: service@blcup.com

这里是对外汉语精品教材的展示平台

汇集2000余种对外汉语教材，检索便捷，
每本教材有目录、简介、样课等详尽信息。

It showcases BLCUP's superb textbooks of TCFL (Teaching Chinese as a Foreign Language)

It has a collection of more than 2,000 titles of BLCUP's TCFL textbooks, which are easy to be searched, with details such as table of contents, brief introduction and sample lessons for each textbook.

这里是覆盖全球的电子商务平台

在任何地点，均可通过VISA/MASTER卡在线购买。

It provides an e-commerce platform which covers the whole world.

Online purchase with VISA/MASTER Card can be made in every part of the world.

这里是数字出版的体验平台

只需在线支付，即刻就可获取质高价优的全新电子图书。

It provides digital publication service.

A top-grade and reasonably-priced brand new e-book can be obtained as soon as you pay for it online.

这里是对外汉语教学/学习资源的服务平台

提供测试题、知识讲解、阅读短文、教案、课件、教学示范、教材配套资料等各类文字、音视频资源。

It provides a services platform for Chinese language learning for foreigners.

All kinds of written and audio-visual teaching resources are available, including tests, explanations on language points, reading passages, teaching plans, courseware, teaching demo and other supplementary teaching materials etc.

这里是沟通交流的互动平台

汉语教学与学习论坛，使每个参与者都能共享海量信息与资源。

It provides a platform for communication.

This platform for Chinese teaching and learning makes it possible for every participant to share our abundant data and resources.